Reconstructing Argumentative Discourse

STUDIES IN RHETORIC AND COMMUNICATION
General Editors:
E. Culpepper Clark
Raymie E. McKerrow
David Zarefsky

Frans H. van Eemeren, Rob Grootendorst
Sally Jackson, and Scott Jacobs

Reconstructing Argumentative Discourse

The University of Alabama Press   Tuscaloosa and London

Copyright © 1993
The University of Alabama Press
Tuscaloosa, Alabama 35487–0380
All rights reserved
Manufactured in the United States of America

∞

The paper on which this book is printed meets the minimum requirements of
American National Standard for Information Science-Permanence of Paper for
Printed Library Materials, ANSI Z39.48-1984.

Library of Congress Cataloging-in-Publication Data

Reconstructing argumentative discourse / Frans H. van Eemeren . . . [et
al.].
    p.   cm.—(Studies in rhetoric and communication)
    Includes bibliographical references and index.
    ISBN 0-8173-0697-8
    1. Persuasion (Rhetoric) 2. Discourse analysis. 3. Speech acts
(Linguistics) I. Eemeren, F. H. van. II. Series.
P301.5.P47R43   1993
808—dc20   93–18082

British Library Cataloguing-in-Publication Data available

Contents

Preface

In contemporary argumentation research, there is an unfortunate division between descriptive and critical work. Those approaching argumentation theory from a social scientific perspective tend to think of their work as "descriptive," and those approaching argumentation theory from humanistic perspectives such as logic and rhetoric tend to think of their work as "normative" or "critical." Social scientific approaches generally claim to be value-free. They generally portray themselves as avoiding questions of how individuals in principle *should* and *should not* argue in favor of simply asking how individuals in fact *do* and *do not* argue. In contrast, critical approaches are often more concerned with the properties of models of ideal argumentation than with features of actual argumentative practice. They tend to emphasize questions of how, ideally, individuals *should* and *should not* argue, seeming to be generally uninterested in questions of how individuals in fact *do* and *do not* argue.

Those on each side of the divide seem to regard the other side as so different in purpose and approach as to be irrelevant to their own concerns. Standing between these two approaches, we see much to be gained from a recognition of the relationship between descriptive and normative theory and much to be gained from their reconciliation within a program of detailed empirical analysis.

To get a sense of what we have in mind, consider an excerpt from Senator Edward Kennedy's nationally televised "Address to the

People of Massachusetts" on July 25, 1969. In the speech, the senator gives an account of his involvement in the drowning death of Mary Jo Kopechne.

What is noticed as important about this text would likely depend heavily on whether a descriptive or a critical approach is taken. A descriptive approach would likely focus on the pragmatic structur-

Example 0.1

01 On Chappaquiddick Island, off Martha's Vineyard, I attended

02 on Friday evening, July 18, a cookout I had encouraged and

03 helped sponsor for a devoted group of Kennedy campaign

04 secretaries. When I left the party, around 11:15 P.M., I

05 was accompanied by one of these girls, Miss Mary Jo

06 Kopechne. Mary Jo was one of the most devoted members of

07 the staff of Senator Robert Kennedy. She worked for him for

08 four years and was broken up over his death. For this

09 reason, and because she was such a gentle, kind, and

10 idealistic person, all of us tried to help her feel that she

11 still had a home with the Kennedy family. There is no

12 truth, no truth whatever, to the widely circulated

13 suspicions of immoral conduct that have been leveled at my

14 behavior and hers regarding that evening. There has never

15 been a private relationship between us of any kind. I know

16 of nothing in Mary Jo's conduct on that or any other

17 occasion—and the same is true of the other girls at that

18 party—that would lend any substance to such ugly

19 speculation about their character. Nor was I driving under

20 the influence of liquor. Little over one mile away, the car

21 that I was driving on an unlit road went off a narrow bridge

22 which had no guardrails and was built on a left angle to

23 the road. The car overturned in a deep pond and immediately

24 filled with water.

ing of the speech (its management of "disagreement space," for example), while a normative approach would likely focus on the deficiencies of the speech as an explicit defense of a clearly articulated claim.

A descriptive approach to argumentation might note, for example, that while much of the excerpt has the character of a narrative recounting of the events leading up to the fatal accident, the senator's story also functions as an argument against potential accusations of misconduct. For one thing, the narrative functions to deny suspicions of sexual misconduct concerning the nature of the party and the drive later that evening. While the denial in lines 11–19 is fairly overt, the argumentative support for the denial is less obvious. It is conveyed through a strategy of suggestion and implication. Notice, for example, the connotations of innocent clean fun—of hot dogs on the grill and outdoor games—that attach to the description of the event as a "cookout." Notice also the formal, paternalistic relationship between the senator and Miss Kopechne that is implied in the description. Senator Kennedy is described as helping to "sponsor" the cookout and as trying to help Miss Kopechne "feel that she still had a home with the Kennedy family." Miss Kopechne is described as "a gentle, kind, and idealistic person," as a "devoted" staff member and campaign secretary for Robert Kennedy (impersonal role categories), as being "broken up" over his death. In other words, Miss Kopechne was not the kind of person who would be likely to entertain thoughts of sexual misconduct with the senator; and the senator was acting out of noblesse oblige toward his fallen brother's staff—a motive incompatible with thoughts of sexual misconduct.

For another thing, the senator describes the accident in a way that insinuates that he was not responsible for the car's going off the bridge into the water. It was "an unlit road." The bridge was "narrow" and "had no guardrails." And it was "built on a left angle to the road." Notice how this reading is further encouraged by describing the car—and not the driver—as going off the bridge. In other words, the narrative builds a case for the argument that the senator was not responsible for the accident because it was such an unsafe bridge that anyone (or anyone's car) could have gone off it.

So, a descriptive approach to materials such as those in example 0.1 could lead to the observation that narratives can serve the kinds of functions and present the kinds of evidence and reasoning usually associated with more overtly argumentative discourse. A descriptive approach might furthermore lead the analyst to notice the strategic value of this way of getting across a case. The tactic allows the senator to convey a rationale to an audience that would justify dismissing suspicions of sexual misconduct while simultaneously suggesting that such suspicions are too unseemly to dignify with a defense. And the tactic enables the senator to provide an account of how he went off the bridge without having to treat the question of reckless driving as an open issue.

Assuming that a critical approach would recognize this excerpt as a case of argument at all, it would almost certainly zero in on the way in which Senator Kennedy's account runs contrary to normative standards for how argument *should* be conducted. For example, the senator's claims in lines 11–19 do more than deny charges of immoral conduct. Kennedy phrases his denial in a way designed to discourage strongly any further critical scrutiny of the charges. Notice that these lines close by describing the charges as "ugly speculation." (Later in the speech, the senator makes reference to "innuendo and whispers.") Moreover, the senator's denials focus not so much on charges leveled against his own behavior as on charges leveled against the behavior of Miss Kopechne and the other girls at the party. There is a not-so-subtle message here: "If you continue to impugn my character, you will also be impugning the character of a dead girl, and of all the other girls at that party. Moreover, you will be feeding ugly, cheap gossip."

Or again, the strategic value of a narrative substitute for open argumentation might be taken to be precisely what is so troublesome about such a tactic. It allows the senator to evade clear argumentative claims. Just what, precisely, is the reasoning that suggests that Miss Kopechne was not that kind of girl and that the senator had no improper intentions? It allows the senator to avoid taking on such argumentative commitments as, for example, the obligation to defend his case against further critical questioning or refutation. (In fact, following the speech the senator has consistently refused to answer further questions about what happened that night.)

But the alternatives of descriptive and critical approaches to this case of argumentation are not as clearly distinct as we may have suggested, and we do not think that they should be construed as genuinely separate and unrelated enterprises. Any description of argumentation is already profoundly connected with normative concepts, whether explicit or implicit. For example, simply to characterize example 0.1 as suggesting or implicating an argument is to hold it up to a standard of overt and explicit argumentation. While this characterization is surely grounded, in part, in certain features of the text and in knowledge of the rhetorical situation faced by the senator (press accounts were filled with suspicions of sexual misconduct and reckless driving), the characterization is also grounded in a normative presumption that the senator's speech is responding to that situation in an argumentatively relevant way.

And to notice certain features of the speech as having strategic value is to compare the speech as given with a picture of what might have been said but was not. Such a comparison is not just with any unrealized possibility but with those of normative interest. That is, the strategy is made visible against a background of expectations that an argument is called for and of how such an argument might be presented.

Likewise, any evaluation of the speech depends on a clear understanding of its pragmatic structuring. Although one can build abstract models of argumentation without regard for practical circumstances, one cannot apply these to the task of evaluation without taking those circumstances into account, and no normative theory can anticipate from the beginning all the ways in which actual practice may depart from normative ideals. In this example, it is the empirical observation of the possibility of argument by suggestion that raises normative issues in the first place. Hence, description depends on some prior normative concept of what is important about the discourse, and evaluation depends on some achieved empirical sense of what is remarkable about the discourse.

We are convinced of the importance of normatively informed description and empirically adequate theorizing. This book is our effort to describe argumentation as it is, but with respect to an image of how it should be.

The book originated in two initially separate projects: the primarily normative work of van Eemeren and Grootendorst embodied in their "pragma-dialectical" theory (esp. van Eemeren and Grootendorst 1982, 1983, 1984, 1990, 1992a), and the primarily descriptive work of Jackson and Jacobs on the organization of conversational argument (esp. Jackson and Jacobs 1980; Jacobs and Jackson 1981, 1982, 1983, 1989). Each position involves speech act theory as an important component, and we have extended our positions independently, though in very similar directions. Our friend and colleague Charlie Willard saw the close alignment in our views and first brought us together at the Third Summer Conference on Argumentation at Alta, Utah. This led to several years of discussion back and forth, culminating in a year of intense collaborative work at the Netherlands Institute for Advanced Study in the Humanities and Social Sciences (NIAS). This book is the product of that work.

Organization of the Book

The first two chapters present the theoretical position on argumentation to be elaborated in the book. Chapter 1 points out the importance of integrating descriptive and normative interests and discusses some of the difficulties involved in doing so. The key to a solution is the concept of a speech act elaborated as a special case of Gricean (1975) cooperativity. In our view, speech act theory should be taken as a description of the natural normative organization of discursive activity. And we believe that argumentation is best understood as a kind of discursive activity.

In chapter 2 we locate normative and descriptive interests in argumentation within a comprehensive program of research and theorizing. We also further develop a speech act conception of argumentation by discussing the argumentative functions of speech acts within an ideal model of critical discussion. This ideal model, a philosophically grounded normative model of argumentative exchange, serves as a point of departure for a resolution-oriented analysis of argumentative discourse.

Chapters 3 and 4 take up methodological issues in balancing the role of empirical and normative influences in the analytic reconstruction of argumentative discourse. Chapter 3 elaborates a general conceptualization of these roles and locates our position in comparison to other theoretical approaches. Chapter 4 illustrates through an extended example how empirical cues and normative presumptions work in reconstructing the "case" in support of or against the conflicting standpoints taken in an argument.

Chapters 5–7 take up several theoretical issues that arise in the process of applying a normative model of ideal argumentation to the situated practices of everyday argumentation. In chapter 5 we examine implications of the pragmatic context of everyday conversational argument for the normative structuring of argument. Specifically, we address the problem of how normative concepts of argumentation as assertions can be reconciled with the empirical observation that people do not conduct argumentation simply through assertives.

In chapter 6 we address implications of taking a pragmatic approach to argumentation for the problem of how to realize the conditions for ideal argumentation in practice. Specifically, we look at programs for third-party dispute mediation as an institutionalized effort on the part of mediators to manage the framework for argumentation without conducting the argumentation.

And in chapter 7 we examine the role of the higher-order conditions presupposed by an ideal model of argumentation and the limits of the ideal model as a procedure for resolving differences of opinion. We do this through analysis of a form of argumentation occurring within the context of religious witnessing and audience heckling, which is particularly problematic as far as the observance of normative standards is concerned.

Chapter 8 points to the ways in which theoretically informed observation opens opportunities for further elaboration of the theory, especially in terms of practical application and a perspective on practicality.

As will be obvious to readers familiar with our prior work, some of these chapters are dependent primarily on the pragma-dialectical theory of van Eemeren and Grootendorst, others primarily on empirical work by Jackson and Jacobs on conversational argument. We would like to think, however, that the ideas developed in the book are a product of an extended critical discussion in which all four contributed equally to arrive at a shared position. Order of authorship is alphabetical.

Acknowledgments

This work was made possible by our appointments at the Netherlands Institute for Advanced Study in the Humanities and Social Sciences (1989–90), by van Eemeren's and Grootendorst's supported leaves of absence from the University of Amsterdam, and by Jackson's and Jacobs's supported leaves of absence from the University of Oklahoma, Office of the Provost. We are indebted to the other members of our NIAS research group on Fallacies in Argumentative Discourse: Agnes van Rees, Agnes Verbiest, Douglas Walton, Charles Willard, and John Woods. For reading and commenting on earlier drafts of the manuscript, we would like to thank Francisca Snoeck Henkemans and Jesse Delia. Portions of the manuscript were read by the students and faculty of a course offered at the University of Amsterdam Summer Institute on Argumentation during the summer of 1990, and we are indebted to them for much useful discussion.

Reconstructing Argumentative Discourse

1

Reconciling Descriptive and Normative Insights

The study of argumentation has at its core several interrelated concerns. These central concerns include an interest in the process of disputation and an interest in standards of reasonableness underlying this process. While it is possible to pursue an interest in the process of disputation in a purely descriptive way, or to pursue an interest in standards of reasonableness in a purely normative way, we begin this book with the premise that it is better to approach the study of argumentation from a perspective that integrates descriptive concerns with normative concerns. This perspective is intended to overcome the limitations of the exclusively descriptive approach exemplified in contemporary linguistics and discourse analysis and the exclusively normative approach exemplified in modern logic. Modern logicians tend to restrict themselves to nonempirical, or "world-independent," regimentation, while contemporary discourse analysts tend to favor nonprescriptive models of discourse. While normative and descriptive concerns need to be kept straight, it seems to us that neither approach to argumentation is sufficient by itself. In our opinion, the study of argumentation should serve as a *trait d'union*. (For a more elaborate discussion of this view, see van Eemeren 1987a.)

Normative models of argumentation should be applicable to actual practice, and descriptive inquiries should cast light on normative concerns. We believe this integration can occur without reducing normative principles for reasonable discussion to anthropologically relative characterizations, and likewise without pre-figuring the categories and principles of descriptive inquiry in a way that makes them immune to empirical disconfirmation. Our approach, based at once in empirical and critical analysis of discourse, can be seen as one component of a general field of study which we will term "normative pragmatics." While we will have little more to say about normative pragmatics as a field of study, the importance of an approach to argumentation that is responsive to both descriptive and normative interests will be a repeated theme.

We have tried to integrate a commitment to empirically adequate description with a critical stance toward argumentative practice. The primary theoretical device used to accomplish this integration is the concept of a speech act. In our view, speech act performance is a real-world phenomenon whose natural organization is normative. In analyzing discourse as speech act performance, we describe actual practices which are themselves embodiments of underlying standards of reasonableness and rationality. While normative issues are fundamental to discourse phenomena generally, they are especially clear in the study of argumentation.

In this chapter, we briefly review central concepts related to the idea of a speech act and sketch the theoretical stance we take toward speech acts in argumentative discourse. We then describe four theoretical/methodological commitments that characterize our approach and that differentiate it from other contemporary approaches.

Speech Act Rules

Our analytic position takes the utterance in context, rather than the proposition, to be the basic unit of analysis. In uttering a proposition, a speaker is always performing a speech act (Austin 1962; Searle 1969). The focus on speech acts emphasizes the way in which communication is a form of rational action. In communication, speakers use language to do things, that is, to create certain effects by acting on the social world. Part of what is involved in understanding what people mean by what they say is not just a recognition of the expressed propositional content but a recognition of what it is they are trying to do in saying something. In speech act theory, this latter recognition amounts to a recognition of the *illocutionary force* of an utterance (Searle and Vanderveken 1985, 12–26).[1]

This intentional and functional framework of interpretation points to the role of utterances in plans for the achievement of individual and social goals (Cohen and Levesque 1990; Cohen and

Perrault 1979; Jacobs and Jackson 1983). In ordinary speech situations, both speakers and hearers give careful attention to the goals behind what is said, to the apparent requirements for achievement of those goals, and to the potential contribution of the speech act itself to the achievement of the goal.

At the level of broader activities, speech acts can be seen as elements in broader plans. Any particular speech act may play a subordinate role in the pursuit of higher-order goals (see Ferrara 1980; Frentz and Farrell 1976; Levinson 1979; Littman and Allen 1987). The requirements of these broader activities help to establish the suitability, pertinence, and appropriateness of particular speech acts as well as provide a broader context of meaning for the interpretation of any speech act.

The communicative success of an individual speech act can be seen to depend on a plan whereby features of the utterance are integrated with background information in a way that leads to recognition of the force of the utterance.[2] Likewise, both the correct performance of a speech act and the achievement of its intended effects depend on a plan whereby contextual and communicative requirements are satisfied.[3]

In our view, the systematic connection between underlying goals and speech acts as components of plans is what is captured in the notion of "felicity conditions" for speech act performance. In the standard treatment (Searle 1969), a speech act is said to be felicitously performed if the following general conditions hold:[4]

1. *The propositional content condition.* The utterance must express propositional content appropriate to its force. For example, promises must refer to future states, while reports of occurrences must *not* refer to future states.

2. *The essential condition.* Making the utterance must "count" as an expression of a certain objective, within some set of social understandings.

3. *The sincerity condition.* The speaker must actually believe, want, and intend anything represented as believed, wanted, or intended.[5]

4. *The preparatory condition.* The speaker must have adequate justification for undertaking to achieve the underlying objective and must believe that performing the speech act itself will help lead to the achievement of the objective.

We can refer to conditions 1–4 as "generic" speech act conditions.

Any particular speech act type will also have a set of special conditions that are tailored to the practical structure of the underlying objective that characterizes the act type. Requests, for example, under ordinary circumstances have conditions something like the following:

1. Propositional content condition: The utterance makes reference to a future action to be performed by the addressee.
2. Essential condition: Making the utterance counts as an attempt to get the addressee to perform some action.[6]
3. Sincerity condition: The speaker actually wants the addressee to perform the requested action.
4. Preparatory condition: The elements associated with the performance of the action (e.g., time, place, objects) exist; the hearer has the ability to do the action; the hearer is willing to do the action; the hearer would not do the action in the absence of the request (i.e., would not do the action as a matter of course); and there is some good reason to perform the action.

Felicity conditions for other speech act types, including grants of requests, have different specific conditions. For example, the sincerity condition attached to a grant of a request is that the speaker actually intends to perform the action agreed to.

Fitting argumentation into the framework of speech act theory means among other things that there must be felicity conditions for arguing, just as there are felicity conditions for requesting, promising, complaining, and so on. A complete discussion of this point can be found elsewhere (van Eemeren and Grootendorst 1984), so we shall confine ourselves here to a very brief summary. Arguments are conducted by means of speech acts, and they therefore exhibit the properties of speech acts. Having an argument is a kind of speech activity composed of speech acts, while making an argument is the performance of a particular kind of speech act. The making of an argument is a complex speech act made up of simple speech acts (of asserting) but structured at a global level by a set of felicity conditions for the act complex. For pro-argumentation, the conditions are as follows:[7]

1. Propositional content conditions:
   a. The speaker, S, has put forward a standpoint (or opinion), O.
   b. S has advanced a constellation of assertives, $A_1, A_2, \ldots, A_n$, in which propositions are expressed.
2. Essential condition: Advancing this constellation of assertives counts as an attempt by S to justify O to the satisfaction of the

hearer, H, i.e., to convince H of the acceptability of O by means of $A_1, A_2, \ldots, A_n$.

3. Sincerity conditions:

   a. S believes that O is acceptable.

   b. S believes that the propositions expressed in $A_1, A_2, \ldots, A_n$ are acceptable.

   c. S believes that $A_1, A_2, \ldots, A_n$ constitute an acceptable justification of O.

4. Preparatory conditions:

   a. S believes that H will not or does not accept O at face value.

   b. S believes that H will accept the propositions expressed in $A_1, A_2, \ldots, A_n$.

   c. S believes that H will accept $A_1, A_2, \ldots, A_n$ as a justification of O.

   d. S believes that either the propositions expressed in $A_1, A_2, \ldots, A_n$ are not already obvious to H, or $A_1, A_2, \ldots, A_n$ constitute a justification of O that is not already obvious to H, or both.[8]

A parallel set of conditions apply to contra-argumentation. Notice that in our position, speech acts are not restricted to the level of the individual sentences, to which they are exclusively related in Searle's standard theory. Starting from Searlean terminology, argumentation can be described as a complex of illocutionary acts on the sentence level which constitute, as a unit at a higher textual level, the illocutionary act complex of argumentation. On the suprasentential level argumentation is typically connected as a subordinate structure with another more or less complex illocution in which a standpoint is expressed (thus condition 1a).

The act of making an argument along with the other acts that may compose the activity of having an argument can all be usefully understood in terms of the role they play in broader plans and activities. As we shall see in chapter 2, this specification of the felicity conditions for making an argument reflects the broader standards and goals of critical discussion. Part of the theoretical task we face in this chapter can be accomplished by noting that speech act conditions for acts of asserting and arguing are codifications of what speakers are held responsible for defending when engaged in argumentative discourse. But speech act rules do not account in a general sense for speakers' obligations to defend their own speech act performances, that is, to enter into argumentative discourse. The residue of our theoretical task requires the embedding of speech act rules within a set of interactional principles.

Interactional Principles of Cooperation and Alignment

As we suggested earlier, speech act theory articulates normative standards of reasonableness and rationality that are recognized and invoked by natural language users themselves. We believe that the felicity conditions for any given speech act are not simply arbitrary conventions. Speech acts occur in interaction against a backdrop of presumptions and strong expectations that serve as a kind of idealized, abstract model of interactional competence, and felicity conditions reflect the operation of this sense of competence. These presumptions and expectations describe beliefs, wants, and intentions that a speaker *ought to have* as a rational agent acting under typicalized circumstances, with a typicalized stock of knowledge and a functionally restricted system of relevancies.[9] Persons are never perfectly rational agents, but the point is that, within the limits of certain idealized assumptions, they can be seen to be treated as such by their fellow interactants and to be held accountable and critiqueable for failing to act as such.

Perhaps the best known among the theoretical models of these presumptions is Grice's Cooperative Principle: "Make your contribution such as is required, at the stage at which it occurs, by the accepted purpose or direction of the talk exchange in which you are engaged" (1975, 45; see also Grice 1989). Grice takes this principle to embody rational conduct in all manner of cooperative interaction and communication—not just in conversation. And he takes it to embody a guide for action on the part of speakers, a presumption on the part of hearers such that they will assume (within limits) that speakers are acting in accordance with the Cooperative Principle, and an expectation on the part of speakers that hearers will make this presumption.

Grice's statement of the Cooperative Principle is somewhat open to interpretation, but on the basis of his discussion of how it operates in conversation, we can take it to encapsulate at least three distinct, logically ordered presumptions (see Jacobs and Jackson 1983).

At a minimum, interactants are presumed to exhibit *instrumental rationality.* That is, we expect their utterances to be means designed to achieve some end and to be responsive to the requirements of the situation.[10] Thus, the sense of an utterance is to be found in relation to its bearing on some goal attributed to the actor and to its adaptation to perceived circumstance.

Second, the Cooperative Principle assumes more than individual rationality—it further assumes coordination among the activities of individuals. Conversational contributions are presumed to occur within *a system of mutual awareness and mutual dependency.* The notion of cooperation suggests that rational interactants will pursue their own goals by taking into account and being responsive to the goals and plans of others. In this way, the sense of an utterance is to be found in the way in which it aligns with the activities expressed in the utterances of fellow conversationalists.

Third, the Cooperative Principle optimally presumes *joint activity.* People are presumed to be helpful, not just taking account of one another's purposes, but actually taking them up. Ideally, interaction occurs within a reciprocity of perspectives and a consensual agreement of purpose of the sort that Goffman (1959, 10) termed a "working consensus."[11] In this way, the sense of an utterance is to be found in the way in which it contributes to the "accepted purpose or direction of the talk exchange."

Taken by Grice and most discourse analysts to be a prerequisite for rational, joint activity, the Cooperative Principle encompasses certain values (sincerity, efficiency, relevance, and clarity) that give rise to the conversational maxims of Quality, Quantity, Relation, and Manner (Grice 1989, 26–27).

The *Quality Maxim* as formulated by Grice requires speakers to try to make their contributions true, refraining from saying anything believed to be false and avoiding statements for which there are inadequate grounds for belief. The *Quantity Maxim* requires speakers to be as informative as is required for current interactional purposes, but not unnecessarily informative. The *Relation Maxim* requires that contributions be relevant to the accepted purposes of an interaction.[12] And the *Manner Maxim* requires speakers to try to make their contributions clear, avoiding obscurity and ambiguity and seeking brevity and orderliness.[13]

The Gricean maxims of Quality, Quantity, Relation, and Manner, extended from the domain of what is properly *informative* to the domain of what is properly *performative,* can account parsimoniously for both speech act rules and rules for speech act sequences in interaction. Within Grice's theory of communication, speakers behaving cooperatively should design their contributions so as to preserve these values. And cooperative hearers should presume that speakers are behaving cooperatively, and so should work to preserve that assumption by constructing an assumptive context in which the other's conversational acts are maximally cooperative.

Thus, when confronted with an apparently uncooperative utterance, rather than assuming that the speaker is simply saying something pointless, false, vague, or otherwise senseless, the hearer should try to construct an interpretation which would be a cooperative message to communicate. In this sense, the maxims operate as standards for testing the adequacy of possible implicatures. The maxims can be described briefly as a set of requirements that maximally rational language users should observe and should expect from others: be honest, be reasoned, be efficient, be pertinent, and be clear.

The relationship between these maxims and the "generic speech act conditions" should be quite clear. The maxims prohibit speech acts which are insincere, unmotivated, unnecessary, pointless, or incomprehensible. These prohibitions correspond roughly to the various classes of speech act conditions, taking somewhat different meanings for different classes of acts.[14]

The Manner Maxim, the requirement of clarity, corresponds to the so-called recognizability conditions for the performance of speech acts: the propositional content condition and the essential condition (van Eemeren and Grootendorst 1984, 40–42).[15] Clarity requires that the speaker formulate the speech act in such a way that the hearer is able to recognize its communicative force and to establish what propositions are expressed in it.

Clarity does not, of course, require explicitness, but it does require that nonexplicitness—like any other effortful behavior—be motivated by some intelligible objective. Hearers assume that speakers will not make it impossible or unnecessarily difficult to infer their objectives, and they interpret speech acts accordingly. In this way, clarity is linked to a preference for standardized and economical usages. Complexity of expression is assumed to convey a complexity of purpose and/or deviation from normal assumptions about context.

The Quality Maxim has two subcomponents, one having to do with honesty and the other with the reasons one has for believing or wishing something. Both subcomponents are tied to the "correctness conditions": the honesty component to what are normally referred to as sincerity conditions, and the reasonableness component to act-specific preparatory conditions. The implication of the honesty requirement is that the speaker may be held responsible for having undertaken the commitments which are associated with the speech act concerned. In performing a directive ("Close the window"), the speaker may be held responsible for wanting the listener to perform the action referred to in the directive; in performing an assertive ("It is raining"), the speaker may be held responsible for believing that the proposition expressed is true; and so on.

The reasonableness requirement is that the speaker have sufficient reason for believing what is believed, sufficient reason for wanting what is wanted, and sufficient reason for believing that what is intended can in fact be successful in achieving its underlying objective. In the case of assertions, the reasonable speaker must have grounds for believing the assertion to be true; in the case of requests, the reasonable speaker must have a need for the requested act and must believe that the hearer is able to satisfy that need through granting the request.

The Quantity Maxim as ordinarily understood provides for adjustment of how informative to be: enough, but not too much. Cast in performative terms, the maxim would provide for performance of speech acts that are necessary for some plan, but would prohibit speech acts that are without such "motivation." The Quantity Maxim requires efficiency in the use of speech acts. Acts that are necessary for the accomplishment of some objective are generated by the first half of the maxim, and acts that are not needed for the accomplishment of the objective are suppressed by the second half. The preparatory conditions for the complex speech act of argumentation exhibit a duality precisely parallel to the duality of the Quantity Maxim—the first condition suppressing unnecessary argumentation, and the second generating as much support as (apparently) needed. Notice that the performance of the complex speech act of argumentation is unnecessary if the speaker assumes that the listener is already convinced of the standpoint being defended (the first preparatory condition). And the performance is pointless if the speaker assumes in advance that the argumentation will under no circumstances lead the listener to an acceptance of the standpoint (the second and third preparatory conditions).[16]

The Relation Maxim requires that any speech act fit into a framework of rational and cooperative conduct. In terms of a minimal presumption of instrumental rationality, the Relation Maxim calls on any utterance to have a point.[17] In this sense, the Relation Maxim provides for the illocutionary point captured in the essential condition of any speech act. In making an utterance, a speaker is assumed to be performing some type of action. But the Relation Maxim also requires that speech acts contribute to a broader context of activity, as elements in broader plans with higher-order goals. In this sense, speech acts are required to contribute to the coherence of the discourse as a whole.[18] Speech acts should be an appropriate sequel to prior discourse in the sense that the performance of a particular speech act should contribute to the underlying purpose of the exchange as constituted in speech acts already performed. The Relation Maxim, then, provides for *uptake and preservation of open interactional purposes* from one speech act to another, whether the succeeding speech acts involve alternation of participant roles or not.

Relevance in a sequence of speech acts by alternating speakers is notoriously difficult to define in general terms. In part, this is difficult because speech acts are required to be relevant not to prior speech acts but to the purposes and plans constructed by prior speech acts. Moreover, the demands for responsiveness allow for the initiation of structurally subordinate goals and plans that build back into the ongoing activity, for the temporary suspension of current concerns, for the initiation of new purposes upon closure of old purposes, and to shifts to various metapurposes.

However, we can say at least this: If the communicative and interactional goal behind a speech act can be specified, what counts as a relevant response will depend on what can make a difference, one way or another, to the accomplishment of those goals. Every speech act seeks to achieve the communicative effect that the listener understands it, and the interactional effect that the listener accepts it. So the performance of a speech act expressing the fact that another speech act has been understood or accepted will be a relevant reaction. The expression of nonunderstanding or nonacceptance is an equally relevant reaction. Giving reasons as to why something is or is not accepted is also relevant.[19] An appropriate reaction is not necessarily a fitting reaction, let alone the reaction that most closely meets the speaker's wishes or expectations.

It is in some ways even more difficult to say what counts as an appropriate sequel to a speech act of one's own; a sequel appears here not as a subsequent utterance but as a continuation of a single speech composed of multiple simple speech acts. As with alternating contributions, a series of acts by a single speaker must preserve purpose from one act to another in order to be mutually relevant. In general, the same principle governs relevant expansions of a single speaker's act as governs response to that act. Expansions must contribute in some fashion to some identifiable purpose or goal, for example, by securing an act against challenges to its validity. As has been shown by Schegloff, Jefferson, and Sacks (1977), giving reasons for a standpoint is considered to be a perfectly normal "repair" of an utterance in the face of actual or anticipated disagreement, and what can serve as a "reason" depends on the nature of the speech act being performed (Jackson and Jacobs 1980; Jacobs and Jackson 1981, 1982).

The Gricean maxims do much the same work, theoretically, as the generic speech act rules, but the Cooperative Principle itself adds a "driver" for the conversational system. Speakers and hearers are obliged by this principle not simply to follow the maxims but to do what is necessary to preserve cooperativity as a practice and as a presumption. Speakers acting cooperatively must treat any apparent departure from cooperativity as a problem requiring solution: either an interpretive problem or a practical problem. To preserve the Cooperative Principle, interactants must *notice and repair* apparent deviations from the maxims.

As will become clear later, the theoretical apparatus provided by speech act rules and conversational maxims can be specialized to the task of analyzing argumentative discourse by adding a purpose overlay. Supposing that the purpose of a dialogue is *to resolve a disagreement*, we will see that the Cooperative Principle and related notions generate a certain idealized method of discussion. This will be the subject of chapter 2.

Four Core Commitments in the Study of Argumentation

We approach the study of argumentation with four basic premises, each of which represents a point of departure for our approach from other contemporary perspectives on argumentation. These premises are methodological or metatheoretical; although they represent fundamental choices about how to study argumentation, they also both reflect and shape our picture of the object of our study. The four premises form the basis for integrating a descriptive model of argumentation in terms of speech act theories of discourse with a normative model of argumentation as critical discussion. By describing argumentation in terms of the pragmatic structures and functions of speech acts and by grounding the acceptability of argumentation in the problem-solving and conventional validity of the rules of a critical discussion, a concept of reasonable argumentation can be developed that is externalized, socialized, functionalized, and dialectified (van Eemeren and Grootendorst 1984, 7–18).

Externalization

Argumentation is conducted through discourse. It involves more than just a situation in which two parties happen to hold incompatible viewpoints, and it involves more than just a process of personal reasoning. For argumentation to occur, disagreement must be externalized, or at least externalizable: incompatible standpoints must be expressed and brought into confrontation with one another. Or, if not actually expressed and brought into open confrontation, this relation between standpoints must somehow be projected in the discourse. Making an argument pragmatically presupposes a standpoint and at least the potential for opposition to that standpoint. And individuals must submit their standpoints to public certification. In this process people find out whether or not their beliefs make sense and whether or not their reasoning is cogent.

For this reason, we see as incomplete any efforts to reduce argumentation to processes of reasoning or to a structure of attitudes and beliefs. While matters of interpretation, inference, belief, intention, and so on certainly underlie argumentation (in the same way that they underlie *any* discursive activity), their influence upon the way in which argument proceeds is channelized by a system of public commitment and public accountability. What people argue over is not so much the actual positions of the parties but the positions that the parties can be held to have expressed, whether directly or indirectly. And the reasons (motives) people may have for holding a belief are not always the same as the reasons (grounds) they will offer and accept in defense of a claim. These distinctions may form the basis for a great deal of frustration and confusion among arguers, but the distinctions are there. In which ways and to what extent reasoning and argumentation diverge and converge are fascinating questions, but they can be asked only if we keep the two concepts separate.

Socialization

It is possible to view arguments as an externalization of an individual thought process, abstracting coherent elements (i.e., data, warrant, and claim; or major premise, minor premise, and conclusion) from the communicative process in which they occur. This way of viewing arguments is typical of positions which are merely concerned with argument "as product" (see Wenzel 1980, for extended discussion of the distinctions among argument as process, product, and procedure). When argument is viewed as product, the central question becomes one of accounting for how the elements of one party's position hold together to support a point of view.

Our view departs from this individualized perspective. We view argumentation as the externalization of a social problem-solving process. Argumentation is not so much a process whereby a single individual privately draws a conclusion as it is a procedure whereby two or more individuals try to arrive at an agreement. We take the properties of argumentation to reflect a collaborative structure that emerges from dialogic interaction—real or projected. Instead of just searching for how the elements of one party's position hold together, we search for how they call out and respond to the questions, doubts, objections, and counterclaims raised by an antagonist.

The distinction between an individualized perspective on argument and a socialized perspective on argument (akin to the distinction between methodological individualism and methodological socialism) should not be confused with a distinction between two different objects of study. O'Keefe's (1977) "two senses of argument"—argument as something one person makes versus argument as something two or more people have—are both possible objects of study from either an individualized or a socialized perspective. From our point of view, both arguments made and arguments had are seen as social and collaborative, as being jointly authored by protagonist and antagonist.

Central to our approach, then, is the notion of participant roles. Argumentation presupposes two distinguishable positions: that of a protagonist or proponent, and that of an antagonist or opponent. Toulmin's (1958) position seems to us to go part of the distance toward a socialized perspective on argument, in seeing each element of an argument as a response to a possible challenge or query. But the characteristic questions Toulmin associates with each element in his model ("What do you have to go on?" etc.) serve only as an explanation of how the argument hangs together, not as a serious description of opposition. Perelman and Olbrechts-Tyteca's (1958) concept of "universal audience" offers an abstract description of opposition, but without any serious commitment to the collaborative involvement of proponent and opponent in argumentation.[20] A genuinely socialized account of argumentation cannot do without a distinction between the role of the protagonist and the role of the antagonist.

Functionalization

Argument is very often described in structural terms, not only in the study of formal and informal logic, but also in the study of fallacies and other aspects of practical argumentation. Although structural descriptions of argument have much to recommend them, structural analyses tend to ignore the functional motivations and functional requirements that underlie the structural design of an argument.

Our view departs from a strictly structural view of argument by emphasizing the function of argument in managing the resolution of disagreements. An emphasis on the functions of argumentation, and on the interactional processes within which it occurs, allows us both to describe and to evaluate argumentation in relation to its purposes. Argumentation arises in response to or in anticipation of disagreement, and particular lines of justification are fitted to meet the nature of that disagreement. The structure of argumentation, the requirements of justification, and the need for argumentation itself are all adapted to the contexts in which opposition, objections, doubts, and counterclaims arise.

Dialectification

A model of argumentation may be attentive to or indifferent to a set of critical standards for rational judgment. Externalization, functionalization, and socialization create pressures on the analyst to describe argument as it occurs, without regard for how it ought to occur. Dialectification counters this pressure. Viewing argument dialectically means that argumentation should be seen as occurring within a critical discussion. Argumentation is then regarded as a regimented procedure for defending a standpoint against the critical reactions of a rational judge.

The dialectical idea of having a regulated critical discussion grounds the acceptability of a standpoint in a principle of reasonableness that is neither absolutistic nor relativistic. In order to avoid the dangers of absolutism inherent in the geometric approach favored by some logicians and the dangers of relativism inherent in the anthropological approach favored by many rhetoricians, our dialectical approach treats argumentation as part of a critical discussion procedure for resolving differences of opinion. This discussion procedure incorporates elements from the logical as well as the rhetorical approach. (For a discussion of geometric, anthropological, and critical traditions, see Toulmin 1976.)

A critical discussion procedure takes its reasonableness from a two-part criterion: problem-solving validity and conventional (or intersubjective) validity (Barth and Krabbe 1982, 21–22; cf. Crawshay-Williams's [1957, 175] distinction between conventional validity and methodological validity). Problem-solving validity has to do with the efficacy of a procedure for serving its purpose. If the purpose of critical discussion is thought to be resolution of disagreements, then the critical discussion model must be designed in such a way as to lead to efficient resolutions and to avoid obstacles to resolution or "false" resolutions. In chapter 2, we will describe an ideal model of argumentation whose problem-solving validity derives from the incorporation of preconditions and discourse mechanisms tailored to the cooperative search for resolution. Intersubjective validity has to do with the conformity between the model's components and the values, standards, and objectives actual arguers find acceptable. One way to establish the intersubjective validity of such a model is by showing that it is a specialized version of more general principles of cooperation, a topic to which we return in chapter 5.

A commitment to a dialectical approach to argumentation does not necessarily mean that we analyze only those exceptional cases in which there is 100 percent rational and reasonable discussion. What it means is that we distinguish between principles and practices, between rules and regularities. A normative model of argumentation should permit us to define the conditions under which rational judgment can take place. But it should also permit us to see when, how, and why ordinary argument deviates from ideal critical discussion.

Speech Acts and the Four Core Commitments

How does a speech act perspective contribute to the externalization, socialization, functionalization, and dialectification of the subject matter of the study of argumentation?[21] Argumentation is aimed at convincing another person of the acceptability of a standpoint. Both the notions of acceptability and disagreement can be given concrete meaning from within a speech act perspective. Rather than being treated as internal states of mind, these notions can be given externalizable meaning in terms of discursive activities. Disagreement in argumentation expresses itself in the form of an opposition among speech acts interlocked into a joint activity. Acceptance can be conceptualized as the performance of a preferred partner to the arguable act. "Being convinced" can be seen as an undertaking of the commitments entailed by the speech act that is accepted, and acceptance can be seen as the verbal expression of this undertaking.[22]

Speech act theory provides for socialization by emphasizing that the performance of a speech act presupposes a set of preconditions for whose satisfaction the speaker can be held publicly accountable. Although it is often supposed that speech act theory is unsuited to analysis of act sequences, we find that a speech act perspective extended to the interactional and textual level achieves socialization as well, by displaying the ways in which substantive "positions" and "cases" in support of positions are developed and given meaning through the collaborative work of interlocking argumentative roles.

A speech act perspective achieves functionalization by organizing the analysis around the practical context in which the disagreement occurs—around an interactionally emergent specification of what is "at stake." To see that argument occurs through speech act performances—and *over* speech act performances—is to see a "disagreement space" organized with respect to interactional purpose and speech function. In this way, the enthymematic quality of arguments can be explained as following from interactional requirements of quantity which serve to localize argument to those issues thought to be controversial and to discourage unnecessary "proof" (Jackson and Jacobs 1980, 261–64). Likewise, a speech act perspective emphasizes the way in which arguments must contribute to the resolution of a dispute. Fallacies may contain deductively valid arguments (e.g., red herring, straw man, begging the question) that are nevertheless irrelevant because they do not address the basis for disagreement between the parties (see van Eemeren and Grootendorst 1992a, for an extended treatment of fallacies from the perspective of speech acts in critical discussion).

Dialectification is achieved within our speech act perspective through the construction of an idealized activity type defined by idealized argumentative conditions and idealized speech act performance. This idealized activity type constitutes a model of the systematic exchanges of resolution-oriented argumentative moves which we term "critical discussion." The idealization involved in the notion of a critical discussion is in some respects comparable to the way in which Searle's (1969) felicity conditions can be seen as an idealized model of an act type or the way in which Grice's (1975) Cooperative Principle and conversational maxims provide an idealized model of conversational practice. The notion of a critical discussion amounts to an adaptation of conceptions of rational and cooperative activity to the restricted domain of relevance provided by the goal of resolving a difference of opinion according to "the merits." In later chapters we offer a more extensive explanation of critical discussion and the relationship between critical discussion as a model and argumentation as a practice accountable to the model.

Notes

1. Recognition of the illocutionary force of an utterance should not be confused with achievement of the intended perlocutionary effect of an utterance. The relationship here is quite complex, depending upon the kind of speech act in question and the broader purposes of the act, but the distinction should nevertheless be maintained. This is the difference between recognizing that the speaker is trying to get the hearer to do something (e.g., is requesting that the hearer do such and such) and the hearer's actually doing it; or between recognizing that the speaker is trying to

convince the hearer of something (e.g., is asserting such and such) and the hearer's actually being convinced. On a slightly different line, speakers can be heard as trying to apologize (i.e., as intending to express sorrow or regret), without having their apology accepted. And speakers can be recognized as undertaking to place themselves under an obligation to do something (i.e., as promising to do something) but yet have no one depend on them to carry out what they promised to do. Or a different kind of failure can occur when, for example, a speaker who does not have the authority to christen a ship is heard as trying to do so and so fails to actually christen the ship.

2. This kind of planning invokes various "illocutionary force indicator devices" and has led to the problem of so-called indirect speech acts. See Bach and Harnish 1979; Clark 1979; van Eemeren 1987b; Gibbs and Mueller 1988; Perrault and Allen 1980; Searle 1975.

3. The relations among the communicative success of a speech act, the correctness of its performance, and the achievement of its intended consequences are complex. Terminology for these distinctions is not uniform. Van Eemeren and Grootendorst (1984, 40–42) distinguish the first two conditions in terms of recognition and correctness conditions, meaning communicative success and correctness of performance. They then argue for the conventional connection between the illocutionary act of arguing and the perlocutionary act of convincing. Vanderveken (1990) distinguishes the latter two conditions as success and satisfaction conditions, meaning successful performance and satisfaction of intended effects.

4. Subsequent formulations differ in respects not important to our purposes, analyzing the essential condition into illocutionary point, degree of strength of illocutionary point, and mode of achievement (Searle and Vanderveken 1985; Vanderveken 1990).

5. An alternative way to see sincerity is in terms of responsibility and commitment. That is, the requirement of sincerity applies not so much to actual mental states as to pragmatic consistency—the speaker can be held liable for not acting in ways consistent with represented beliefs, wants, and intentions. See van Eemeren and Grootendorst 1984.

6. It should be noted that only rarely is the point of a request to get the hearer to perform some action without consideration of the state of affairs that such an action would bring about. This relation is usually understood in the expression of a request. The "action" thus need be no more specific than "bringing about" some desired state of affairs. Requests are also distinguished by their mode of achievement (Vanderveken 1990). The hearer must have rights of refusal, so that a request is satisfied by virtue of the hearer's deciding to undertake to bring about the requested state of affairs.

7. For a quite different understanding of the relation between speech acts and arguments, see Jacobs 1989.

8. A discussion of most of the items on this list can be found in van Eemeren and Grootendorst 1984, 42–46. Condition 1a is added because it is a pragmatic presupposition of condition 2. Condition 4d is added, following Ferrara's (1980) lead, as an "obviousness" condition akin to Searle's (1969, 1975) treatment. The preparatory condition 4c might also be further extended by taking into account the grounds for *H*'s failure to accept *O* at face

value. To be fully pertinent, S must believe that $A_1, A_2, \ldots, A_n$ will overcome H's grounds for doubting O.

9. See Schutz's (1973, 40–47, 245–59) discussions of rational theorizing in the social sciences as well as Dennett's (1990) discussion of intentional systems as technical refinements of folk psychology.

10. These two aspects of instrumental rationality fit more or less with Schutz's (1973, 69–72) "in-order-to" and "because-of" motives.

11. See also Searle's (1990) discussion of joint intentions and Jacobs and Jackson's (1982) discussion of George Herbert Mead's notion of the social act. This latter, optimal sense of cooperativeness perhaps leads Grice (1975) to question whether or not the Cooperative Principle applies to arguments. It seems to us, however, that while there may be a lack of consensus at one level, at a higher level argumentation as critical discussion can be seen as a cooperative, joint effort to arrive at such a consensus. In this sense, it is optimally cooperative.

12. This often-criticized maxim is really little more than a restatement of the Cooperative Principle itself. Perhaps for this reason Sperber and Wilson (1981) argue for reducing the entire system to a single Principle of Relevance.

13. Searle's (1975) observation that indirect speech acts are more readily inferred from idiomatic or conventionalized usages than from nonidiomatic or unconventional forms can be seen as a special case of the Manner Maxim.

14. For a somewhat different approach to extending Grice's maxims beyond assertives to speech acts generally, see Bach and Harnish 1979, 62–65.

15. Van Eemeren and Grootendorst distinguish between those felicity conditions that describe communicative success and those that describe correct performance of an act. A speech act can be recognized as such, even though its performance does not satisfy sincerity and preparatory conditions. Failure of recognizability conditions results in a misfire; failure of the correctness conditions results in an abuse (Austin 1962). Aspects of some preparatory conditions, however, also seem to enter into the recognition and identification of the speech act being performed. The difference between an argument and an explanation, for example, has to do in part with whether a listener fails to understand or to accept a standpoint. A command differs from a simple request in depending on the authority of the speaker rather than the willingness of the hearer. See also Bach and Harnish's (1979, 55–57) discussion of the difference between success conditions and felicity conditions.

16. Notice also that the Quantity Maxim as applied to the speech act of argumentation also calls for the kind of adjustment discussed in note 8 above. Arguments should be made that are responsive to the grounds the hearer has for doubting a standpoint; arguments that are not responsive to those grounds are superfluous. See Jackson and Jacobs 1980.

17. This reading of the Relation Maxim is suggested by Nofsinger's (1975) submaxim of pertinence.

18. The relevance of a speech act is defined with respect to its contribution to the goals of an overall activity. The coherence of a discourse depends on the relevance of its constituent speech acts. On relevance as a goal-

related concept, see van Eemeren and Grootendorst 1992b, and on the conceptual connection between the relevance of an utterance and the coherence of discourse, see Jackson and Jacobs 1989.

19. Experimental research (Jackson, Jacobs, and Rossi 1987) has shown that the judged relevance of conversational replies is a function of the directness with which the reply addresses the underlying goals.

20. For a discussion of the merits and demerits of Toulmin's and of Perelman and Olbrechts-Tyteca's contributions to the study of argumentation, see van Eemeren, Grootendorst, and Kruiger 1987.

21. For a more elaborate answer to this question, see Grootendorst 1987.

22. For a general discussion of the conventional and rational relation between the illocutionary act of making an argument and the perlocutionary act of convincing, see van Eemeren and Grootendorst 1984, 47–74, and Jacobs 1987, 231–33.

2

A Starting Point for Normative Description

Our project is to give a theoretical explanation of argumentative practices and to create a framework for the criticism and evaluation of those practices. Argumentation has an underlying normative organization, related to commonsense concepts of reasonableness, and our project depends to some extent on our ability to describe this underlying normative organization. However, the development of a model of argumentation which is suitable for criticism and evaluation of practice cannot simply be a process of mirroring the "naive argumentation theories" of ordinary arguers. A perspective must be constructed from which the argumentative conduct subject to those theories may be critically examined. An adequate model of argumentative discourse will draw, at a minimum, on philosophical concepts of rationality and reasonableness and on theoretical understandings of discourse, as well as on empirical analysis of argumentative practices.

In this chapter we build the general framework that informs and motivates the analyses presented in later chapters. We begin by explaining the nature of our project, positioning it within a comprehensive research program in argumentation. Then we present an ideal model of argumentative discourse to be used in later chapters as a normative framework from which to analyze actual argumentative practice.

Five Components of the Study of Argumentation

To give an analysis of argumentation that is both empirically adequate and critically insightful requires a comprehensive research program. On the one hand, a philosophical ideal of reasonableness must be developed that articulates the assumptive framework for a theoretical model of acceptable argumentation. On the other hand, actual argumentative practice must be investigated empirically and compared with the ideal. It may be necessary to develop special analytic instruments to allow a translation between actual interaction and the normative ideal.

To integrate descriptive and normative purposes is a complex problem, and the complexities lead us to construe the study of argumentation as having five interdependent components. A comprehensive program of research in argumentation encompasses a philosophical component, a normative component, an empirical component, an analytic component, and a practical component (van Eemeren 1987a). These components form a framework that encompasses normative and descriptive work.

Philosophical Research: Argumentation and Reasonableness

Various alternative accounts of reasonableness are possible. Our own philosophical orientation reflects a dialectical conception of argumentation. Rather than looking for standards of reasonableness in the substance or form of argument, we locate reasonableness in procedural, goal-oriented standards for the conduct of discussion and the appraisal of substantive reasons and inferential form.[1]

Whether tacitly or reflectively, any analysis of argumentation will imply some philosophical position on reasonableness. If we choose not to confront the problem reflectively, treating argumentation strictly as a user-organized activity, we have adopted a tacit but still specifiable stance toward reasonableness, one which will be recognizable as some form of relativism. One difference between a purely descriptive approach to argumentation and a critical descriptive approach is that the latter calls attention to the need for a standard against which argumentative practice can be judged.

A relativist view of reasonableness centers on the acceptability of argumentation for some particular audience or community. A critical view centers on standards of reasonableness that may or may not coincide with the actual practices in any given case or for any particular community.

Our philosophical position is closer to the second of these alternatives than to the first. We assume that argumentation is to be judged not only in terms of its success in gaining assent but in terms of the "rightness" of the procedures by which this assent is gained. Argumentation considered ideally is not simply a set of practices that happen to settle disputes—that is, to "terminate" the dispute in some way or other—but a set of methodic procedures that enable discussants to really resolve disputes "on the merits."[2] Reasonable argumentation maximizes the opportunity for discussants to do just that. But we are attentive to the possibility that "the merits" may be evaluated by participants in ways that are tied to the practices of a particular social group sharing certain values and background assumptions, and that what merits assent is itself subject to argumentative scrutiny.

Normative Research: Models for Reasonable Argumentation

On the normative level, scholars of argumentation express their ideals of reasonableness by presenting a particular model of what is involved in acting reasonably in argumentative discourse. A normative model presents a picture of argumentation as it *should* or *could* be conducted.

An ideal model aims at providing an adequate grasp of argumentative discourse by specifying, in accordance with a certain philosophical conception of reasonableness, which modes of arguing are acceptable to a rational judge. Such a model serves both analytic and critical functions.

A normative model will specify such things as argumentative roles, argumentative moves, and procedural rules that organize and constrain the conduct of disputation so as to contribute to a resolution of a difference of opinion. Our particular choice has been to develop a model that construes argumentation as a methodical exchange of speech acts among cooperative discussants. We return later to a specification of our theoretical commitments and a sketch of our model.

Empirical Research: Describing Argumentative Practice

On the empirical level, scholars of argumentation describe and explain the actual practices by which people produce, identify, and evaluate argumentative discourse, and they try to identify the factors which influence these practices. Empirical research leads to a descriptive representation in the sense that a picture is presented of argumentation as it is in fact conducted.

Empirical research can be quite diverse in both topic and method. Depending on the theoretical framework, the central empirical questions might range from factors accounting for individual differences in argumentative competence, to principles and practices that organize institutional forums and fields for dispute resolution, to cognitive processes and discourse structures for producing and interpreting arguments. Within a program of research based on speech acts, the most fundamental questions are those having to do with pragmatic structures, in particular, with factors that play a part in the process of accepting (or not accepting) a point of view.

It is important to see that empirical argumentation research is guided by normative concerns as well as by a descriptive theoretical framework. Indeed, many so-called questions of empirical description already have a normative component implicitly built into them (e.g., questions of competence or of possible institutional forums). Without a prior normative framework, descriptive theory runs the risk of allowing superficial, peripheral, or incidental characteristics of argumentation to dominate the analysis. Good empirical research should enable the analyst to address questions of whether or not people are arguing as they should and what factors facilitate or inhibit meeting normative standards.

Likewise, empirical research can provide an important basis for evaluating the validity of normative models of argumentation. Normative models can be evaluated against the two criteria of problem-solving validity and conventional validity mentioned in chapter 1. Both concepts of validity have empirical implications. Problem-solving validity depends on the adequacy of the model as a description of effective practice—its ability to discriminate good argumentation from poor. To the extent that actual argumentative practice follows the standards of a normative model but results in intuitively questionable procedures or to the extent that actual argumentative practice departs from the standards but results in intuitively acceptable procedures, we should be skeptical of the model's problem-solving validity.

Conventional validity depends on the fit between the model and accepted notions of reasonableness, rationality, and so on. To the extent that actual discussants can be shown to reject the standards of the model or to accept other standards, we should be skeptical of the model's conventional validity.

Analytic Research: Reconstructing Argumentative Discourse

The reconstructive component of a general program of argumentation research is concerned with the analysis of particular argumentative texts in their own right. Here, actual argumentative practice is held up to critical scrutiny in terms of the standards of a normative model. Analytic research assesses the individual case in light of argumentation theory rather than assessing normative or descriptive models in light of empirical cases or inducing from particular cases a general pattern or principle.

In a dialectical analysis like ours, which hinges on reconstructing argumentative discourse as an attempt to counter doubt regarding the acceptability of a standpoint, an attempt is made to provide insight into the aspects of the discourse which are relevant to the resolution of the dispute. A central problem for critical analysis (both for particular cases and in general) is how to reconstruct argumentative discourse for the purposes of the analysis without distorting the nature of the phenomena to be analyzed. Not all of what occurs in argumentative discourse will be relevant to our critical interests. Actual argumentative discourse often requires substantial interpretation and transformation before the argumentative content can be recovered.

Reconstruction of argumentative discourse aims for a normative description, one that can be defended empirically while being useful critically. The task of reconstruction is to recover from discourse its underlying argumentative organization (i.e., to find the elements to which the standards and categories of the ideal model apply), but to do so without constructing a self-confirming artifact.

Practical Research: Improving Argumentative Practice

Practical research in argumentation is aimed at implementing philosophical, theoretical, empirical, and analytic insight within argumentative practice. It is designed to empower ordinary discussants to engage in argumentation that more closely approximates ideal standards. The guiding question is how one can methodically improve argumentative practice, whether through improvement of individual competencies or through alteration of the social and institutional conditions for argumentation.

As will become clear, the approach taken in practical research depends directly on the theoretical perspective from which research is conducted. Our theoretical perspective directs our practical interests in two directions. The first direction is individual-level; its thrust is the elevation of individual competence through development of a discussion-minded attitude. The second direction is social- or institutional-level; its thrust is the development and examination of means by which social structures can constrain argumentative practice for good or ill.

These five components are tightly interwoven. Not only does the approach taken to one task depend upon the approach taken to other tasks, but the tasks themselves overlap and interpenetrate. In the chapters that follow, all five components are addressed in one fashion or another, though rarely one at a time. In the remainder of this chapter, we sketch a model of ideal argumentative discussion that is an embodiment of our philosophical commitments, a result of our normative theorizing, a companion to our empirical research, a constraint on our analytic research, and a foundation for our practical research.

An Ideal Model of Argumentative Discourse

Argumentation is a special sort of disagreement-regulating mechanism, related in various structural and functional ways to a wide range of other activities involving conflict and disputation. Seen in terms of critical discussion, argumentation differs from other ways of handling disagreement in that it seeks not mere acquiescence or mere settlement but resolution of the dispute. Let us begin by trying to design a discursive system for the resolution of disputes. Such a system amounts to an ideal model for disagreement-resolution, one important function of which is to allow us to examine actual disputation practices critically for suitability to this presumed function.

A system built for resolution of disputes must operate in such a way as to satisfy both parties to the dispute. A system that results in mere settlement of a dispute (e.g., through externally imposed choice of one position over another) does not *resolve* the disagreement but only ends the discussion of the disagreement. Any resolution-oriented system is structured in such a way as to assure that if it comes to any settlement at all, the settlement is one recognized by both parties as correct, justified, and rational. Hence, one characteristic of the ideal model is an unlimited opportunity for further discussion; an ideal system does not constrain the possibilities for expansion of a discussion. In a resolution-centered system, there is no judge other than the participants themselves; it is they who must decide when one position or another is no longer tenable. Another characteristic of the ideal model is symmetry in the argumentative status of the participants; whatever rights and responsibilities are assigned to the advocate are also assigned to the adversary. No participant should be restricted in exploring available standpoints or the basis for competing standpoints. Any decision concerning the merits of a standpoint should be a consensus decision, not one based on differential authority, status, or power.

The term "critical discussion" denotes this ideal system (elaborated more fully in van Eemeren and Grootendorst 1984). The critical discussion model is a theory of how discourse would be structured if it were purely resolution oriented. It is not a theory of how discourse *is* structured, nor is it a claim about what functions are or are not pursued in actual argumentation. Nevertheless, it plays an important role in the analysis of actual argumentation, as we will shortly see.

Stages in Resolving a Dispute

An ideal system for resolution of disputes must be capable of (1) identifying disagreements; (2) establishing agreements between two parties as to the means by which the disagreement will be settled; (3) providing for indefinite exploration of the merits of the competing positions, as needed; and (4) ending with either a resolution of the disagreement or a mutual recognition that no agreement is (currently) attainable. These four subtasks to be managed by the model can be considered stages in an ideal argumentative discussion, though it should be stressed that the stages are ordered only logically, not necessarily temporally. The second stage presupposes the first, the third presupposes the second, and the fourth presupposes the third; but actual discussion may or may not make an overt pass through these stages, and even if it does, it may repeatedly double back for another pass.

We call these four stages the confrontation stage, the opening stage, the argumentation stage, and the concluding stage. (See van Eemeren and Grootendorst 1984 for a complete discussion of argumentation stages.) In the *confrontation stage,* the disagreement is identified through some form of expression: it becomes clear that there is a standpoint which meets with doubt or contradiction. The confrontation stage—which is nothing more than a kind of affirmation that two parties disagree about something—can obviously have all sorts of sequels, ranging from a coercive imposition of one party's views on the other to a passive acceptance of the fact that there is disagreement.

In the *opening stage,* the parties try to find out whether there is sufficient common ground to make resolution-oriented discussion profitable. This common ground will include not only shared background assumptions concerning facts and values but also a sort of social contract consisting of argumentative obligations and procedural agreements as to the manner in which the discussion is to be conducted. In essence, participants must agree that there is some hope of resolving the disagreement through discussion and must enter into a cooperative search for resolution within a set of shared expectations about the way the search will be conducted. Assuming that the initial conditions are found to hold, one party indicates preparedness to defend the standpoint at issue, thus taking on the role of protagonist; the other party indicates preparedness to respond critically, thus taking on the role of antagonist.[3]

In actual argumentative dialogue, participants may repeatedly cycle back through this opening stage as deviations from procedure are identified and repaired, or as participants otherwise find the need to discuss how to proceed. Such a possibility is essential to the possibility for reasonable discussion—there must be the possibility for self-correction, not simply for the purposes of achieving consensus at the substantive level of differences of opinion, but also at the pragmatic level of procedural moves. In this sense, the opening stage can be seen as representing both a "repair" function and a reflexively open possibility of metadiscussion.

In the *argumentation stage*, argumentation is advanced and reacted to. The protagonist adduces arguments for the purpose of overcoming doubts about the standpoint. If not yet wholly convinced of part or all of the protagonist's argumentation, the antagonist elicits new argumentation from the protagonist, and so on. As a consequence, the protagonist's argumentation can vary from extremely simple to extremely complex, so that the argumentation structure of one argumentative discourse may be much more complicated than that of the next. An important feature of the ideal model is that it describes a mechanism that can be applied recursively; each contribution to the discussion can become the subject of disagreement and further argumentation. There is no prior limit on the depth or breadth of the discussion.

The *concluding stage* fixes the outcome of the discussion: either a resolution or a decision that no resolution can be reached. Resolution requires that both parties come to agreement; this means either that the protagonist withdraws the challenged standpoint or that the antagonist withdraws the objections to the standpoint. Only if both parties can agree on the outcome can the dispute really be regarded as having been resolved. In principle, discussion can continue indefinitely, delving ever deeper into the bases for the difference of opinion. In practice, a difference of opinion may not be resolvable within the limits of what is currently known or within the limits of the participants' own perspectives. In such cases, the concluding stage marks not the resolution of the dispute but the recognition that no resolution is (currently) possible.[4] Because participants always have the right to explore further the basis for their standpoints in light of new arguments and evidence, any resolution is always tentative, for all practical purposes, and relative to the considerations raised in that discussion. After the concluding stage has been completed, the discussion of the standpoint at issue is over. But this does not mean that the same discussants cannot embark upon a new discussion. This new discussion may relate to a more or less drastically altered version of the same dispute or to a quite different dispute, and the discussants' roles may switch or may be the same. Likewise, more limited discussions can be embedded within a broader dispute, in which case the four stages may be reproduced in miniature.

Distribution of Speech Acts

Within these four stages of discussion, what sorts of communicative acts would be ideally suited to the resolution of disagreement? It is easy to say what sorts of acts are unsuited to resolution. One thing that is clear is that a disagreement in views cannot be resolved through strategies that end a discussion without mutual consent. Commands, threats, and similar sorts of acts are thus rather clearly unsuitable. Likewise, the mutual consent must be based on the merits of the case, not on the participants' personal stake in any particular standpoint. So various commissives having to do with offers, bargains, and bribes will likewise be unsuitable to critical discussion. Resolution, in contrast, depends on some collaborative exploration of the grounds for competing viewpoints, so the most central argumentative functions will be seen to be dependent on acts of asserting.

An amended version of Searle's (1976) taxonomy of the types of speech act is taken as the starting point (see also Searle and Vanderveken 1985; Vanderveken 1990). The classification divides speech acts into five types: assertives, directives, commissives, expressives, and declaratives. We consider each type and examine how acts of each type might contribute to the resolution of a difference of opinion.

All acts within the general class of *assertives* have the common characteristic that they commit the speaker to recognizing the acceptability of a proposition: to believing the proposition and defending it if necessary. Asserting is the prototype for this class, but other acts such as claiming, affirming, negating, objecting, predicting, supposing, and opining function similarly within an argumentative discussion. Different types of assertives may vary in terms of the strength of belief expressed or the definiteness of the commitment to defend. As noted before, assertives are central to argumentation, not only as conveyances for standpoints, but also as the means by which arguers put forward the grounds for their standpoints.

Directives are characterized by an attempt to get the listener or reader to do something or refrain from doing something. Included in this class are requests, commands, questions (information requests), threats, prohibitions, and the like. However, not all directives are appropriate within such a discussion.[5] Where directives occur within a critical discussion, their role must be either to challenge a standpoint, to request argumentation in defense of a standpoint, or to request information so as to clarify some issue. A critical discussion does not contain directives such as orders and prohibitions. Neither can the party that has advanced the standpoint be challenged to do anything else than give argumentation for his or her standpoint.

The defining feature of *commissives* is that they commit the speaker or writer to do something or refrain from doing something. Examples are offers and promises. In critical discussion, commissives fulfill the roles of accepting the standpoint, accepting the challenge to defend the standpoint, accepting the argumentation, deciding to start a discussion, agreeing to take on the role of protagonist or antagonist, agreeing on the rules of discussion, and, if relevant, deciding to begin a new discussion. Some of the required commissives can be performed only in cooperation with the other party.

Expressives are characterized by expression of feelings. They include such acts as airing one's fears, gratitude, joy, sorrow, or grief. Expressives play no part in critical discussion; this is not to say that they do not occur, but only that they are not argumentatively relevant acts. They do not create any commitments for the speaker or writer which are directly relevant to the resolution of a dispute; the mere expression of feelings cannot be an argument in support of a standpoint. Avowals of feelings are neither true nor false, only sincere or insincere. They differ from the actual assertion that one has certain feelings. Such feelings can be relevant to a standpoint only by way of some asserted connection.[6]

Declaratives are acts performed in specific institutionalized contexts to bring a state of affairs into being. Examples are christening, marrying, divorcing, naming, and so on. One subclass of declarative-like speech acts are "usage declaratives": speech acts such as definitions, precizations, amplifications, and explications whose purpose is to facilitate or increase the listener's or reader's comprehension of other speech acts. Although declaratives play an important part in institutionalized forms of argumentation such as court proceedings, they play only a limited role in a system designed for resolution. Declaratives function to terminate argumentation, not to resolve a difference of opinion, because they depend on an authoritative pronouncement by someone uniquely entitled to perform the declarative. Within a critical discussion aimed at resolution, the only declaratives with any positive contribution are the usage declaratives, which can be used to announce what a speaker is going to mean in using some expression or to clarify what a speaker meant in having used some expression. Usage declaratives prevent unnecessary discussions about spurious "verbal" disputes from arising, or real disputes from terminating in spurious resolutions. They can occur at any stage of the discussion (and they can be requested at any stage).

To sum up: In an ideally structured, resolution-oriented discussion, all kinds of assertives can be used to express standpoints and argumentation and to establish the results of the discussion; directives are suitable only for challenging somebody to defend a standpoint and for requesting argumentation in support of a standpoint; commissives are used to accept a standpoint or argumentation and to agree upon the division of dialectical roles and upon the discussion rules; and language usage declaratives are helpful in avoiding misunderstandings. Restricted are certain uses of directives and commissives; prohibited are expressives and declaratives other than usage declaratives. The distribution of these various act types across subtasks in critical discussion is shown in table 2.1, where acts appropriate to each functional stage are listed.

Higher-Order Conditions

The system described above assumes that certain conditions hold. Together with an appropriate set of rules for conducting a critical discussion, the system defines a discussion procedure ideally suited to the resolution of a difference of opinion.[7] It is not, of course, a model of any actual phenomenon; the system presumes ideal participants and ideal conditions along the lines discussed in chapter 1. In fact, the system assumes at least two levels of "higher-order" conditions that would have to hold in order for the system to lead to resolution. Let us think of the ideal discussion procedure as a "code of conduct" for rational discussants. What sort of people could adopt

Table 2.1 Distribution of Speech Act Types Across Functional Stages in Discussion

Stage in Discussion	Speech Act Type
Confrontation	
1.1	expressing standpoint (assertive)
1.2	accepting or not accepting standpoint (commissive)
Opening	
2.1	challenging to defend standpoint (directive)
2.2	accepting challenge to defend standpoint (commissive)
2.3	deciding to start discussion; agreeing on discussion rules (commissive)
Argumentation	
3.1	advancing argumentation (assertive)
3.2	accepting or not accepting argumentation (commissive)
3.3	requesting further argumentation (directive)
3.4	advancing further argumentation (assertive)
Concluding	
4.1	establishing the result (assertive)
4.2	accepting or withholding acceptance of standpoint (commissive)
4.3	upholding or retracting standpoint (assertive)
(Any stage)	
5.1	requesting usage declarative (directive)
5.2	defining, precizating, amplifying, etc. (usage declarative)

such a code? In what situations would such a code be possible? As we will see later, we can explain real-world departures from ideal structures by reference to real-world constraints.

When we consider the ideal discussion procedure as a code of conduct for persons who wish to resolve a disagreement by means of discussion, we have in mind an idealized set of attitudes and intentions. The code of conduct presumes, most basically, that both parties wish to resolve, and not merely to settle, the disagreement. If we think of the code itself as a set of "first-order" conditions for the rational resolution of disagreements, we can think of the presupposed attitudes and intentions of the arguers as "second-order" conditions.[8]

The first-order conditions, if satisfiable, provide certain guarantees against things that could go wrong in the search for a resolution to a disagreement. For example, the first-order conditions assure that both parties to a dispute will have unlimited opportunity to cast doubt on standpoints and that both parties to a dispute will be obliged to respond to such doubts.

The second-order conditions correspond, roughly, to the psychological makeup of the arguer. These conditions stand outside the discourse as constraints on the way it is conducted. Second-order conditions include internal states of arguers having to do with their motivations to engage in critical discussion. The sincerity conditions for making an argument are specific manifestations of these sorts of conditions. Although such states can be represented, asserted, or expressed in discourse, they are not contained in discourse. They are pragmatic preconditions for such discourse. Second-order conditions also include dispositional characteristics of arguers having to do with their abilities to engage in critical discussion.

Second-order conditions require that participants be disinterested in the outcome of the discussion, in the sense that they are willing in principle to give up a position if it is shown to be indefensible or if a competing position is shown to be more defensible. An ideal participant has no stake in the outcome; considerations of gain and loss, winning and losing, are irrelevant if the objective is to resolve the disagreement "on the merits." Second-order conditions require that participants be able to reason validly, to take into account multiple lines of argument, to integrate coordinate sets of arguments, and to balance competing directions of argumentation. The ideal model assumes skill and competence in the subject matter under discussion and on the issues raised. In principle, an ideal participant will not exclude potential arguments from considerations because of difficulties in analysis and evaluation; sophistication, complexity, and subtlety of an argument should not be negative considerations against considering that argument.

Abilities and motivations are interrelated in complex ways. Defects in motivation may reflect various sorts of constraints on ability. For example, failure to maintain an impartial point of view may reflect difficulties in decentering from one's own concerns and taking the perspective of other parties. To a certain extent, heightened motivation can offset limited abilities to, say, follow complex arguments or to engage in impartial reflection on the issues. The important thing to see about second-order conditions is that in order to fulfill the first-order condition, which says that parties must not prevent each other from advancing viewpoints or casting doubt on viewpoints, the people concerned must, among other things, have a second-order discussion attitude that involves the willingness and ability to express their opinions, to listen to the opinions of others, and to change their own opinions when these fail to survive critical examination.

But there are still higher-order conditions. Not only must participants be willing and able to enter into a certain attitude, they must be enabled to claim the rights and responsibilities associated with the argumentative roles defined by the model. To say that in an ideal discussion everyone should have the right to advance his or her view to the best of his or her ability is to presuppose a surrounding sociopolitical context of equality and an overall parity in psychophysiological capacities. The ideal model assumes symmetry in the status of the participants; neither party can be dependent, subordinate, or inferior.[9]

Likewise, the ideal model assumes the absence of practical constraints on matters of presumption in standpoints or time allowed for deliberation. The goal of resolution of differences "on the merits" is incompatible with situations in which one standpoint or another may enjoy a privileged position by virtue of representing the status quo or being associated with a particular person or group. Presumption is a matter to be decided in the opening stage of discussion, not a matter to be imposed on a discussion. Similarly, practical demands such as the need to come to a decision now or an artificial limitation on the range of standpoints available for consideration will restrict the principle of open exploration of possible standpoints and the grounds for those standpoints.

Where first-order conditions represent constitutive elements of a code of conduct aimed at the resolution of disputes, the second-order conditions refer to a "discussion-minded" attitude and an argumentative competence. The third-order conditions stress the importance of political ideals such as nonviolence, freedom of speech, and intellectual pluralism as well as practical constraints and resources for empowering critical discussion.[10]

It should be noted that, for the purposes of critical evaluation, many though not all of these higher-order conditions have a moral or ethical dimension to them. Thus, we ordinarily hold people responsible for holding certain attitudes and values, and for having certain purposes and intentions. We require of people that they have the proper motivations in a way that we do not apply to deficits in ability. Likewise, we hold people responsible for "taking advantage of the situation" when that is a decision that is under their control. For example, we view differently distortions of critical discussion arising from an explicit appeal to power (threats) or authority (declarations) compared with distortions arising from simple perceptions of power or authority imbalances. And we can hold institutions responsible for guaranteeing certain third-order conditions (e.g., political and social rights), but not necessarily others (e.g., constraints due to time or presumption).

Ideal Model and Actual Practice

When analyzing argumentative discourse, the normative ideal of a critical discussion serves as a kind of template against which experience can be compared and a kind of standard against which it can be judged. As we will see, actual human interaction is not "naturally" resolution oriented. People involved in disagreement are not normally disinterested in the outcome but have a heavy interest in one outcome or another. They do not generally enter into discussion willing to subject all of their thinking to debate but treat certain things as so fundamental as to be beyond challenge. They have deficiencies of skill. They argue within social conditions that virtually assure some degree of inequality in power and resources. And the same circumstances that often give rise to argument also place practical demands for settlement and practical constraints on the ability to truly resolve disagreement. Actual argumentative practices are shaped by these constraints, and institutions developed to control argumentation are built to overcome or compensate for these constraints. This will be a guiding theme throughout the book.

The model exists as an abstraction, a theoretically generated system for ideal resolution-oriented discussion. Actual practices are not described by such a model, but certain of their features can be given interesting explanations in terms of the model. The model can provide a framework for interpreting and reconstructing the argumentative features of actual discourse, whether dialogic or monologic. It can provide a framework for the evaluation of argumentative conduct and can serve as a standard for guiding improvement in the practice of argumentation.

Notes

1. Looking for standards of reasonableness in the substance of arguments corresponds to the rhetorical emphasis on grounding proofs in "good reasons" (Fisher 1978; Wallace 1963). Looking for standards of reasonableness in the form of arguments corresponds to the logical emphasis on formal validity of propositional structures (Copi 1965, 2–4). See Wenzel's (1980) discussion of three views of argument.

2. *Settling* a dispute means that the difference of opinion is simply set

aside or is suspended, temporarily or forever. This can be done in ways ranging from more to less civilized (calling in a referee, ombudsman, judge, or arbiter; compromising; tossing a coin; or fighting it out). A dispute is *resolved* only if the doubt about the standpoint expressed by one party is retracted because the argument offered to support it is convincing or if the other party withdraws the standpoint by virtue of realizing that it cannot stand up to the criticism leveled against it (see van Eemeren and Grootendorst 1992a, 34).

3. To doubt a standpoint is not necessarily to adopt a standpoint of one's own. The role of antagonist, however, can easily coincide with the role of protagonist of another—and contrary—standpoint. In that case the dispute and the discussion are "mixed."

4. See Fogelin's (1985) notion of "deep disagreements" and Woods's (1990) "standoffs of force five." It may not even be possible for participants to "agree to disagree," in which case the possibility of any sort of conclusion becomes extremely problematic. For more on this possibility, see chapter 7.

5. It is not clear, either, that any utterance that counts as some sort of assertive is an acceptable move in a critical discussion. Insisting, for example, seems to imply a degree of commitment that may foreclose openness to rebuttal. Likewise, a criticism, while classified as an assertive by Searle and Vanderveken (1985), is an act whose point can be to express disapproval of the addressee—which is exactly the sort of thing that can sidetrack a discussion (see Jacobs, Jackson, Stearns, and Hall 1991).

6. This observation has implications for problems of reconstruction. See the discussion of a parallel case for commissives in example 5.1 in chapter 5.

7. For a discussion of the rationale for the rules in terms of their problem-solving and conventional validity and a discussion of the rules themselves, see van Eemeren and Grootendorst 1988, 1989.

8. Cf. Barth and Krabbe's (1982, 75) distinction between discussion rules which are rational of the first order and discussion-promoting rules which are rational of the second order.

9. Although Habermas's (1970, 1979, 1981) ideal of consensus in a speech situation of communication unimpaired by power relations rests on philosophical starting points that are different from our own, in some respects his ideal is not dissimilar to ours. In view of our Popperian conception of intellectual doubt and criticism as the driving force of progress, however, we eventually seek not consensus but a continual flow of ever more advanced opinions.

10. The reader will no doubt recognize this classification of higher-order conditions as corresponding, roughly, to Heider's (1953) discussion of a naive theory of action as involving personal force (effort and ability) and environmental force (difficulty). There are other ways to organize the factors influencing the success and failure of actions. Not a great deal hinges on this particular set of differentiations, but it is a useful expository tool. For example, from a slightly altered framework, it might be useful to distinguish fourth-order conditions which relate to normal input and output conditions (as Searle [1969] calls them), specifying among other things that, for analytic purposes, the basic model of a critical discussion situation

assumes that people have a normal communicative capacity and are in a physical situation that allows the transmission of interpretable signals. Nonfulfillment of these conditions, however, would affect communication in general, not just argumentation, and therefore these conditions can be left out here.

3

Principles and Procedures for Normative Reconstruction

For many, the raison d'être of argumentation studies is the critical analysis of argumentative discourse—the interpretation and evaluation of actual cases of argumentation in light of normative standards for argumentative conduct. This interest is certainly deeply implicated in the other components of argumentation research; it provides a substantive grounding for philosophical and normative research and gives direction to empirical and practical research.

A central problem for critical analysis is how to represent argumentative discourse in a way that is both relevant to the interests of normative analysis and faithful to the intentions and understandings of the ordinary actors who produce the discourse. Critical analysis of argumentative discourse is always a confrontation between the ideal and the real. Actual practice is evaluated against a normative standard, and the adequacy of the current version of this standard is simultaneously tested for its "problem validity." In this chapter, we provide a framework for conceptualizing the process of representating complex dialogue, and we discuss some methods that may be used to extract standpoints and lines of argument in support of those standpoints.

Normative Reconstruction

We use the term "reconstruction" to refer to a representation of discourse fashioned to fit a specific analytic perspective. Any reconstruction of argumentative discourse approaches a text in terms of a particular viewpoint and is motivated by a particular interest. Analytic reconstruction always takes place in terms of a theoretical framework that concentrates on certain aspects of the discourse to the exclusion of other aspects. While an analytic reconstruction of argumentation is not really a "coding" of individual utterances, it is similar to coding in that it represents discourse in a way that highlights various features of the discussion process to the exclusion of other features.

The form of reconstruction most suitable for our theoretical purposes is one which orients to disagreement resolution, making more visible those things relevant to the resolution of the disagreement. The ideal model serves as a heuristic tool for a systematic resolution-oriented reconstruction of the various relevant speech acts and stages in an argumentative discourse (van Eemeren and Grootendorst 1990), allowing for an abstraction from actual discourse to the "case" offered in support of a standpoint. To reconstruct an argumentative discourse as a critical discussion is to construct a model or representation of that discourse *as if it were* a critical discussion. That is, textual structure, propositional content, pragmatic functions, and so on are all imputed to the discourse with reference to what would be relevant to the resolution of the dispute.

Ordinarily, the primary interests of a normative reconstruction of argumentative discourse are to recover the propositions that make up the substance of the arguments, to determine how the arguments are used to justify or refute the standpoints at issue, and to examine how the performance of speech acts can function at a particular stage of discussion to help resolve a dispute.[1] Normatively reconstructing the discourse enables the analyst to see better how these functions might be performed and to evaluate the discourse against a normative standard.

Interpretive Problems in Reconstruction

When analyzing everyday argumentation, the analyst faces the obvious problem that little in actual everyday discourse directly corresponds to the ideal model of critical discussion. From the point of view of ideal argumentative conduct, much remains unsaid in ordinary discourse. For example, a speaker or writer does not often state explicitly the purpose of his or her contribution, and new stages in the discussion are hardly ever announced explicitly. Likewise, argumentative roles, presumptions, procedures, and similar matters are usually taken for granted rather than explicitly discussed.

Or again, any variety of utterances and forms of expression may serve as paraphrases for one another, in effect repeating the same point. Argumentation may occur by means of speech acts quite different from those envisioned by the ideal model of critical discussion, as standpoints may be introduced through offers or expressives; arguments may be made by questioning, taunting, or complaining; acceptance may come in the form of a grant or a thank you. And much else goes on besides argumentation. A variety of acts, activities, and aspects of expression may occur throughout an argumentation that are designed to pursue goals, topics, and concerns that are only incidentally related to the purpose of rationally resolving a difference of opinion.

Despite all of this, it may still be intuitively apparent that argumentation is taking place in a way that functions more or less along the lines of critical discussion. We would not want to say that argumentation is not occurring or that it is somehow defective just because what is said and done does not openly, directly, and completely correspond to an ideal model of critical discussion. But then again, neither should the discourse be reconstructed in a way that overinterprets its argumentative potential. Normative reconstruction is not simply a blindly optimistic force-fitting of ideal categories onto actual conduct. After all, much of the point of critical analysis is to evaluate whether or not and to what degree actual argumentative conduct lives up to ideal standards.

Here, then, is the problem for normative reconstruction. The reconstruction should highlight and recover our intuitions about how the discourse can be seen to have an argumentative function, but it should maintain a sensitivity to the way in which any argumentative potential in the discourse is communicated. Reconstruction must identify the components and lay out the structure of the argumentation in a way that makes the discourse susceptible to critical tests for validity and acceptability. At the same time, it should provide a comparative basis for exposing and evaluating defects in the actual conduct of the argumentative discourse as it has occurred.

Empirical Grounding for Reconstruction

How do we justify reconstructing a discourse in a way that more openly and clearly fits the ideal model of argumentation through critical discussion? Part of the justification for any reconstruction is empirical. That is, the reconstruction imputes structures, functions, and content to the discourse that the participants themselves and natural-language users in general intuitively recognize. In other words, the analyst's representation is meant to call attention to features of the discourse to which natural-language users themselves orient, and which they expect others to recognize. Part of the job of arguing for the acceptability of a reconstruction involves assembling evidence that the reconstruction is "intersubjectively" valid. Consider the exchange in example 3.1 that occurs when two Mormon missionaries (M1 and M2) come to visit at the home of a non-Mormon (L).[2]

There are several empirically grounded claims that can be made about the argumentative structure, function, and content of this exchange, claims that go beyond simply repeating what is openly and directly said. For example, we can see that the content of the claim summarized in 01 (that the Mormon church is different from other churches because Mormons believe everyone must be baptized) is not offered simply as information that is interesting in its own right, but is offered to provide an argument for accepting the higher-order standpoint that Mrs. Lee should convert to the Mormon faith. Likewise, we can see that Mrs. Lee's response in 02 is not an act of affiliation and agreement but is an argument for rejecting M1's higher-order standpoint.

A primary grounding for these claims comes from ethnographic evidence. This dialogue occurs in the context of a visit by Mormon missionaries to the home of a non-Mormon. There is an unstated purpose to such visits that permeates the ensuing discussions: proselytization, aiming for conversion to the Mormon faith. Even where that is not the immediate intention of the missionary, most recipients of these visits treat what is said as having some relevance to an underlying standpoint to the effect that the recipient should convert to the Mormon faith. That, presumably, is what hinges on the issue of whether and how the Mormon church differs from other churches. The missionaries need to establish some reason to switch churches, and that reason would most naturally be found in a difference between the churches.

This ethnographic background also allows us to see the questioning in 03, 05, 07, and 09 as an effort to elicit premises that might be used to build arguments to reestablish this higher-order standpoint. That is, we have reason to believe that when M1 asks, "Uh, well what do you believe?" he has not abandoned his initial purpose or standpoint in order to elicit information for some newly emergent purpose—as we might infer if this were simply a casual "get to

Example 3.1

(M1 is responding to Mrs. Lee's question of how the Mormon church differs from other churches. M1 has just finished explaining that "Mormons believe that everyone must be baptized.")

01 M1:   Okay?   So there's one- one difference.   ((Pause))   Okay?
         We believe every-
         [

02 L: My church believes that too.

         ((Pause))

03 M1:   Uh, well what do you believe?

         ((Pause))

04 L: I don't believe that.

05 M1:   You don't believe the Bible?

         ((Pause))

06 L: No:- not- ((Pause)) Well I don't believe that uh, uh,
         uh, put into the context of our times that that's true.

07 M2:   Wellll, does Jesus Christ change from age to age? Does
         he change?

         ((Pause))

08 L: The world has changed.

09 M2:   Does Jesus Christ change?

10 L: No, but that doesn't mean that the meaning of his words
         doesn't.

11 M2:   *Oh*, but it does.

12 L: Uh- Heh-heh-heh ((Nervous giggle))

13 M2:   Mrs. Lee, I think you need to find out what you believe,
         first of all.   ((Pause))   You've got to find out- reach
         down inside of yourself and find out what you believe.
         'Cause it sounds like you're not even sure of what you
         believe yourself.

know you" visit in which reciprocal self-disclosure were the expected pattern.[3]

We can also reconstruct from the text certain propositions that are implicated but not expressed. For example, turn 05 ("You don't believe the Bible?") communicates the unexpressed premise that the Bible says that everyone must be baptized and claims in effect that when Mrs. Lee says that she does not believe that everyone must be baptized, she is committing herself to claiming that the Bible says something that is not true. The reconstruction of this unexpressed information illustrates a different source of empirical grounding: knowledge of conventional structures and strategies of discourse. At least part of this inference is warranted by the patterning of cohesive devices in turns 01 through 05 (Halliday and Hasan 1976). Specifically, in 04, Mrs. Lee uses an anaphoric pro-term together with a parallel sentence construction to refer back to M1's cutoff claim in 01: "We believe every[one must be baptized]." In 04 "that" replaces "everyone must be baptized." Then in 05 M1 again uses the cohesive device of parallel construction ("you don't believe" paralleling "I don't believe") to create a frame for highlighting an anaphoric substitution: "the Bible" substitutes for "that" in this slot, which was a substitution for "everyone must be baptized." The cohesive devices, then, signal the following equivalence: to deny "I believe everyone must be baptized" is equivalent to denying "I believe the Bible." Seeing that this equivalence is being signaled leads to the construction of the unexpressed premise, "The Bible says everyone must be baptized."[4]

Or again, presumably any native-language user can intuitively recognize that the questions by the Mormons are more than just a series of distinct and independent information questions. They can be heard as a concerted effort to elicit answers that would make a case for the claim that everyone should be baptized (and therefore that people should convert to the Mormon faith). And while it is not altogether clear what that case amounts to, the questioning seems to anticipate something like the following chain of argument: Since Jesus Christ does not change from age to age, his teachings do not change from age to age and will apply to the context of our times. The Bible reports that Jesus Christ taught that everyone must be baptized. So, if we believe in Jesus Christ's teachings and we believe that the Bible reports his teachings, we must believe that the teaching that everyone must be baptized applies to the context of our times. And that conclusion contradicts the assertions behind Mrs. Lee's avowals in 04 and 06.

This attribution is surely intuitively available to any reader. But it is an intuition that can be empirically grounded by the analyst.

(Indeed, this intuition is available to any reader precisely because it is empirically grounded.) In part this attribution is grounded in cultural knowledge about the Bible and about plausible premises (e.g., that M1 and M2 expect Mrs. Lee to believe in Jesus Christ already, since she has announced that she is already a member of a chuch and has never directly denied the authority of the Bible or of Christ). But this attribution can also be partly backed by pointing to the parallelism between this pattern of questioning and a very general strategic pattern of argumentation called confrontation.[5]

In the standard pattern of confrontation, the confronter—in this case, the "tag team" of M1 and M2 (see Brashers and Meyers 1989)—first isolates and targets an assertion made by the confronted (in this case, Mrs. Lee's claim that not everyone must be baptized). Confronter then questions confronted in a way that elicits premises which can later be seen to contradict the original claim (e.g., what the Bible says is true; Jesus Christ said everyone should be baptized; biblical mandates are timeless and unchanging in application). The confronter then expressly presents the obvious inconsistency in a kind of "punch line" (e.g., in the form of a rhetorical question: "Then how can you say such and such?") that is designed to get the confronted to back down from the original standpoint taken.

While this pattern does not "come off" completely in the case above, it bears a striking resemblance to other cases documented in the literature. And this comparison allows us to attribute to M2's comments in turn 13 an argument that might not otherwise be apparent. What M2 is in effect asserting is that Mrs. Lee's answers are inconsistent with her denial that everyone should be baptized—which is the standard type of claim made in this slot of a confrontation sequence. We can also notice that this assertion is based on a kind of evidence that parallels what is ordinarily the case for confrontation sequences. Ordinarily, the self-contradiction consists of showing that the targeted assertion is contradicted by assertions that the confronted has either agreed with or supplied through the answers to the questioning. Here, however, the self-contradiction is attributed to the pragmatics of Mrs. Lee's answers: Mrs. Lee is obviously uncertain about her answers. She is answering as she does, not because she has thought her position through and is answering what she believes to be true, but because she does not really have a position and is simply anticipating what answer is needed to avoid contradicting her original claim. She therefore has not reasonably defended the claim she put forward in 04.[6]

Especially in cases of dialogue, another source of empirical grounding may come from various cues that indicate how the participants themselves understand the argumentative force of the discourse. For example, there is good reason to believe that the participants themselves understand the argumentative trap that this pattern of questioning leads to. The pauses, fillers ("uh" or "well"), cut-offs, and restarts are all characteristic vocal features of an orientation toward dispreferred turns in conversation (Heritage 1984b, 265–80; Levinson 1983, 332–36). Notice also the way in which Mrs. Lee's answers in 06, 08, and 10 fail to provide a direct and straightforward answer to the Mormons' questions. In 08 and 10 Mrs. Lee seems to deny an anticipated implication of accepting the proposition in question. Or notice how in 09 M2 simply repeats his question from 07 when Mrs. Lee fails to give a direct answer in 08.[7] All such clues suggest that the missionaries are trying to maneuver Mrs. Lee into giving answers that will contradict her prior standpoint and that Mrs. Lee sees this strategy and is trying to avoid giving those answers.

Several sources of empirical evidence thus can come into play: ethnographic evidence, comparative information about discourse in general, and reflexively organized cues to how the participants themselves understand what is going on. This evidence can be assembled both to justify the analyst's intuitions empirically about what is being argued and to augment those intuitions so as to go beyond a naive reading of the discourse. These various sources of information are interdependent in subtle and complex ways. None of these sources works alone, and all work against the background of the analyst's and reader's own cultural knowledge and intuitive competence as a native speaker. Ultimately, the acceptability of any particular reconstruction of a discourse will depend on its overall coherence, its accountability to the details of the text, and its consistency with other information about how this case works in particular, how related cases of this type work in general, and how discourse in general is known to work. (For more extended discussion of empirical methodology in discourse analysis, see Jackson 1986; Jacobs 1986, 1988, 1990.)

Normative Warrants for Reconstruction

Empirical grounds, taken by themselves, are not sufficient to provide a complete and unequivocal reconstruction of argumentation in terms of the ideal model. Even in the most clear-cut cases of filling in missing premises, we must *assume* that the speaker is being cooperative—that is, that the speaker is orienting to contributions of interlocutors, is taking up the evident purposes of the exchange, and is making a contribution that fits with those purposes. This is more than just an empirical attribution. It is a normative presumption in the sense that we expect of interlocutors that they will act in reasonable, cooperative ways, and we hold them accountable for meeting such expectations.[8]

In accordance with their own specialized interests, argumentation analysts hold participants to a refined version of this normative presumption of cooperative communication. In this respect, the ideal model for critical discussion serves as a heuristic tool in the analysis, which can be seen in two ways. First, the empirical qualities of any discourse suggest multiple meanings and are compatible with multiple forms of representation, not all of which are equally relevant to a critical analysis. Those aspects of the discourse relevant to a reconstruction are determined, in part, by the critical rationalist perspective of the ideal model. The philosophical background of the model dictates an interest in those aspects of discourse that are relevant to a resolution-oriented analysis.

Empirical considerations suggest meanings and functions other than the argumentative functions and structures that are of interest to a critical reconstruction. In the example above there are social and relational meanings that could also be selected out for reconstruction and analysis. For instance, Mrs. Lee's utterance in 02 does not merely argue against the missionaries' standpoint, it also disaffiliates with them socially. She casts her church as an alternative to the Mormon church, and she places herself in an antagonistic relationship with its representatives. Or again, M1's question in 05 is phrased in a way that is laden with implications for Mrs. Lee's moral identity (and not just with argumentative implications for what will and will not be taken as an acceptable assertion). At least as far as the Mormon missionaries are concerned, to admit openly to not believing the Bible is to place oneself into a category of moral alien that is quite different from being a non-Mormon who still confesses faith in the Bible. Likewise, M2's comments in 13 indicate a social categorization of Mrs. Lee as a lost and confused soul. Those comments claim for M2 a role in which he has the authority to impute personal beliefs to Mrs. Lee, to counsel her, and to pass judgment on her.

Pointing to the social functions of these turns does not deny their argumentative functions and implications. But the point to see is that a dialectical reconstruction selects those qualities of the discourse that isolate the argumentative structures, functions, and content of the discourse and ignores other aspects that do not clearly bear on those considerations.[9] The warrant for this selectivity is a normative one based on the interests of the analyst.

An ideal normative model also serves as warrant for reconstruction in a second way. While empirical features of the text suggest multiple meanings and multiple forms of representation, empirical features do not always provide an analyst with decisive clues to any particular meaning, or they underdetermine the most appropriate form of representation.

Sometimes the problem of underdetermination can be side-stepped, resolution of the issue not being crucial to the analyst's purposes in conducting a given analysis. For example, many spoken and written texts do not straightforwardly produce arguments but instead frame the argumentation in an act of reporting (cf. Goffman 1974). In such a case, the person reporting is not openly intent upon resolving a dispute by convincing someone else. Most newspaper items containing speeches and elements of discussions are officially intended to be taken by the reader simply as information about what someone else argued. But that does not mean that the materials cannot be usefully construed as argumentation. Example 3.2 is fairly typical of a newspaper report in which a dispute is fought out among opponents who are not clearly identified.

It is not quite clear who is the antagonist here, though the potential for an antagonist is clearly projected in the opening reference to a possible debate. Nor is it absolutely clear what the main standpoints are on the question of "who is actually receiving a so-called 'genuine minimum' income."

And it is unclear whether or not the article itself should be analyzed as argumentation or only as a report of a (potential?) argument. In the former case, the roles of protagonist and antagonist would have to be imputed to the author and the reader respectively. But that imputation is conditional on a decision to treat the article itself as argumentation, a decision which is not strongly grounded in any empirical evidence one way or the other.

Part of the ambiguity arises from the use of the phrases here italicized: "the Local Authorities' Association *has demonstrated that, at any rate,* they include many elderly people." On the one hand, this statement could be intended simply as a report of the status of one line of argument made by the association in support of some higher-order standpoint on the question of "who is actually receiving a so-called 'genuine minimum' income." The qualifier "at any rate" suggests that there is more to the debate than this claim alone. On the other hand, this phrasing could be intended as an argument from authority on behalf of the claim that many elderly people receive a genuine minimum income. The conclusionary judgment implied by the verb "to demonstrate" suggests this latter interpretation. A similar ambiguity occurs later in the text in which a reported claim is qualified as "the Association believes"—where

Example 3.2

Real low incomes for elderly

Should a new debate brew up in the coming weeks about who is actually receiving a so-called "genuine minimum" income, the Local Authorities' Association has demonstrated that, at any rate, they include many elderly people. The Association has carried out a survey of those applying for the Christmas bonus. The survey covered 114 districts and found 506,000 people applying for the bonus. Most of them were either elderly or members of ethnic minorities. The Association believes that with more preparation (with information aimed more carefully at particular sections of the community) more of the elderly and more foreigners would have applied, since the survey also showed that it is precisely these groups who have most difficulty finding out about and applying for the bonus.

"believes" contrasts with the later phrase "the survey also showed that," which refers to the basis for the association's belief.

In spite of these complications, however, we can still recognize a train of argument that is part of a critical discussion. It is fairly easy to identify the dialectical stages that have to be passed through in the resolution of the dispute. The first sentence signals the confrontation stage as it introduces the dispute (or potential dispute). As quite commonly happens, the opening stage is less clear-cut, but in the first sentence we are told that the Local Authorities' Association will act as protagonist with respect to the proposition that the elderly are among those receiving a "genuine minimum" income. The argumentation stage contains the results of the association's survey and is located further in the future ("Should a new debate brew up in the coming weeks . . ."). The concluding stage is left unilaterally to the association ("has demonstrated"). Moreover, the categories of protagonist and antagonist are clearly projected by the discourse, even if it is not altogether clear exactly who has taken on these roles. The normative commitments associated with those roles can be applied conditionally to anyone who was to occupy those roles. It should be clear that, for the purposes of analyzing these aspects of argumentative structure and function, an identification of who is actually filling the roles of protagonist and antagonist and a decision on whether or not the writer in fact intends to be arguing as well as reporting are incidental issues that need not be resolved in order to carry out the analysis.[10]

There are, however, a variety of cases in which empirical ambiguity and vagueness in meaning can pose an obstacle to analysis. In such problematic cases, a critical reconstruction should tend toward the strongest possible reading, providing the best fit with the normative model. Since the point of a normative analysis is to find out how conflicts can be resolved in a reasonable way, the reconstruction should represent the discourse in maximally reasonable terms.

From a critical rationalist perspective, acting reasonably to manage disagreement implies taking part in a critical discussion. This means that the analyst will try to reconstruct the problematic parts of the discourse as part of a critical discussion, presuming that, in the absence of decisive clues to the contrary, the discourse is designed to resolve a difference of opinion in a reasonable way. The speaker or writer is then given the benefit of the doubt, and the analysis is favored which is most beneficial to the resolution of a dispute. The analyst opts for assigning to a questionable utterance the communicative force which is the most congruent with the distribution of speech acts in the ideal model of a critical discussion, and where the content of the discourse is incomplete or otherwise equivocal in meaning, the analyst makes sense of the discourse by filling in propositional content as would be most reasonable in making an argument.

For an analysis of speech acts belonging to the argumentation stage, this means that if the communicative force is not completely clear, an argumentative interpretation should be tried reconstructing those parts of the discourse that serve as argumentation. (See van Eemeren and Grootendorst 1992a, 49, for this strategy of *maximally argumentative interpretation*.) In such an analysis it is of special importance that argumentation be clearly and justly distinguished, not only from communicative acts like advancing a standpoint and accepting or rejecting it, but also from act complexes which may just as well be performed in that stage of a critical discussion but which aim at different interactional effects and create different kinds of commitments, such as those usage declaratives of definition, precization, amplification, explication, and explicitization.

In the case of precization, for instance, one should not ask if it is an adequate defense of a standpoint but if it indeed restricts the possible interpretations of what is precised. If, however, a speech act is not considered as an argumentation but mistaken for some sort of usage declarative, it will fail to be judged properly and adequately as a contribution made by the speaker or writer in resolving the dispute at issue. This strategy of maximally argumentative interpretation applies not ony to speech acts belonging to the category of assertives but also to implicit speech acts which at first sight appear to be commissives, directives, expressives, or declaratives but which fulfill a constructive part in the critical discussion only if reconstructed as argumentation.

Speaking more generally by way of a legal metaphor, it might be said that in analyzing a discourse satisfactorily, judgment must be made and pronounced by a rational judge who assumes that disputants are themselves reasonable in a dialectical sense. This judgment may in fact have to be made in the absence of indisputable facts and in spite of a lack of proof, starting from circumstantial evidence. It must take into account all extenuating or aggravating circumstances. In interpreting the communicative force of speech acts, this rational judge is required to apply the strategy of *maximally dialectical analysis* (van Eemeren and Grootendorst 1992a, 105). Discussants are given the benefit of the doubt and are presumed to be acting reasonably insofar as this judgment is consistent with the available evidence.

In other words, the analyst applies an interpretive strategy that can be seen as a normatively specialized version of applying the Gricean presumption of cooperativity in generating implicatures. This strategy implies that a discourse which may or may not be conceived of as a critical discussion is conceived of as such. In applying the strategy of maximally dialectical analysis, the point of departure is the presumption that the discourse is meant to resolve a dispute. On such a presumption all speech acts performed are, in the absence of contrary indications, interpreted as a potential contribution to this goal. In this way, the language users are given maximal credit where credit is due.

A maximally dialectical analysis of this sort is chosen only where such an analysis is not ruled out by empirical considerations and where the dialectical force ascribed to an utterance remains compatible with other obvious functions of the utterance. An aside that is clearly simply an aside remains an aside. And the relevance of a question that is clearly a question naturally remains a question, regardless of whether or not it could also be construed as being an argument. The strategy of maximally dialectical analysis just prevents speech acts which play a potentially crucial part in resolving a dispute from not receiving acknowledgment. This is why in a dialectical analysis certain speech acts are, for example, substituted by the assertive standard form of a standpoint or an argument for that standpoint.[11] Applying the strategy of maximally dialectical analysis, a normative reconstruction of the discourse can be achieved which may be properly described as a dialectification.

Approaches to Analysis and Reconstruction

So far, the framework for the analysis of argumentative discourse used by the analyst and the framework for the interpretation of argumentative discourse used by an ordinary-language user do not seem to be much different. In chapter 5 we will give more detailed attention to what we will term "naive reconstruction," meaning interpretive procedures used by ordinary-language users to accomplish an ongoing "reading" of the situation. Although we will argue that elements reconstructed analytically must be accessible *in principle* to naive reconstruction, this does not mean that naive reconstruction is in fact identical to analytic reconstruction, even under ideal conditions of cooperation and reasonableness. To reconstruct what a certain conversational move contributes to a case in support of a standpoint addresses a technical problem that is different from the problem of explaining, say, the overall functional organization of that move in the conversation, its communicative design, or its structural positioning with respect to other moves. The perspective of analysis and the perspective of interpretation should be clearly distinguished.

In this section, we attempt to position our own perspective with respect to other typical approaches to the analysis of discourse. We draw several distinctions among discourse analytic approaches, none intended to be more than a way of relating our approach to other approaches. The first distinction is between what we term "analytic" and "interpretive" approaches. The second distinction is between a priori and a posteriori approaches. The third distinction is among contrasting concepts of organization, which we term sequential, conventional, and rational.

Analytic vs. Interpretive Approaches

Pike's (1967) distinction between an "etic" and an "emic" perspective on language use captures much of what we mean when we speak of a distinction between analytic reconstruction and naive reconstruction (see also Taylor and Cameron 1987 and Wootton 1976). According to Pike (1967), an emic approach attempts to describe the particular interpretation procedures that the language users themselves in fact apply: their labeling and classification of discourse units, implicit recognition rules, and so on. In an etic approach, the discourse is methodically analyzed from an external perspective. Starting from objective verbal and nonverbal cues, the analyst aims at identifying what is going on in the discourse by applying an explicit decision procedure. In an etic approach, analytic decisions are made from within a scheme that is both systematically articulated and comprehensively applicable. That is, an etic scheme of reference is designed to reflect a theoretically principled order of classification and to be capable of subsuming the emic system of any particular speech community. In principle, the critical analyst adopts an etic approach to argumentative discourse because of the purpose-overlay implied in the critical discussion model. At the same time, concepts fundamental to the model (such as standpoint) draw attention to arguers' own perspectives.

All approaches to discourse in which a purely emic perspective is chosen we shall call interpretive, and all approaches in which a purely etic perspective is chosen, analytic. Both perspectives find adherents among discourse analysts.

Exemplifying interpretive approaches are forms of analysis that describe or explain participant perspectives on interaction. Symbolic interactionist approaches generally and most theories of strategic message production and message design can be classified as interpretive (see Blumer 1969; Burleson 1989; Delia, O'Keefe, and O'Keefe 1982; Maines 1981; O'Keefe 1988; Sanders 1987). Efforts to construct participant-oriented typologies of illocutionary acts also qualify as interpretive (Clarke 1983; Kreckel 1981; Rosaldo 1982).[12]

The most clear-cut examples of analytic approaches are those that focus entirely on analyst-defined features of discourse. Interaction analysts such as Duncan and Fiske (1977) and Cappella (1979, 1980) concentrate on objective physical features of the discourse, describing patterning and organization in terms of features which may or may not have any clear relevance to participant perceptions of the organization of discourse.[13] More relevant to our current purposes are analytic approaches involving functional features of discourse, for example, approaches based on theoretical systems of speech acts (Edmondson 1981; Searle 1975, 1976; Searle and Vanderveken 1985; Vanderveken 1985, 1990). We group Searle and Vanderveken's speech act theory with analytic approaches, not only because the categories for their taxonomy of speech acts are self-consciously derived from a set of theoretically based ordering principles, but also because they openly deny that the procedure for deriving indirect speech acts may be considered to be a description of the actual interpretive procedures of language users. Likewise, we group Edmondson with analytic approaches because in his system, the language user's own perceptions are discounted, and even the use of the ordinary illocutionary verbs as names for the various types of speech act is rejected. But it is perhaps clear that the grounding of such analyses in ordinary-language intuitions about speech act types introduces interpretive elements.

In establishing a procedure for identifying what is relevant to the resolution of a dispute, we opt for such an analytic approach which includes interpretive insights. Such an analytic approach is captured by Schutz's (1973, 6) notion of "constructs of the second degree." By this phrase, Schutz means that the objects of human studies have intrinsic meaning apart from the interests and relevancies of the analyst.[14] The constructs of the human studies refer to and are founded upon the commonsense constructs of everyday actors. Rather than being first-order constructs, the constructs of the analyst are constructs about constructs—and part of the task of any analytic model is to select and codify that preexisting system of relevancies. At the same time, however, Schutz insists that the constructs of the human studies must necessarily reflect the specialized analytic problems of the social scientist and be developed in accordance with the technical ordering principles and the requirements of systematization of the discipline. The categories and principles of an analytic model cannot, and should not try to, correspond to the commonsense constructs of everyday actors. For this reason, while an analytic model is accountable to the structure of everyday discourse, it is never simply a reproduction of the perspective of an ordinary-language user; nor is it governed by the interests and categories of an ordinary-languge user.

A Priori vs. A Posteriori Approaches

Cutting across the distinction between interpretive and analytic approaches is a distinction between a priori and a posteriori approaches. An a posteriori approach to discourse is inductive: the theoretical insights are gained by way of empirical observation. An a priori approach starts from certain theoretical premises concerning the way discourse is conducted.

A posteriori approaches may be interpretive or analytic. A posteriori interpretive positions include most ethnographers of speaking and many conversation analysts. Ethnography of speaking aims for description of the participant-defined features of the diverse speech events they encounter in the communities they study and the social conventions that govern them. A common theme in writing about ethnography is that the analyst must be prepared to see the speech event as organized in terms of the constructs of the participants.[15] Conversation analysts following the ethnomethodological tradition of Garfinkel (1967) adopt an initially atheoretical, inductive approach in an effort to establish empirically the methods by which orderliness is created in ordinary discourse—in other words, the methods used by the conversationalists themselves in order to reach a shared interpretation (cf. Heritage 1984b; Schegloff 1988; and Zimmerman 1988).[16]

A posteriori analytic approaches are also inductive, but they do not focus on discovery of the meanings participants bring to situations. A good example is interaction analysis, which generally applies analyst categories to the description of interaction but aims for inductive model-building based on regularities in the association of one act type and another (Bakeman and Gottman 1987; Cappella 1979, 1980; Duncan and Fiske 1977). Interaction analysts frequently describe their approach as starting without theoretical preconceptions and searching for a "grammar" of conversation by noting regularities in the sequencing of act types within interaction (Jose 1988; Stech 1975).

A priori approaches differ from a posteriori approaches in that they start from a theoretical stance taken toward the phenomena, such as a theoretically generated classification of illocutionary acts. Leading examples are members of the Birmingham school (Coulthard 1977; Stubbs 1981, 1983), who study the structure of verbal exchanges; speech act analysts, who try to describe the deep structure of speech acts (Ferrara 1980; Gibbs and Delaney 1987; Hancher 1979; Searle 1969; Vanderveken 1990); and the Griceans, who formulate conversational principles (Brown and Levinson 1987; Horn 1984; Leech 1983; Sperber and Wilson 1986).[17] Although these approaches are more analytic than interpretive, it is also possible to take an interpretive a priori position (e.g., Clarke 1983).

No position is purely a posteriori, for at a minimum the observer begins with constructs embedded in ordinary communicative competence. Likewise, no position is purely a priori, for theoretical concepts must come from experience with the phenomena unless they are entirely devoid of content. The distinction is not meant to be more than a contrast in emphasis and research direction, a rough distinction between theory as a summary of observation and theory as a structuring of observation.

Our position is a priori in the sense that it begins with a model of critical discussion, worked out abstractly as a description of what discourse would look like if ideally tailored to the task of disagreement-resolution. But the model obviously depends upon some understandings of the structuring of discourse that are experientially and observationally based.

Concepts of Organization: Sequential, Conventional, and Rational

Among the a priori, analytic approaches (the approaches most similar to our own), there are still important differences. An important difference between the members of the Birmingham school, on the one hand, and the Searleans and Griceans, on the other, is that the former concentrate on the surface level of discourse, whereas the latter try to grasp its "deep structure." Stubbs (1981, 1983), Coulthard (1977), and other members of the Birmingham school analyze the structures of verbal exchange by describing the acts which constitute the discourse by their interactional function. They try to distinguish between structurally well-formed and ill-formed sequences. Essentially, their approach amounts to a form of distributionalism. The function of an utterance is determined by its regular sequential positions within a system of co-occurrences and alternatives. Like certain a posteriori analytic approaches (such as Duncan and Fiske 1977), their analysis is driven by a "sequencing rules" approach.[18]

Unlike for the Birmingham school, for the Searleans function is determined by conventional devices such as "felicity" conditions and by the intentions of the speaker. Verbal utterances are goal-directed speech acts that further the interests of actors in a certain speech event. Verbal utterances can serve this function because they are recognizable realizations of certain speech acts. Their recognizability is due to the common knowledge among language users of the conventions that govern the performance of speech acts. The conventional felicity conditions determine when an utterance may be taken as a certain speech act. By virtue of the conventionality of the felicity conditions, it is possible to identify which intention may be ascribed to the speaker.

Labov and Fanshel (1977, esp. chap. 3) extend speech act theory by formulating rules of discourse that specify how analysts can identify speech acts at a deep level. These rules have the following form: "If S produces an utterance and the conditions $C_1, C_2, \ldots, C_n$ apply, analyze this utterance as a speech act belonging to category X." In their view, the sequencing of speech acts is governed by quasi-grammatical rules. The speech acts that play a part at the deep level may, at the surface level, be realized by various kinds of other speech acts. A sequence of speech acts that is orderly at the deep level may seem incoherent at the surface level.

The organization of verbal interaction can be regarded as a product of sequencing or as a product of conventional structures, but it can also be regarded as a product of deeper rational principles. A sequential view of organization assumes that order in discourse is to be found at the level of behavioral regularities that may or may not be recognized by the language users themselves. On this view, the meaning of acts is constituted by their probability of occurrence in a particular interactional context.

According to conventionalists, order in discourse is to be found at the level of more or less arbitrary agreements that serve as the basis for shared normative expectations. On this view, the meaning of acts is constituted by rules that serve as stipulative definitions for any given act type.

According to rationalists, order in discourse is to be found at the level of principles for practical action that serve as guides for the calculation of strategic action and as interpretive presumptions for the construction of inferences. On this view, the meaning of acts is constituted by communicator intentions and a process of inference to the best explanation.[19] Searleans tend to emphasize the conventionality of language use; Griceans favor a rationalistic view.[20] For Grice (1975, 1989), the Cooperative Principle and conversational maxims are not merely rules that conversationalists do in fact follow but principles that are reasonable for them to follow.

We have argued elsewhere that a rational model can subsume and explain much of what is wanted from a conventional or sequential approach (Jacobs 1985; Jacobs and Jackson 1983, 1989). We see these three approaches to organization as representing successively deeper levels of structure.

As far as the empirical justification of a normative reconstruction of argumentative discourse is concerned, in our view, an integration of Searlean insights into the communicative aspect of discourse and Gricean insights into the interactional aspect provides the most adequate approach. In ordinary discourse, the communicative and the interactional aspects are closely interwoven. In principle, the communicative effect of understanding is aimed for only in view of achieving the interactional effect of accepting, and these two effects are simultaneously pursued by the same speech act.

The integration of Searlean and Gricean insights, because of its combination of conventional and rationalist views, brings together in a harmonious way the rules and regularities of actual discourse and the normative principles of goal-directed discourse. Hence, we would characterize the approach developed in this book as more analytic than interpretive, as more a priori than a posteriori, and as built on a rational model of discourse structure.

Notes

1. The critical analysis of argumentative dialogue may be concerned with aspects of argumentation other than the structure and substance of a completed "case" made for or against some standpoint. One could, for instance, be interested in how a case emerges through dialogic interaction, in the properties of argumentative gambits that rely on timing and order of presentation, or in the communicative structure of strategies for alluding to arguments or hinting at cases. See the analyses in chapters 5 and 6 for some of these concerns.

2. From Jacobs 1986. All examples use an adaptation of Gail Jefferson's transcription notation (see Atkinson and Heritage 1984): Single parentheses ( ) indicate material that was not clearly audible to the transcriber or not audible at all. Brackets [ ] indicate beginning and endpoints of interruption and overlap. Equal signs = mark a continuous stream of talk between two speakers or by the same speaker. Double parentheses (( )) contain editorial descriptions. Italics indicate special stress. Words spelled in all capital letters indicate increased loudness. Colons and repeated letters indicate stretched sounds. Dashes at the end of partial or completed words indicate cutoff sounds. Punctuation marks usually indicate vocal intonation rather than grammatical form.

3. The use of "well" by M1 in 03 and by M2 in 07 is also a conventional means of marking the relevance of an utterance in a context where expectations of upcoming coherence have been upset (Schiffrin 1987). That is, the questions in 03 and 07 are not *just* questions but questions addressing something problematic in the continuation of the discourse.

4. There is more to the construction of this missing premise than a simple follow-through on the cohesive cues in the text. See van Eemeren and Grootendorst 1982, 1983.

5. See Bleiberg and Churchill 1975; Jacobs 1986; also discussion of turns 037–46 and 095–99 in example 6.4. An example of the standard pattern is the following case, from an initial psychotherapy session between a young female patient and a middle-aged male therapist (from Bleiberg and Churchill).

01 Pt: I don't want them ((parents)) to have anything to do with my life, except ((Pause)) security(?)
           [
02 Dr: You live at home?
03 Pt: Yes.
04 Dr: They pay your bills?

05 Pt: Yeah.
06 Dr: How could they not have anything to do with your life?

6. Perhaps more precisely, Mrs. Lee has called into question her commitment to part of Grice's (1975) Quality Maxim: Do not say that for which you lack adequate evidence. For a more elaborated discussion of this example as an instance of "confrontation," see Jacobs 1986.

7. Nofsinger (1975) discusses the occurrence of repeated turns as evidence for failure of responsiveness on the part of the recipient of the initial turn.

8. Normative and empirical aspects of interpretation are inextricably bound together. Just as normative presumptions such as Grice's (1975) Cooperative Principle are empirically grounded in the sense that ordinary-language users orient to such a principle, so also any empirical grounding for interpretation will be normatively warranted by the assumption that the actor is reasonable, cooperative, knows "what anyone should know," and so on. No normative principle for reconstruction would thus be acceptable to the analyst if it could not be shown to be intersubjectively valid (i.e., empirically grounded). And no empirical cue or background information is interpretable or relevant outside a framework of normative standards and presumptions.

9. A very difficult issue is what is and is not relevant to the conduct of the argumentation. At present there are no principled answers to that question. For example, some of the so-called fallacies of argument may not involve arguments at all (e.g., argument *ad baculum* [i.e., appeal to force] or certain emotional appeals). Or what is objectionable are the argumentatively irrelevant qualities (e.g., some cases of argument ad hominem or cases of loaded language). But those aspects of the discourse should still be retained in a reconstruction. Nevertheless, we should not confuse this issue with the related issue of what kinds of information should be taken into account when deciding on the most appropriate argumentative reconstruction. The information that is represented in the reconstructed argument is not the same as the information that needs to be taken into account in deciding just how the argument should be represented in a reconstruction. More on this topic in chapter 5.

10. These issues might prove important for other considerations. For example, the fact that a writer can use the reporting frame to evade argumentative responsibilities while putting forward an argument is a danger that a critic might wish to point out. Clearly, however, when claiming that the writer was in fact doing so and should be held accountable for it, one should bear in mind that the absence of strong empirical grounding cannot be compensated for by emphasizing the analyst's strong normative interest in critical discussion. The problem here is that empirically there is a normative expectation that news reporters will not engage in advocacy (for a similar situation, see norms for mediators in chapter 6). About all that could be said is that *if* the writer was making an argument, certain argumentative responsibilities *would* follow from that, and that *if* the writer had the intention of forwarding an argument without owning up to it, that

intention *could* be satisfied through the textual presentation in question. But neither "if" leads to a bona fide critical evaluation or judgment, since here the benefit of the doubt calls for a nonargumentative reading.

11. A specific problem of analysis arises when it is unclear whether an argumentation is multiple or is coordinatively compound. Then it is possible that the speaker or writer sees the single arguments individually as conclusive of his or her standpoint, but it is equally possible that the speaker or writer takes them to be a conclusive defense only when seen in concert. In dialectical analysis multiple interpretation of the argumentation structure is a strategy to start with. That way, at least there are guarantees that each single argumentation will be examined as to its justifying or refuting capacity in relation to the proposition to which the standpoint being defended refers. Since in this way we attribute a maximum of argumentative force to each individual, single argumentation, this recommendation leads to the strategy of *maximal argumentative analysis* (van Eemeren and Grootendorst 1992a, 81).

12. We see Clark 1983 as exemplifying an interpretive approach by virtue of assuming performative verbs to be indicative of the language users' categorization of discourse.

13. Duncan and Fiske (1977, 10) mention as a defining strength of their approach the use of data generated "through observations demanding a minimum of inference by the rater (in part by avoiding the ascription of 'meaning' to actions)." Cappella (1979, 1980) takes this strategy to its logical extreme, concentrating on the analysis of patterns of the purely physical features of talk and silence.

14. We use the term "human studies," even though Schutz referred only to the social sciences and had specifically in mind the discipline of economics. His point, however, is not restricted to these disciplines.

15. E.g, Saville-Troike (1982, 4) describes ethnography as follows: " 'Doing ethnography' in another culture involves first and foremost field work, including observing, asking questions, participating in group activities, and testing the validity of one's perceptions against the intuitions of natives. Research design must allow an openness to categories and modes of thought and behavior which may not have been anticipated by the investigator."

16. In the conversation analytic approach, agreement on the rules of discourse is regarded as something for the conversationalists themselves to work out. The methods they use in negotiating this agreement are based on the principles of accountability and intersubjective understanding. Conversation analysts thus do not assume a universal and preprogrammed communicative competence; instead, they start from the methods displayed by ordinary-language users in their conversational negotiations. The conversation analytic approach aims to provide insights into the interpretive categorization of events and sequences of utterances by the conversationalists. Notions such as "preference system," "adjacency pair," "preferred pair part," "dispreferred pair part," and "markedness of dispreference" (pausing, token agreement, etc.) play a crucial role in their description. However, for a view contrary to the a posteriori analysis of such constructs see Coulter 1983.

17. Edmondson (1981) goes one step further in following an analytic and a priori line of approach. He also considers the exchange of speech acts as the fundamental discourse unit, but he does not want to rely on a taxonomy of speech acts which is in any way derived from ordinary-language use and instead proposes his own taxonomy based on theoretical considerations. In his taxonomy, each utterance has, by definition, only one force. Unfortunately, it is not quite clear why he chooses the specific acts that are included in his taxonomy.

18. See also interaction analysts following in the tradition of Watzlawick, Beavin, and Jackson 1967.

19. Various aspects of these contracts are discussed in greater detail in the chautauqua debate between Cappella (1990) and Jacobs (1990) as well as in Akmajian, Demers, Farmer, and Harnish 1990, chap. 9, and Kauffeld 1987.

20. Among positions built on a concept of organization as "rational," the best known are Brown and Levinson's (1987) theory of politeness, Clark and Haviland's (1977) Given-New Contract, Leech's (1983) Tact Maxim and Principles of Interpersonal Rhetoric, and Sperber and Wilson's (1986) relevance theory.

4

Dialectical Reconstruction

In dialectically reconstructing argumentative discourse, the analyst is building an analytic overview of those aspects of the discourse that are crucial for the resolution of the dispute. Such a reconstruction is guided by a search for the following:

1. the points at issue,
2. the different positions that the parties concerned adopt with respect to these points,
3. the explicit and implicit arguments that the parties adduce for their standpoints,
4. the structure of the argumentation of each of the parties.

Identifying the points at issue entails determining the propositions with respect to which standpoints are adopted and called into question. Identifying the positions of the parties in the discussion amounts to determining who plays the part of the protagonist of which standpoint and who takes the role of the antagonist. In identifying the arguments that are being advanced in an argumentative discourse in favor of a standpoint, implicit or indirect aspects must be identified and represented in explicit form. Identifying the structure of argumentation entails determining how the arguments put forward relate to one another in their support for the standpoint. In the simplest case, a standpoint is defended by only one argument. Generally, however, the argumentation structure is more complex because speakers or writers believe they need more than one single argument to defend their standpoint and because the information presented may function as support for multiple claims. The nature of the complexity depends on the precise relationship between the component arguments.

Reconstruction Transformations

We might think of the relationship between an ordinary presentation of discourse (as, say, written text or written transcription of oral discourse) and a dialectical reconstruction of that discourse in terms of transformations of deletion, addition, permutation, and substitution that are applied to ordinary discourse. While these transformations do not necessarily correspond to actual steps that an analyst takes in reconstructing the arguments expressed in a discourse, they do provide a useful way of thinking about how critical analysis works with a selective idealization of a discourse.[1]

The dialectical transformation of *deletion* entails a selection of elements from the original discourse that are immediately relevant to the process of resolving the dispute; elements that are irrelevant for this purpose, such as elaborations, clarifications, and sidelines, are omitted. Any repetitions that occur in the text, even if slightly differently worded, are also omitted. This transformation, in other words, amounts to the removal of information that is redundant, superfluous, or otherwise not relevant for the presumed goal.

The dialectical transformation of *addition* entails a process of completion which consists of the supplementation of the given discourse with those elements immediately relevant to the resolution of the dispute but left unexpressed. Only elements that are instrumental in achieving the resolution of the dispute are made explicit. This transformation is partly a matter of making implicit elements explicit, partly a matter of filling in unexpressed steps. Supplying missing elements in the various stages of discussion might include assuming that someone who advances a contrary standpoint is thereby also indicating doubt about the original standpoint. Another example is the explicitization of a premise or a conclusion that has been left unexpressed in the discourse.

The dialectical transformation of *permutation* entails the ordering or rearranging of elements in the original discourse in such a way that the dialectical process of resolving the dispute is made as clear as possible. The various stages in the resolution process must be distinguished, and at the same time the overlap between different stages and the anticipation of steps to come, or a reference back to steps already dealt with, must be readjusted. Those parts of the confrontation stage, for example, which are postponed to the argumentation stage or even the concluding stage must be put in their dialectically "ideal" place. In contrast to a purely descriptive record, a dialectical reconstruction need not necessarily follow a real-time, linear ordering of events. Sometimes, the actual chronology can be retained; sometimes some rearrangement is called for. In the latter case, the elements are (re)arranged in a way that directly reflects the process of resolving a dispute in our ideal model.

The dialectical transformation of *substitution* entails an attempt to produce a clear and explicit presentation of elements fulfilling a dialectical function in the discourse. It results in a uniform notation for elements which fulfill the same function. For example, some elements which are formulated as rhetorical questions may function as arguments and must therefore be represented as arguments. Different formulations of the same standpoint are reduced to one (standard) formulation. Ambiguous or vague formulations must be replaced by well-defined standard-phrases that are unambiguous and clear, whereas different formulations of elements with the same function are represented by the same standard-phrase. This translation amounts to a replacement of the pretheoretical formulations of colloquial speech with theoretical standard-phrases.

An Extended Example

Example 4.1 can be used to demonstrate the plausibility of dialectical reconstruction and to illustrate just what it does and does not entail. The following transcript comes from a court-ordered mediation session between a divorcing couple in dispute over custody arrangements for their children. The mediation agency in question is officially referred to as a "conciliation court," although reconciliation of the divorcing couple is not a purpose of the session.[2] The official purpose of such sessions is for the couple, with the aid of the mediator, to arrive at a mutually agreeable arrangement for visitation and custody of their children. M is the mediator, H (Fred) is the husband, W (Genie) is the wife.[3] The transcript starts shortly after the couple's lawyers have discussed the case with the mediator.

In this discussion, there is a difference of opinion between Fred and Genie, although what exactly this difference of opinion amounts to, and whether or how exactly Fred and Genie's argumentation is meant to support their respective standpoints, is not immediately obvious. On the face of it, the exchange sounds like a chaotic

Example 4.1

01 M: How do you un- you understand why you're here today?

((Pause))

02 M: Both of you yeah

03 H: We're going to file divorce suits

04 M: Okay, but do you know why you're here in conciliation court and not in the uh, the court though

05 W: Because of the child.

06 H: Yeah

07 M: Anytime there are differences that parents have regarding the children, um before the judge or commissioner hears the case, parents are first given a chance to come here and talk about the child in this case it's Jonathan and um, because most of the time you as the parents, are the ones who know what what Jonathan needs what would be good for him more than than most people, the judge won't know, Jonathan the judge also won't know you very well

08 W: Mhm

09 M: uh so the, the plan is to first see if there's a way that you can work something out for Jonathan, uh if not then the court will help you make the decision for Jonathan and and=

[   ]

10 W: Mhm

11 M: =issue order. If you're able to agree, and we come up with a plan, we can write that down have that signed (   ) by attorneys, the judge will sign that, making that a court order. It carries the same weight that anything that the judge himself or herself might issue

12 W: Mhm

13 M: But uh what other concerns about Jonathan what would you like for Jonathan

14 W: Well I want Jonathan with   Now my husband has filed a custody suit that my twelve year old son from a previous marriage beats the five year old, and that I stand by and don't do anything about it.   Now this is very untrue, they are both   my   children

[   ]

15 M: Let me, let me back up a little bit and ask you what you would really like for Jonathan and Gregg, not not for yourselves but for them.

Example 4.1 (Continued)

16 H: Want 'em to have everything that I been tryin' to give 'em =

17 M: = Okay, what what ha been try- what have you been tryin' to give 'em.

18 H: Good life

19 M: Good life

20 H: Everything physical and, mind can give you, 's what I've tried to do for the past since he's been born and before that I tried to (deal) with my other one also.

((Pause))

21 M: S—is it Jenny, Genie

                     [

22 W: Genie

23 M: Genie, what what else would you want for Jonathan and Gregg. What would you want to give them

24 W: Well I wanta give 'em the best of everything I'm able to, I'm working

25 M: Mhm

26 W: I don't want Jonathan taken away from me, and to go with his father because I don't think that would be right, his father is on drugs, he's an al he he drinks, he lies, all this is very untrue what he's been saying. He can have visitation rights, what what I know he will do is I know the minute he gets ahold of Jonathan I won't see Jonathan again. He eh he's not working, he has nothing to hold him here he has told me time and time again that if he and I ever separated, he would take Jonathan and I would never see him again. Now he's turned around and said

                                [   ]

27 H: That's not true

28 W: That is true

        [

29 H: No it's not true

30 W: What you have said about about Gregg

                     [   ]

31 H: I'm   not   working because I had an accident okay

              [   ]

32 W: Because you were driving under the influence and went off a cliff Fred

Example 4.1 (Continued)

```
                          [    ]
33 H:                     I    had not been cited for any such violation
         I did have an auto accident, and at the bottom of the cliff
         where I laid for two and a half hours, I did have beer and
         the lady that found me, also had a beer sitting on the side
         of the cliff before they got me up in a basket on the side
         of the cliff I went off a cliff four hundred and fifty
         feet, and I'm not on drugs
                     [                    ]
34 W:                two    hundred   feet, two hundred feet =

35 H:    = Four hundred and fifty

36 W:    Two hundred feet I have the police report
                     [                          ]
37 M:                     Fred   Fred what happened I mean how did
         the accident occur?

38 H:    I was nervous I was upset, I have been evicted from my home
         which I had s- paid for, supported, all the time that we'd
         been there, I was abruptly woken in =
                     [  ]
39 W:                Ahh!

40 H:    = the middle of the night told to pack what little my
         personal effects that I wanted, and leave.
                [    ]
41 W:           you

42 W:    Alright   he   was
                     [        ]
43 H:                Forthwith, in the middle of the night.
                               [   ]
44 M:                          Okay                    Okay.

45 W:    He was served divorce p-
                     [
46 M:                     Do you do you know that I don't I'm not a
         judge and that I don't make the recommendations.
                          [            ]
47 W:                     Oh           okay

48 H:    Okay so I'm just telling you how my accident happened
                               [   ]
49 M:                          Okay
         Okay =

50 W:    = and I'm telling you he was driving under the influence I
         have the police report *in* my purse.
```

Example 4.1 (Continued)

51 M:	[ ] Alright Okay

52 W: He was under the influence =

53 H: = I had not been cited

54 W: He took he has not been cited
       because there was no one to see him behind the wheel. =
       [   ]

55 H: and   I   wasn't under any drugs

56 W: = He was served papers on five twenty a. m. on May
sixteenth, it was said in the papers that you do not remove
anything from the house he took everything he could get his
hands on, drove up to Lake Loyola, driving under the
influence and drove his truck off a two hundred foot cliff
and lost everything. And then he turns around
                      [   ]   [   ]

57 M: Okay   Okay
((Pause))

58 W: just let me finish, and then he turns around, and says to
his lawyer that my twelve year old son is beating the five
year old, that is a *downright DIRTY LIE* and I am not going
to stand by and let him get away with it.

---

squabble filled with mean and petty accusations (Fred lies, drinks,
and is on drugs), pointless digressions that have nothing to do with
the issue at hand (How did the accident occur? Was Fred drinking?),
trivial bickering over inane points (Was the cliff 200 feet or 450 feet
high?), and repetitive clashes of assertion, denial, and reassertion
that seem to go nowhere. Genie seems more intent on establishing
the low character and blameworthiness of her former husband than
on resolving the question of custody of Jonathan. And Fred seems
preoccupied with defending himself against the charge that he drove
off a cliff because he was drinking. The mediator has clearly lost
control of the discussion. It is just the sort of worst-case scenario in
which we might test the plausible limits of dialectical reconstruction.

The strategy of maximally dialectical analysis directs the analyst
to try to construct the most charitable representation consistent
with the empirical evidence, under the presumption that the discussants are engaged in a critical discussion designed to resolve a
difference of opinion and are making contributions relevant to the

pursuit of that objective. This construction can be done regardless of the fact that the content of the standpoints and the structure of the supporting argumentation is not altogether obvious, and despite the fact that it is not altogether obvious that Fred and Genie take resolution of their differences to be the organizing purpose of their discussion. But then, dialectical reconstruction of argumentation would be of very little interest if it applied only to cases in which the purposes were manifestly in accord with those of a critical discussion, where the content and structure of the argumentation were explicit or transparently obvious, and where the attitudes and conduct of the discussants plainly resembled what could be expected from an ideal rational discussant.

Despite the rather severe and apparent defects in argumentative procedure in this discussion, we can still extract readily enough an initial formulation of the basic standpoints in dispute and a partial case for and against those standpoints. The difference of opinion between Fred and Genie has to do with custody and visitation arrangements for their son, Jonathan. The confrontation stage of this dispute was initiated long ago. In this discussion it is presented only through allusion (as in 03, when Fred answers, "We're going to file divorce suits," or in 07, when M alludes to "differences that parents have regarding the children . . . in this case it's Jonathan") and through report and restatement (as in 14, when Genie reports that she wants Jonathan with her and implies that Fred has filed for custody of Jonathan; in 26, when Genie says that she does not want Jonathan to go with Fred).

So, as indicated in figure 4.1, Fred has adopted something like the standpoint that "Fred should have custody of Jonathan." Genie has adopted something like the standpoint that "Genie should have custody of Jonathan." Fred has also adopted the standpoint that "Genie should not have custody of Jonathan," and Genie has also adopted the standpoint that "Fred should not have custody of Jonathan." Moreover, in the opening stage, Fred takes on the role of protagonist for the dispute in the first row, while Genie takes on the role of antagonist; Genie takes on the role of protagonist for the dispute in the second row, while Fred takes on the role of antagonist. Opposition in each row is indicated by a negated arrow ($\leftarrow/\rightarrow$).

But there is more to the structure of this confrontation stage than simply the semantic opposition of the standpoints. It is also clear from the discussion that both Fred and Genie take it that by denying the other's positive claim, they have established their own positive claim, and vice versa. In other words, by arguing that Genie should not have custody of Jonathan, Fred supports his claim that he should have custody of Jonathan, and by arguing that she should have custody of Jonathan, Genie supports her standpoint that Fred should not have custody of Jonathan. These relationships are indicated in the figure by arrows pointing from the supporting argument to the standpoint; in this particular case, since either of the two positions taken by a party can be considered a standpoint supported by his or her other position, the arrows go in both directions. This dispute, in other words, is not simply *mixed;* the standpoints of the two parties are taken to be mutually exclusive, and for each party his or her two standpoints are taken to be mutually implicative (see also chapter 2 and van Eemeren and Grootendorst 1992a).

Parts of this episode are recognizably argumentation for or against those standpoints. In 14 and 58 Genie reports Fred's basic case for custody: "that my twelve year old son from a previous marriage beats the five year old, and that I stand by and don't do anything about it." Genie then denies this charge in 14 and 26 ("this is very untrue"), and again in 58 ("that is a *downright DIRTY LIE*"). Fred's case could simply be reconstructed as "Gregg beats Jonathan" and "A parent should not have custody of a child if they allow that child to be beaten" and "Genie allows Jonathan to be beaten by Gregg." The evidence for this latter premise is that "Genie stands by and doesn't do anything to stop Gregg from beating Jonathan." These are straightforward substitutions and additions to what has been said. But it would not be the best reconstruction because it is not consistent with the full sense of what Fred has said.

Fred's utterance is informationally dense in the sense that his reported characterization calls out a context of moral obligation. To say that someone "stands by and doesn't do anything about it" is to imply that something should be done to change an undesirable state of affairs and to charge that person with willfully abstaining from acting on a moral duty to do so. Such a statement implies that the person has the opportunity and ability to do something, is somehow obligated to act on that ability and opportunity, but chooses not to

Figure 4.1

H: Fred should have custody of Jonathan.	←/→	W: Fred should not have custody of Jonathan.
↑↓		↑↓
H: Genie should not have custody of Jonathan.	←/→	W: Genie should have custody of Jonathan.

[Either Genie should have custody of Jonathan or
Fred should have custody of Jonathan, but not both.]

act. At least tentatively, we will entertain the hypothesis that Fred's case is based on the claim that Genie should not have custody of Jonathan on criteria having to do with moral character. As we shall see, this seems to be recognized as a pivotal decision rule by both Fred and Genie. A reconstruction of his case based on this hypothesis is presented in figure 4.2.

The fact that Fred's case is presented as a report by Genie creates certain irresolvable ambiguities on other points, however. Notice that Gregg is described as a twelve year old and Jonathan as a five year old. Why use these descriptors? We can assume that these descriptors are argumentatively relevant, but at least two possible lines of relevance could be at work here, depending on the authorship of the descriptors. Are these Genie's own descriptors, or is she simply repeating Fred's forms of reference? If authored by Genie, these descriptors could be taken as possibly emphasizing that Gregg and Jonathan are just kids, so that the charge that Gregg "beats" Jonathan sounds exaggerated. If authored by Fred, the descriptors could be taken as possibly suggesting such an age difference that the fighting is unfair and dangerous—Jonathan is so much younger that he cannot defend himself, and Gregg has reached an age where he is strong enough to inflict physical harm on a young boy.

Likewise, it is unclear what to make of Gregg's being described as Genie's child "from a previous marriage." Numerous possibilities might be entertained, but none seems to have strong enough empirical grounding to be entered into a reconstruction. If the description is taken to reflect Genie's point of view, it could point to an explanation of why the children might fight. It might also imply a reason why custody of Gregg is not at issue—natural parents have a presumptive custodial claim to a child over stepparents. If the description is part of Fred's case, repeated but not authored by Genie, it might also point to a reason for his special interest in Jonathan, but not Gregg.

Or again, it is unclear just what part(s) of Fred's case Genie claims to be "very untrue." That Genie follows up her denial in 14 by starting to elaborate a defense with "they are both my children" makes it sound like she would follow up with something like "and I wouldn't let either one get hurt." But her argument gets cut off before it can be fully developed and responded to in a way that would explore what she is claiming. She pretty clearly means to be suggesting that she is concerned with protecting the health and welfare of both her children. And it seems unlikely that she would want to deny something like the claim that Gregg and Jonathan fight. But it is not clear whether she is denying that she does not act to stop Gregg from beating Jonathan, or denying that Gregg beats Jonathan

Figure 4.2

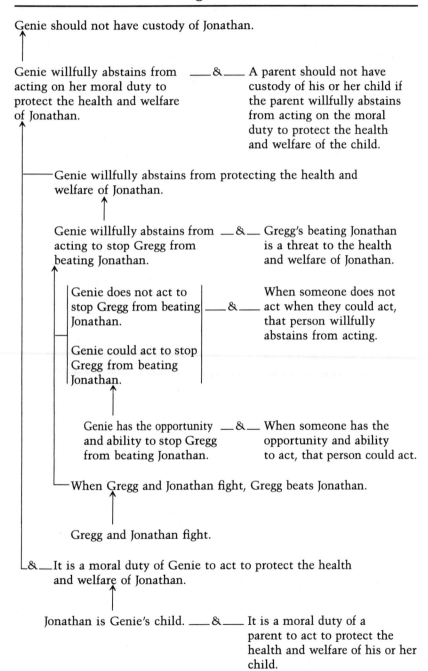

in the first place, or denying both. About all we can say is that Genie seems to be making an argument along the lines of the one reconstructed in figure 4.3. In any case, it should be seen that even where there is a presumption of argumentative potential, that presumption may not lead to a clear reconstruction of who is arguing what.

In providing this initial, tentative, and partial reconstruction, several transformations have already been implicitly performed. For example, in suggesting the equivalence of material in several of the turns, we have implicitly suggested transformations of substitution and deletion. Substitution is implied by the fact that equivalence requires that there be a common, standardized formulation for the slightly different wordings in the expression of Genie's standpoint in 14 and 26; of Fred's standpoint and case in 14 and 58; and of Genie's denial in 14, 26, and 58. Deletion is implied by a common substitution. Repetition of these assertions is noninformative and can be deleted in assembling the structure of each discussant's case. In a similar way, substitution occurs in the unpacking of the statement "my twelve year old son from a previous marriage beats the five year old" into "Gregg and Jonathan fight, and Gregg hurts Jonathan" or changing "I stand by and don't do anything about it" into "Genie does not act to stop Gregg from beating Jonathan." Likewise, permutations have occurred. We have implicitly treated all expressions of Fred and Genie's standpoints as occurring in a normalized, initial position for the confrontation stage of the discussion, despite their appearance at diverse points in time. And we have permuted Genie's report of Fred's assertion of a standpoint into Fred's assertion of a standpoint. And finally, we have engaged in addition by attributing mutual exclusion to Fred's and Genie's standpoints. Fred is not simply asserting the standpoint, "Fred should have custody of

Figure 4.3

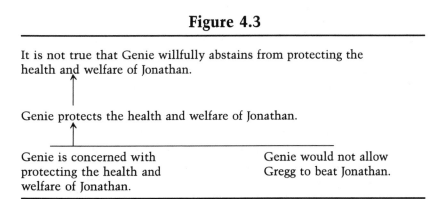

Jonathan"; he is also negating the standpoint, "Genie should have custody of Jonathan." Likewise, in elaborating Fred's case, we have added numerous unstated premises as well as semantic and pragmatic implications from what was said.

Dialectical transformations are thus implicit in this much of our reconstruction. But what about the rest of the discussion? What should be done with it?

Some turns can be effectively ignored and deleted from a reconstruction because they are cut off before they can make a point (41, 42). And a large set of turns contain utterances that function primarily as management acts without argumentative force or substantive content. Genie's "just let me finish" in 58 can be deleted. The exchange in 21 and 22 and the mediator's question in 37 appear to serve simply information functions. The use of "Mhm" by Genie in 08, 10, and 12 and by the mediator in 25 can be deleted for purposes of reconstruction. The mediator's use of "okay" and "alright" in 17, 44, 49, 51, and 57 can also be treated this way. These moves all function as management moves that withhold taking a stand on what has been said.

However, such moves cannot simply be mechanically erased. For example, in 47 Genie's use of "Oh" is a "change of state token" that, together with her subsequent "okay," acknowledges that she had been treating the mediator as a judge but now knows better (Heritage 1984a). And a move like Genie's "Ahh!" in 39 should not be deleted. While not containing overt propositional content, it is an evident disagreement with Fred's claim that he had supported their home all the time that they had been there. Rather than deletion, a negative proposition should be substituted.

One large class of utterances seems best placed in the opening stage of a critical discussion, rather than being treated as elements belonging to either the confrontation stage or the argumentation stage. Specifically, material in turns 01 through 12 concerns straightforward matters of purpose and procedure. In turns 07 and 09, for example, the mediator seems to be alluding to two specific rules common to divorce mediation cases concerning custody and visitation disputes: any arrangement should be in the best interests of the child, and any arrangement should be a consensus decision of both parents. But elements of the opening stage occur elsewhere in this episode, needing some permutation. In 46 the mediator raises an issue of argumentative roles, denying that he serves as a judge of the arguments. And in 47 and 48 both Genie and Fred reply in ways that accept that denial, Genie acknowledging a change of state, and Fred claiming to be simply "telling" what happened—not arguing a case to the mediator (though the subsequent exchange, and especially Genie's use of third-person reference to Fred, makes it clear that the mediator continues to be treated, if not as judge, at least as an audience for their arguments).[4]

Seen as moves in the opening stage, the mediator's questions in 13, 15, 17, 19, and 23 are sensible efforts to gain commitments on the part of Genie and Fred to the decision rule that any arrangement should be in the best interests of Jonathan. In their answers both parents suggest a more concrete criterion for what is best for Jonathan, namely, that what is best for Jonathan is, at least, being in the custody of someone who will be a good parent. And, it seems, a good parent is a good provider with a good character. Interestingly, while the answers that Genie and Fred provide can be partially reconstructed as affirmations of the mediator's decision criterion, this is not altogether the case. Here we have a situation where the answers seem to serve both to affirm an opening stage rule and to provide premises for the argumentation stage. Both Fred and Genie implicitly affirm that they want to do what is best for Jonathan, but they do so by treating the mediator's questions as prompts to show why they would be a good parent for Jonathan and also (in Genie's case) why the other parent would not be (see turn 26).

This latter function of the answers, like the vast bulk of the discourse, appears to belong to the argumentation stage.[5] In fact, Genie cuts off her answer in 14, and the rest of the turn appears to be best placed as establishing her standpoint and initiating argumentation in support of it, not as an affirmation of any decision rule at all. This seems to be why in turn 15 the mediator interrupts Genie's argument, suggests that he "back up a little bit," turns to Fred, and asks what he and Genie "would really like for Jonathan and Gregg, not not for yourselves but for them." Here, the mediator is in effect ruling as premature Genie's shift into argumentation over the case for Fred's suit.

While Fred's answers in 16, 18, and 20 can be reasonably treated as affirming a commitment to wanting what is best for the children, his reference to what he has been "tryin' to give 'em" and his elaboration in 20 seem to serve multiple functions. Fred has been a devoted, capable caretaker of both boys in the past. And so, perhaps it might be reasoned, he would be a good parent to Jonathan in the future. Likewise, in 24 Genie's answer echoes Fred's own formulation in 16. It serves to affirm her commitment to wanting what is best for the children. But Genie adds, "I'm working," an assertion that seems to have an argumentative function. Since, as is later revealed, Fred is not working, one might reason that Genie would be better able to give Jonathan "the best of everything." Both of these interpretations suggest transformations of addition, of inferred content not directly stated in the text; deletion and substitution, accomplished by identifying common statements (e.g., 16, 18, 20); and permutation, in the form of placement of material within stages of the discussion.

Conversely, some of the claims argued by Genie have the function not only of providing substantive support for her standpoints but also of addressing issues that are properly part of the opening stage. When Genie claims in 58 that Fred is telling a lie about Gregg's beating Jonathan while Genie stands by, and when she implies in 26 that Fred's claim for custody is motivated by a desire for reprisal against Genie, she not only is raising issues that have a substantive bearing on the truth of Fred's claims; she is also challenging Fred's commitment to satisfying the role requirements for a good-faith effort at argumentative engagement. In recognizing this latter function, the analyst has implicitly performed a transformation of permutation, identifying acts that normatively occur in the opening stage.

This identification of the various stages of a critical discussion in the example shows once again that we really are dealing with analytic distinctions. True, we can expect the concluding stage, if it occurs, to come at a later point at the end of this mediation session, and this projected final stage will be preceded by the argumentation stage. But the argumentation and opening stages are intermingled, and the confrontation stage, while it occurred at an earlier time, resurfaces during the discussion. Thus, we can see how the permutation transformation is necessary for a dialectical reconstruction.

The rest of the discourse seems to belong simply to the argumentation stage. The problem is what to make of the argumentation. There is clearly claim and counterclaim throughout, but it is difficult to see how the content of the assertions connects in any reasonable way to the issue in contention: Who should have custody of Jonathan?

Let us first try to make sense of Genie's apparent argumentation in turn 26. Upon inspection, the manifest content of her argument, together with plausible premises in arguing for and against custody, suggest a rather complex case. Genie begins by claiming that Fred should not gain custody of Jonathan "because I don't think that would be right." Why not? Genie seems to lay out two lines of argument for why Fred should not gain custody. The first line has to do with a set of attacks on Fred's character: he is on drugs; he drinks; he lies. And while this latter charge may function to undermine the credibility of Fred's charges against her, it also contributes to a case for the implicit claim that Fred would not be a worthy parent. Presumably these charges are signs of an inability to provide properly for Jonathan—which was the issue raised in response to the mediator's questioning in 13–23. And, presumably, these are also signs of moral character—an issue that might reasonably be thought to count in deciding who would be a good parent. This line of argument is reconstructed in figure 4.4.

The second line of argument (see figure 4.5) is that if Fred gains custody, Genie will not see Jonathan again. Her evidence for this assertion is that Fred has repeatedly threatened to take Jonathan away if he and Genie divorced. Since Fred is not working, he has nothing to hold him in the area; there is thus no external constraint against him following through on his threat. By contrast, Genie suggests that if she gains custody, Fred can have visitation rights. Moreover, the claim that Fred is not working contrasts with Genie's earlier assertion that she is working. In other words, Genie can better provide for Jonathan. This latter line of argument can also be reasonably seen to provide further support for Genie's other implicit line of argument, that Fred is neither able nor morally fit to be a good parent.

Figure 4.4

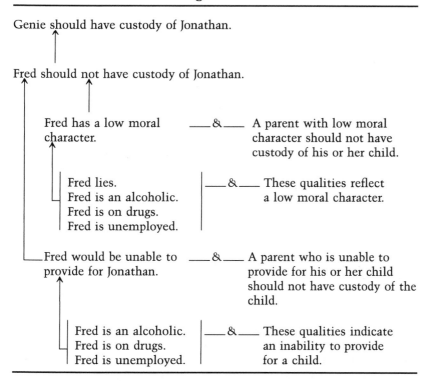

Genie should have custody of Jonathan.

Fred should not have custody of Jonathan.

Fred has a low moral character. ___&___ A parent with low moral character should not have custody of his or her child.

Fred lies.
Fred is an alcoholic.
Fred is on drugs.
Fred is unemployed. ___&___ These qualities reflect a low moral character.

Fred would be unable to provide for Jonathan. ___&___ A parent who is unable to provide for his or her child should not have custody of the child.

Fred is an alcoholic.
Fred is on drugs.
Fred is unemployed. ___&___ These qualities indicate an inability to provide for a child.

Figure 4.5

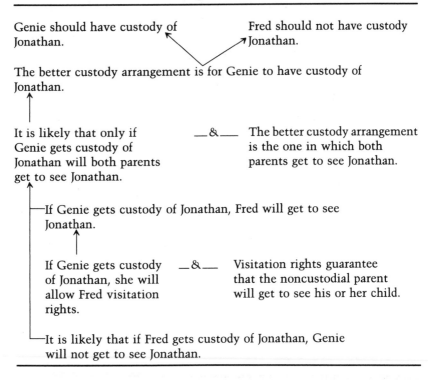

Genie should have custody of Jonathan.

Fred should not have custody Jonathan.

The better custody arrangement is for Genie to have custody of Jonathan.

It is likely that only if Genie gets custody of Jonathan will both parents get to see Jonathan.

___&___ The better custody arrangement is the one in which both parents get to see Jonathan.

If Genie gets custody of Jonathan, Fred will get to see Jonathan.

If Genie gets custody of Jonathan, she will allow Fred visitation rights.

___&___ Visitation rights guarantee that the noncustodial parent will get to see his or her child.

It is likely that if Fred gets custody of Jonathan, Genie will not get to see Jonathan.

Turn 26 ends with a cutoff sentence that seems to hark back to what Fred has said about Gregg's beating Jonathan and Genie's standing by and not doing anything about it. In turn 30 she seems to try to restart the utterance but is again cut off by Fred. But the implication seems clear: Fred's whole case is just a trumped-up effort to retaliate at Genie for getting a divorce. This implication follows both inferentially and sequentially from the report of Fred's earlier threats: "Now he's turned around" and is trying to carry out his threats by making up a lie to gain custody of Jonathan. It is a claim repeated later in turn 58. In 27 and 29 Fred seems to anticipate this implication and deny it, while Genie reasserts it in 28 and 30.

Notice here that Genie seems to be using the same arguments to support multiple, interrelated claims. By asserting that Fred is unemployed, Genie can support the claim that Fred will take Jonathan away if he gets custody, the claim that Fred would be unable to provide for Jonathan, and perhaps also the claim that Fred is of low moral character. Her argument that Fred will take Jonathan away from her if he gains custody is a way to show that Fred should not have custody of Jonathan; but it is also a way to attack the credi-

Figure 4.5 (Continued)

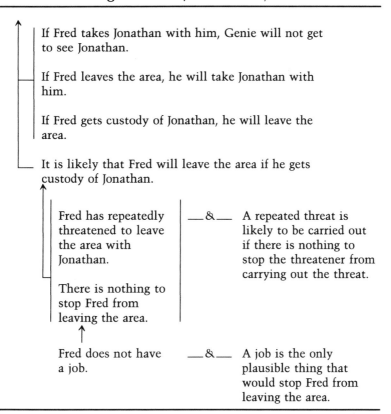

If Fred takes Jonathan with him, Genie will not get to see Jonathan.

If Fred leaves the area, he will take Jonathan with him.

If Fred gets custody of Jonathan, he will leave the area.

It is likely that Fred will leave the area if he gets custody of Jonathan.

Fred has repeatedly threatened to leave the area with Jonathan.   &   A repeated threat is likely to be carried out if there is nothing to stop the threatener from carrying out the threat.

There is nothing to stop Fred from leaving the area.

Fred does not have a job.   &   A job is the only plausible thing that would stop Fred from leaving the area.

bility of Fred's claim that Gregg beats Jonathan and Genie stands by and does not do anything about it. In similar fashion, establishing the claim that Fred is a liar serves as a sort of all-purpose argument to undermine the credibility of any claim he makes. We return to this point below.

Once again, several dialectical transformations have been implicitly performed in arriving at this interpretation. Fred's denial and redenial in 27 and 29 would be consolidated through substitution and deletion into the single assertion that his charges against Genie are true and well motivated. Likewise, a single charge by Genie would substitute for the last sentence in 26, her reaffirmation in 28, and the restart in 30. This would involve considerable addition of explicit information as well as deletion of repetitive turns. And Genie's case as a whole requires addition of implicit premises, unstated conclusions, implied comparisons, and unfinished propositions (e.g., he's an al[coholic]). It is important to note that, although this case may all seem plausible once presented, its main warrant is a set of presumptions attached to maximally dialectical analysis, and not any empirically determined or textually communicated information. Explicit structuring of the content and organization of Genie's argument is thin at best.

A similar plausible structure of reasoning can be attributed to the subsequent exchange concerning the accident. At first glance, it may seem that this whole issue is a non sequitur and a blatant appeal to sympathy on Fred's part. It would appear to involve simply a digressive chain of personal attacks and defensive excuses and quibbling over irrelevant facts. This may be true, but a rational reconstruction can also be arrived at. Following a strategy of maximally dialectical analysis, the facts as presented in Fred's narrative and the objections raised by Genie do have a commonsense bearing on the pivotal issues already implied in the discussion. Once these issues have been identified, they can be called upon to anchor a further reconstruction of each party's case.

We can isolate four apparent points of dispute in the subsequent discussion. The first arises in 31, 32, and 33 and is subsequently recycled in 50, 52, 53, and 54 and is mentioned again in 56. Fred claims he is not working because he had an accident. Genie claims he is not working because he was driving under the influence and went off a cliff. Fred claims that he was not cited for driving under the influence. He claims that he had beer after the accident with a lady who found him. Genie claims that she has the police report.

The second point of dispute arises in 33 and 34, is recycled in 35 and 36, and is mentioned again in 56. Fred claims the cliff was 450 feet high. Genie claims it was only 200 feet high.

The third point of dispute arises in Fred's account of how the accident occurred (38, 40, 43) and in Genie's turns in 45 and 56. Fred claims he was upset because in the middle of the night he was forced to pack up his things and leave the house. Genie claims that he was served papers which told him that he could not remove anything from the house, and instead "he took everything [from the house that] he could get his hands on" and then "lost everything" when he drove off the cliff.

We may also note a fourth point of dispute, although it seems to be dropped. Fred denies Genie's earlier charge (in 26) that he "is on drugs." Fred claims in 33 and 55 that he was not and is not on drugs. But Genie never responds to this direct denial.

We can isolate these points of dispute relatively easily, permuting these claims into common clusters, deleting repetitions, and adding implicit argumentation. One is tempted to ask at this point, What in the world does any of this have to do with who should get custody of

Jonathan? Whatever else we would want to say about these arguments, we certainly would want to acknowledge the lack of any clear connection to the standpoints at issue.

Nevertheless, these arguments can be assigned relevance if we attribute to both Fred and Genie cases based on impugning aspects of the other's moral character and establishing their own good character. This theme has proven relatively successful in sensibly reconstructing the argumentation so far. Fred's accusation (in 14) and Genie's counteraccusation (in 26) have clear moral overtones. This is likewise true of Fred's self-portrayal (in 16, 18, 20) and of Genie's self-portrayal (24, last line of 14). It turns out that this theme provides a reasonable basis for reconstructing the relevance of these other points of dispute.

In 31 Fred responds to Genie's claim that he is not working ("I'm not working because I had an accident"). His response does not deny the practical consequences of this fact for his ability to provide for Jonathan, nor does it address its role as evidence that he will act on his threat to take Jonathan away. Yet these seem to be the main points behind Genie's making this claim. Fred's excuse, of course, could simply be a non sequitur. We could just assume that Fred is not following Genie's argument very well or that he is having trouble thinking of a strong reply in the heat of the moment. But the importance of moral character to both parties' cases suggests another sort of relevance to Fred's excuse, one reconstructed in figure 4.6.

Specifically, given Genie's earlier charges, it would be easy to infer that Fred does not want to hold down a job or that he is the kind of person who, for morally culpable reasons (like alcoholism), cannot hold down a job. Having an accident is an external cause for failure that contrasts with internal causes for failure. It thus seems reasonable to assume that the point of Fred's argument is to deny that his being out of work should be taken as a negative reflection on his moral character. It is not his fault.

Seen in this frame, Genie's charge that Fred was driving under the influence is not just a petty, local refutation with no bearing on broader issues; it is a way of reestablishing the moral implications of his being out of work. By claiming that he was driving under the influence, Genie is arguing that Fred was the cause of the accident, and therefore he is at fault for being out of work. Moreover, she has turned Fred's excuse into concrete evidence that he drinks.

In turn 33 Fred does not directly deny that he was driving while under the influence. Instead, he asserts two facts that invite the inference that he was not under the influence. He claims that he was not cited for driving while under the influence (a claim repeated in

Figure 4.6

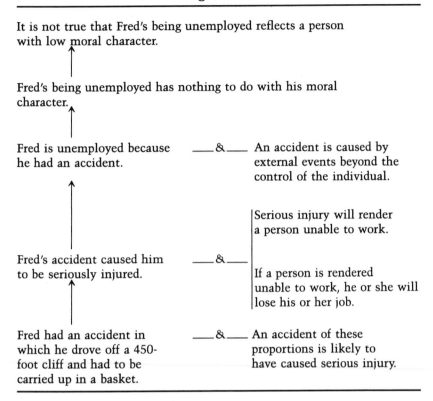

It is not true that Fred's being unemployed reflects a person with low moral character.

↑

Fred's being unemployed has nothing to do with his moral character.

↑

Fred is unemployed because he had an accident.   ___&___ An accident is caused by external events beyond the control of the individual.

Serious injury will render a person unable to work.

Fred's accident caused him to be seriously injured.   ___&___ If a person is rendered unable to work, he or she will lose his or her job.

↑

Fred had an accident in which he drove off a 450-foot cliff and had to be carried up in a basket.   ___&___ An accident of these proportions is likely to have caused serious injury.

53). And he claims that he did have beer with the lady that found him while they were waiting for help.

Here the strategy of maximally dialectical analysis suggests that we not assign to Fred's response an indirect denial that he was driving under the influence. We could do so. It would be a strong position to claim, and ordinarily that would be the inference a person would make. But adding this indirect denial does not explain why Fred does not just openly deny Genie's charge when that would be the most forceful way to respond. He has two opportunities to do so, in 33 and then again in 53. But he twice withholds a direct denial, even though he twice produces a bald, unmitigated negation ("I had not been cited"). Instead, we might assume that Fred may not actually be denying the charge because the charge is true, and so Fred is taking a weaker line of defense: Genie cannot make the charge stick. That line makes sense, given that this particular discussion is being conducted in the shadow of a custody suit before the court.

For the first claim, rather than adding the conclusion that Fred was not drinking while driving, we can add the conclusion that Genie cannot prove that Fred was driving under the influence (which is what she responds to in 54). Assigning that more limited inference suggests a related implicature from the second claim; namely, by claiming that he had beer with someone after the accident, Fred is implicating that he has an alibi. He can show why someone might wrongly think he had been drinking before the accident, and he can corroborate his explanation with eyewitness testimony.

Notice that Genie seems sensitive to this evidentiary tactic as well. In 50 she backs up her claim that Fred was driving under the influence by asserting, "I have the police report *in* my purse." Again, we could add the missing premise that the police report states that Fred was driving under the influence, which ordinarily would be the inference a person would draw. But Genie does not claim that the police report charges Fred with driving under the influence. In fact, in 54 she admits that Fred had not been cited, but the reason was "because there was no one to see him behind the wheel." Instead, the dialectical addition suggested by the strategy of maximally dialectical analysis seems to be the more limited implicature that the police report contains (unspecified) evidence that will corroborate Genie's account of the accident.

Turn 33 initiates a second point of contention. Was the cliff 450 feet or 200 feet high? In reconstructing this exchange, standard propositions can be readily substituted for the content of Fred's and Genie's assertion and counterassertion. And the repetition in 35 and 36 can be deleted. But a problem arises in assigning relevance to these assertions. What difference does it make? What is the argumentative force of these assertions? For Fred, reporting the fact that he was pulled up in a basket from the base of a 450-foot cliff can be taken as graphic evidence that Fred had a bad accident. While this detail may be part of a simple appeal to sympathy, a dialectical reconstruction would suggest that it also has a more relevant argumentative function. Fred is out of work, not because he does not want to work, but because he was so seriously injured that he cannot work.

Whether the cliff was 450 feet or 200 feet high makes little difference to this line of argument. Both distances are a pretty long way to fall. But Genie's denial can serve to bolster a claim that is crucial to her case: Fred lies.[6] It thus becomes important for Fred to stick to his original story.

In the third point of dispute, Fred explains to the mediator how the accident occurred. Once again, the way the story is told might be taken simply as an illicit appeal to sympathy, or as a pointless digression instigated by the mediator to cut off the seemingly petty squabbling in 33–36. But Fred's account is filled with details that also excuse his driving off the cliff as not his fault, that portray Genie as a morally suspect character, and that cast Fred's character in a positive light. We can add the premises required for two causal chains of reasoning. First, Fred reports, "I was nervous I was upset." Being nervous and upset causes a person to make driving errors that result in accidents. Therefore, being nervous and upset caused Fred to make a driving error that resulted in his accident—and this can be presented as a plausible alternative cause of the accident. The second causal chain has to do with the reason why Fred was nervous and upset. He claims he was "abruptly woken in the middle of the night," was told to pack his personal effects, and was "evicted from my home." Presumably, this experience would be enough to make anyone nervous and upset.

Fred's description suggests that, without warning, he was kicked out of his own home and sent packing "in the middle of the night." We might add the premise that only a person of bad character would do such a thing. Presumably, the person who did this was Genie. The conclusion: Genie is a person of bad character. The details of the story, then, function not only to excuse Fred's accident but also to generate a claim that may counter Genie's claim that she should have custody of Jonathan. Presumably, a person who would do this sort of thing would not be a morally worthy parent.

In his story Fred also suggests that he supported the home all the time they had been there (something which Genie scoffs at). While Fred does not explicitly make the argument, this need not be seen as simply a gratuitous interjection. One of the claims he makes in 16, 18, and 20 is that he has been a good provider for his family. This fact can be taken as evidence for his claim to being a good provider. Fred's story can thus be plausibly reconstructed to have multiple argumentative implications for the kinds of moral issues that seem to preoccupy the disputants.

In turns 45 and 56 Genie can be taken as trying to refute central elements of Fred's account. Once again, the point seems to be the question of Fred's and Genie's characters. In claiming that Fred was served divorce papers at 5:20 A.M., Genie is presumably contradicting Fred's claim that he was "abruptly woken in the middle of the night" and may be considerably softening all of the moral implications that might follow from this scenario. The event does not indicate an act reflecting Genie's bad character, but an administrative procedure she had to invoke in order to get Fred to leave. It seems likely that if Fred had been served papers, that Fred knew this was coming some time in advance, and so he could not fairly suggest that he was kicked out of the house without warning and that, in fact, it could be fairly said that he provoked this unseemly incident by not acting ahead of time to leave the house in a timely and orderly fashion.

But the main point of Genie's report in 45 and 56 seems to be that the papers ordered Fred not to remove anything from the house, and instead "he took everything he could get his hands on" and "lost everything" when he drove off the cliff. The fact that Fred has twisted the story suggests once again that he lies. And the fact that he took all the household possessions and drove them off a cliff is further evidence of Fred's irresponsible if not actually malicious character, and evidence that Fred's primary motive in filing a custody claim for Jonathan is one of reprisal. We have, once again, an elaboration of one of the main lines of argument in Genie's case. Taken collectively, Genie's argument seems to be a series of refutations to a series of possible objections to her main point: Fred's case for custody of Jonathan and his efforts at refutation should not be believed.

Figure 4.7

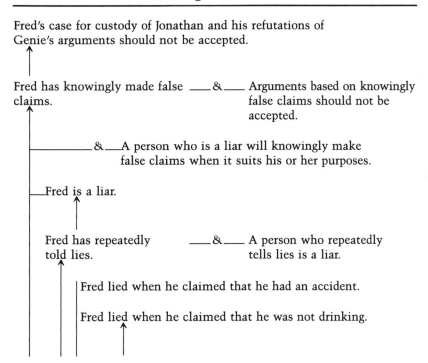

Fred's case for custody of Jonathan and his refutations of Genie's arguments should not be accepted.

Fred has knowingly made false claims. ___&___ Arguments based on knowingly false claims should not be accepted.

___&___A person who is a liar will knowingly make false claims when it suits his or her purposes.

Fred is a liar.

Fred has repeatedly told lies. ___&___ A person who repeatedly tells lies is a liar.

Fred lied when he claimed that he had an accident.

Fred lied when he claimed that he was not drinking.

Figure 4.7 (Continued)

Fred was drinking.

↑

The police report supports the claim that Fred was drinking.

Fred lied when he claimed the cliff was 450 feet high.

↑

The cliff was 200 feet.

↑

The police report supports the claim that the cliff was 200 feet.

Fred lied when he claimed that he was thrown out of the house without warning or cause.

↑

Fred was served ____&____ Divorce papers can be
divorce papers.   reasonably anticipated and
                       are based on justifiable
                       cause.

It suits Fred's purposes to argue for custody of Jonathan.

↑

Fred has the purpose of getting revenge on Genie for divorcing him.

↑

Fred has expressed this purpose.

↑

Fred has repeatedly threatened to leave the area with Jonathan if Genie divorces him.

Fred has acted in the past on the purpose of getting revenge on Genie for divorcing him.

↑

When Fred was evicted ____&____ Fred took everything he
from the home, he took   could get his hands on in

Figure 4.7 (Continued)

everything he could
get his hands on.

order to get revenge on
Genie.

Arguing for custody of Jonathan is part of a plan for Fred
to get revenge on Genie.

If Fred wins his arguments, Fred will get custody
of Jonathan.

If Fred gets custody of Jonathan, Fred will leave
the area.

If Fred leaves the area, Fred will take Jonathan
with him.

If Fred takes Jonathan with him, Genie will not
see Jonathan anymore.

If Genie does not see Jonathan anymore, Fred will
get revenge on Genie.

There is no plausible way to stop Fred from carrying out
his plan if he gains custody of Jonathan.

&————If Fred gains custody of Jonathan, a job
or a court order are the only plausible
means to prevent Fred from carrying out
his plan to get revenge on Genie.

It is not true that Fred's job will prevent him from
leaving the area.

Fred does not have a job.

It is not true that a court order would keep Fred
from leaving the area with Jonathan.

Fred has disobeyed ——&—— A court order would have
court orders in the   no more force in the

Figure 4.7 (Continued)

past in order to get revenge on Genie.	current case than it had in the past.
When Fred was evicted from the home, he took everything he could get his hands on in order to get revenge on Genie.	When Fred was evicted from the home, he was ordered by the court not to take anything.

The Analytic Overview

In this example we have presented a tentative reconstruction of the episode so as to illustrate the way in which dialectical transformations relate the material in a normative reconstruction to what is presented in the ordinary discourse. In doing so, we have presented a kind of analytic overview of the discussion. We have not placed the entire discussion in analytic overview, nor have we always presented the most explicit analytic overview possible. But we have selected enough of the discussion and analyzed it in enough detail that it should be clear how ordinary discourse may be transformed in a manner consistent with the interests of a dialectical reconstruction. In any particular case, what in a discussion gets reconstructed at what level of explicitness in what form will depend on the purpose of the analysis.[7]

In constructing an analytic overview, we have clarified the argumentative functions of various parts of the discussion, showing how they contribute to various stages of critical discussion. We have teased out in more or less explicit fashion a context of claims, assumptions, and lines of reasoning that lend substance to the dispute. By showing the point of various moves in the discussion, we have uncovered a degree of strategic and inferential coherence in the dispute that might not otherwise have been appreciated.

An analytic overview has great advantages in terms of oversight and discernment, especially in more complex discourse. Furthermore, the points that are included in an analytic overview are of direct relevance to the evaluation of the argumentative discourse. In order to understand an argumentative discourse properly, to explain its coherence, and to respond to it in an adequate way, an analytic overview is indispensable.

If it is unclear what standpoint is being defended, there is no way of telling whether the argumentation that has been advanced is conclusive. And if more than one standpoint is being defended in a discussion, it must be perfectly clear which language users are acting as the protagonist of which standpoint and who is the source of the various arguments that have been advanced to defend each one. Otherwise, it will also be impossible to tell whether the various arguments for the same standpoint actually constitute a coherent whole.

In developing an analytic overview of this dispute, we are able to see what sorts of premises are shared and taken for granted by the discussants, and what points are in dispute. For example, it becomes clear that both parties have taken issues of character to be central to the main issue of who should have custody of Jonathan—though exactly how issues of character relate to a decision is sometimes left vague. Moreover, a major part of Genie's case rests on the claim that Fred is arguing in bad faith—that he is lying and arguing out of a motive for revenge. It is important to identify these aspects of the argument because both issues, in their own way, have a corrosive influence on the conduct of the discussion. Raising issues of character often turns the discussion into a moral struggle to establish the other party's blameworthiness and to defend oneself against moral censure rather than a cooperative search for a workable custody arrangement that is in the best interests of the child. This is one reason why mediators commonly try to create a "no-fault" framework for discussion of custody. Similarly, Genie's claim that Fred is acting in bad faith effectively challenges a crucial precondition to argumentative engagement.

It should be noted, however, that just because we can identify reasonable cases does not mean that those cases have been entered into the discussion in a way that promotes reasonable argumentation concerning those cases. By following the strategy of maximally dialectical analysis, we have been able to put the best case forward for both discussants. This is not to say that the discussants themselves have put forward their cases in the best way. The expressive insufficiency of the case as presented by Genie and Fred in part shows that they have not. Empirically, while what Genie and Fred say does not really contradict the reconstruction presented here, it does not strongly support it either. Consider simply the interactional shifts of focus throughout the dialogue.

For example, in order to come to a reasonable reconstruction of the turns from 26 through 31, we have to make sense of both Fred's and Genie's indefinite reference to what is and is not true. With Genie, we can reasonably take it that she believes what is at issue is something about what Fred has said about Gregg—presumably her point at the end of 26, that Fred is making trumped-up charges simply to get revenge by getting Jonathan. But what about Fred? If that is also his point, we must assume that in turn 31 he has dropped this dispute and has started on a new point. If turns 27 and 29 anticipate his claim in 31, we must assume that he is overtly responding to a claim that is at best deeply embedded in the inferential consequences of what Genie has expressed in turn 26 and that he is largely unresponsive to the point Genie is trying to make.

Or again, while Genie's contradiction in turn 34 ("two hundred feet, two hundred feet") is propositionally relevant to what Fred has argued, it is not pragmatically responsive to Fred's point in any direct way.

An analytic overview reflects the particular interests of the analyst as much as it reflects the argumentation of the discussants. In a certain sense, the reconstructed presentation of the argumentation stands as an ideal contrast to the actual presentation of the discussants. Rather than dissolving the apparent disorder, irrelevance, seeming vagueness, and lack of explicitness in the argumentation, an analytic overview can be seen to highlight it. What we have shown in analytic overview is how a maximally dialectical analysis can be constructed. The reconstructive framework of the analyst minimizes the role of communicative obligations by maximizing the burden of interpretation placed on the analyst.

In a dialectical reconstruction, relevance connections are sought for in a calculated and systematic way. In view of the specific insight that the analysis must provide, the interpretation of the discourse is, as it were, programmed by putting the text fragment to be analyzed into the perspective of resolving differences of opinion, and then by checking whether the speech acts that are performed are functional within this framework. According to the ideal model, not all speech acts are functional at every stage of the process of resolving a difference of opinion; their relevance is linked to a specific stage in the resolving process and to the specific (sub)goal that is aimed for in that stage.

In carrying out a dialectical reconstruction, certain constraints on idealization do apply. The legitimacy of any transformation will be based on the normative resonance of the argumentative portrayal with the ideal model, and on the compatibility of that portrayal with the empirical evidence. This tension between empirical and normative adequacy can be captured in the formulation of certain adequacy conditions. As a dialectical reconstruction is aimed at bringing the discourse into the appropriate standard-form of a critical discussion, the dialectical transformations have to satisfy the following general conditions of efficacy, well-foundedness, and parsimony.

The efficacy condition obliges the analyst to make sure that any proposed transformation unambiguously leads to a standard formulation of a speech act represented in the ideal model. The well-foundedness condition guarantees that any proposed transformation be motivated by a pragmatically sound empirical observation concerning the discourse. The analyst should keep in mind that a dialectical reconstruction is not meant to deal with parts of the discourse not intended to play a part in resolving a dispute. It should likewise be kept in mind that the reconstruction ought not render the discourse incoherent. The parsimony condition requires the analyst to change only as much of the discourse as is necessary to produce a critical discussion. These conditions always apply within an analytic context of possible alternative portrayals of the argumentation. Any particular reconstructive transformation will always be tentative, subject to its consistency with an overall reconstruction and relative to the plausibility of those alternative portrayals entertained by the analyst.

Notes

1. In describing this relationship, we do not mean to imply that the ordinary discourse is some sort of pure textual reality, nor do we wish to imply that these transformations are unique to dialectical reconstruction. They are logically required possibilities for *any* representation. Transcription of conversation, for example, involves the same types of transformation: *deletion* of most paravocal qualities of utterance, background sounds, and the whole range of visually available expression, activity, and setting; *addition* of background information, editorial description, and such transcription notation as turn identification; *permutation* of simultaneous talk into a linear arrangement on the page; and *substitution* of standardized orthographic forms for phonetically varied words and utterances.

2. Details of the institution of mediation are described more fully in chapter 6.

3. Transcription notation is explained in note 2 to chapter 3. Mediations analyzed in this chapter and in chapter 6 were selected from transcribed audiotapes of twenty pre- and post-divorce custody and visitation mediation sessions conducted by the Los Angeles County Family Mediation and Conciliation Court. The mediation service is described in Pearson and Thoennes 1984. The transcripts were prepared by Deborah Weider-Hatfield (School of Communication, University of Central Florida) and were made available to us by William A. Donohue (Department of Communication, Michigan State University). The audiotapes were part of approximately eighty collected by the Divorce Mediation Research Project (1981–84),

funded by the Children's Bureau of the United States Department of Health and Human Services (90-CW-634) and administered by Jessica Pearson, director of the Research Unit of the Association of Family and Conciliation Courts, Denver. All names in the transcription have been changed.

4. Notice that Genie's use of "and I'm telling you," while parallel to Fred's usage, does not mean that she is *just* telling rather than arguing. Rather, the phrase is used to add an insistent force to her contrasting position—Fred did not simply have an accident; he was driving under the influence.

5. We should note that there is no concluding stage present in this episode. The episode continues for some time past turn 60, and no overt resolution is ever achieved. The argument becomes so heated that the mediator simply cuts off further discussion by having Fred and Genie call their attorneys back into the room.

6. Notice that here we would ordinarily infer that Genie's claim "I have the police report" implicitly suggests that the police report says the cliff was 200 feet high. She may also be implying that she can prove her case in court.

7. A different analytic overview could be supplied that would highlight other aspects of the argumentation in terms of its contribution to a critical discussion. The patterns of representation chosen here obviously emphasize premises and conclusions and neglect, for example, the interactional structure that might be captured by a flow-sheet representation. Other patterns of representation might, for example, better portray the open-ended way in which the discussants seemingly use materials to support and refute multiple points simultaneously.

5

The Pragmatic Organization of Conversational Argument

In the preceding chapters we have provided a normative framework for the reconstruction of conversational argument. The dialectical model of critical discussion specifies what sorts of speech acts may be performed at various points in the discussion for various specifiable functions. In particular, both standpoints and the arguments that support or refute those standpoints are restricted to speech acts that fall within the general class of assertives. Consistent with this theoretical picture, it can be shown readily enough how natural conversational argument occurs through the exchange of speech acts. Both the object of conversational argument and the means of conversational argument are speech acts. Manifestly, however, arguments are often about speech acts other than assertives, and the argumentation is often conveyed by means of speech acts other than assertives. What are the implications of such facts for dialectical analysis?

In this chapter, we return to the problem of how speech act concepts can be applied to the analysis of conversational argumentation. In doing so, we hope to clarify the pragmatic properties of argumentation as it is conducted in everyday discourse and the relation of the pragmatic organization of argumentation in actual discourse to the pragmatic functioning of argumentation in the context of an ideal critical discussion. Specifically, we will focus on two points:

1. Conversational argumentation is pragmatically organized by the speech acts in which it occurs and by the practical activities in which it plays a role.

2. How we reconstruct the pragmatic functioning of conversational argument as a contribution to the resolution of a difference of opinion in a critical discussion depends upon locating its pragmatic functioning in the context of the practical activities and situated speech acts in which it occurs in actual discourse.

Normative and Naive Reconstruction

To some degree, conversational acts playing a part in an argument can always be "reconstructed" in the form of assertives; the point of this reconstruction is to lay out the structure of each arguer's case. But the analytic work involved in extracting these assertives from argumentative discourse, in seeing how they hang together as a case, and in seeing how they are responsive to elements of an opposing case depends upon an intermediate analytic step that is sensitive to the speech acts being performed and the practical activity context in which they are performed.

The outcome of a normative reconstruction in the dialectical sense will be to recover from a sequence of practically organized speech acts a set of argumentatively relevant moves. The main constraint on such a reconstruction is that the argumentatively relevant moves must be assertives with some identifiable propositional content connected in some accountable way to the speech acts actually performed in the dialogue. The fact that speakers are committed to the acceptability and relevance of the speech acts they are intentionally performing means that those speakers will also be committed to the acceptability and relevance of any assertives that can be reconstructed from that speech act, as pragmatic presuppositions, felicity conditions, or implicatures.

Although a dialectical reconstruction is not an attempt to model natural interpretive processes, it should be clear that any reconstruction offered as an account of the properties of an interaction must have some correspondence with what the participants themselves make of the interaction. If an analytic account of a sequence is given in which certain reconstructed commitments of a protagonist are used to explain the sense and force of an antagonist's response, the account implies that the antagonist has performed or could perform a similar sort of reconstruction. If interactants are assumed to be reconstructing their partners' standpoints, arguments, and cases from the discussion, the work that goes into this "naive reconstruction" is part of what must be explained by a dialectical reconstruction.

Any assertive that can be identified within a dialectical reconstruction of discourse must also be accessible, in principle, to naive reconstruction by the arguers themselves. Any reconstructible commitment associated with an utterance, if it can be retrieved through dialectical reconstruction, must also be retrievable by interactants. As we shall see, the organization of argumentation in conversation depends upon an ongoing process of naive reconstruction by both interactants. This reconstruction is guided by certain deep-background analyses of situation and purpose. Naive reconstructions are visible in the conduct of the discussion, though they are not always explicated. A dialectical reconstruction of an argumentative discussion as a series of assertive moves is not generally possible without attention to these naive reconstructions and the issues that give rise to them.

As an initial way of orienting to the problem of dialectically reconstructing argumentation from the practical contexts of activity in which it occurs, consider the relatively simple case of example 5.1.[1]

There is not much to the argument here, but there is considerably more than appears in a straightforward, literal reading of the text. A starting point for any reconstruction is an identification of standpoints. In this example, C adopts something like the standpoint that B should use one of the display pens on the nearby counter to write her check. In turn 02, B argues against this standpoint, giving as a reason for not accepting it that if she did, she would have to drop out of line and thereby would lose her place in line. In turn 03, C seemingly denies the main claim in B's argument, asserting in effect that she won't lose her place in line. And in turn 04, B seemingly accepts this denial.

Example 5.1

(B and C, who are strangers to one another, are standing next to each other in a checkout line. B is writing out a check when her pen runs out of ink. C points to several display pens on a nearby counter.)

01 C: Why don't you use one of those?

02 B: I'd lose my place in line.

03 C: No you won't.

04 B: Okay. Thank you.

But why does C's denial carry any weight for B? Taken simply as an assertive, C provides no better grounding for his denial than B has for her assertion that she would lose her place in line. Presumably, both B and C are aware of the cultural practices which lead to her claim. At least in crowded American college bookstores, when people drop out of line, they are not allowed back in. In turn 03, C communicates nothing to deny that this norm would not apply. So, what is C's basis for denying this argument?

To answer this question, we have to point to the context of practical activity from which this argumentation has been extracted. B is trying to figure out how to write her check and stay in line at the same time. Part of what is going on in this exchange is not simply argumentation, but argumentation designed to negotiate the force of the speech act in which C's standpoint is initially expressed. Is he just making a suggestion for what B should do, or is he offering to help her? B's objection in 02 does more than make an argument; it provides an opportunity for C to offer to help solve her dilemma (e.g., to hold her place in line). And C's response in turn 03 is not primarily an assertive at all. It is a commissive, an offer. Or perhaps, more accurately, C's denial makes it clear that his initial question was intended all along to be taken as expressing an offer to hold B's place in line. In fact, C's standpoint and subsequent denial are embedded in a commissive that guarantees the truth of his claim that B will not lose her place in line. That is why in turn 04, B does not simply accept C's standpoint but accepts his offer and thanks him.

The most important thing to notice about this brief dialogue is that although it is possible to arrive at a reconstruction in which all of the individual contributions have canonical assertive form, it is not possible to do so without paying attention to the pragmatic organization of the dialogue. That is, C's assertion that B will not lose her place in line has the argumentative relevance that it does because of the force of the speech act in which it occurs. Should the truth of C's assertion be challenged, the assertion would be shown to depend for its truth not on other more basic assertions but on C's having undertaken to bring about a certain state of affairs.

The pragmatic grounding of argumentation in broader conversational activities is quite common. Arguments are frequently performed through speech acts other than simple assertives, and the argumentative force they have depends on the characteristics of the speech events in which they occur. Likewise, the standpoints that get expressed and taken up for argument have their sense and relevance established by the purposes of the activity in which they occur.

Virtual Standpoints and Disagreement Space

Among the materials available to a participant in an argumentative discussion are the discourse itself and the surrounding context of practical activity. From these two components it will always be possible to infer an indefinitely large and complex set of beliefs, wants, and intentions that jointly compose the perspective of one's partner. Any component of this perspective may be "called out" and made problematic within the discourse, if it has any sort of relevance to the underlying purpose of the exchange. When this occurs, the problematized element functions as a "virtual standpoint" in need of defense. Any reconstructible commitment associated with the performance of a speech act can function as a virtual standpoint when it is in fact reconstructed and challenged by an interlocutor. The entire complex of reconstructible commitments can be considered as a "disagreement space," a structured set of opportunities for argument.

Argument in ordinary interaction does not typically occur as an independent, self-organized activity type, but as a subordinate activity laid over other activities of all sorts. Argument can be seen as a kind of regulative mechanism that has relevance to every performance of a speech act of any kind. Argument, as a repair mechanism, selects disputable standpoints in a way that is ever attentive to the purposes of the interaction and to the contributions of individual speech acts to accomplishing those purposes. Every speech act performance creates a structured but indefinitely expandable disagreement space, an open-ended set of virtual standpoints, any one of which, on being "called out," might require defense. So argument is not limited to interactions in which one person makes a claim and another disputes it or to interactions in which two parties enter into a certain sort of dialogue. Argument normally emerges from other sorts of activities, and it can occur in response to any sort of speech act whatsoever, for example, when one party makes a request and anticipates that the other will refuse it or challenge its justification, when one party complains and the other refutes the complaint or questions its legitimacy, or even when one party offers a compliment and the other unexpectedly finds it offensive. Likewise, it can be conveyed by any sort of speech act that can evoke the substantive grounds for disagreement.

The conversational act giving rise to disagreement is often some steps removed from any standpoint or virtual standpoint reconstructed from it; indeed, any speech act will normally imply some large set of associated beliefs that *could* be treated as standpoints.

These are termed *virtual* standpoints to emphasize that they are not, in the performance of the arguable act, put forward *as* standpoints. As they represent commitments the speaker has already accepted implicitly in the performance of the arguable act, however, they function within a limited exchange as the equivalents of standpoints put forward as such.

Any presupposed belief or intention associated with an act can be challenged and can give rise to argument. And any conversational act is potentially arguable in terms of some virtual standpoint. Unlike standpoints put forward as such, virtual standpoints are determined collaboratively in conversation, through acts of naive reconstruction. Any speaker may find that he or she is responsible for defending a standpoint at any moment, when an interactional partner chooses to call out and challenge some previously submerged issue.

We can see both the process of naive reconstruction and the functioning of virtual standpoints in the argumentation contained in example 5.2. The conversation took place in the living room of a college apartment, among four young male roommates.[2] A is taking inventory of the stock of marijuana purchased by C, D, and himself. B only occasionally smokes from the stash and never helps to purchase it.

There is an argument going on in this exchange, and as with example 5.1, there is much more to it than obviously appears in the text itself. B's statement in 16 is not simply an informative comparison with A's report in 01–05. It is an argument against a standpoint imputed to A (and perhaps also to C and D). Nor is C's statement in 17 simply an elaboration or amplification of B's comparison. It is not an agreement with B's point. Somehow, it is a refutation of it. In the subsequent exchange (19–21) B is not just digressing irrelevantly about himself or correcting C's quantification but is defending his argument against C's counterargument. Turns 16, 17, 18, and 19 all can and should be considered arguments of some sort. But how do we make sense of what these arguments amount to, and how do we account for the fact that argumentation is going on at all?

One analytic problem posed by this exchange is how to construct the standpoints that are at issue. The participants themselves seem to be orienting to virtual standpoints inferred from beliefs and intentions embedded in the practical activities in which they are engaged. Tentatively, we might formulate the standpoint to which B's comment in 16 is a challenge as "It is appropriate for the three of us (A, C, and D) to smoke on a regular basis one ounce of marijuana every two or three days." And presumably B is taking the opposite standpoint that it is inappropriate to do so. B seems to have retrieved

Example 5.2

01 A: We have eight ounces left. That should last us
for a couple of days a least
[
02 B: Heh yeah, I guess *so.*

03 A: Twenty-four days I would estimate.

04 B: Eight *ounces*?!

05 A: Sure. We smoke a lid in two or three days.

((Intervening discussion deleted))

16 B: That's like- that's like drinking eight or nine kegs
every week.

17 C: Or smoking two packs of cigarettes every day.

18 D: EHHH-heh-heh-heh-heh

19 B: Yeah (.) Only I don't smoke two packs
of cigarettes every-
[
20 C: Three? Four?

21 B: No. Not nearly that many.

---

this virtual standpoint from the exchange in turns 01–05, but how?

Notice that the virtual standpoint as formulated above does not correspond directly to any of the particular speech acts that A performs over the course of turns 01–05. In 16, B does not seem to find anything problematic about the particular speech acts per se. B is not challenging A's report that there are eight ounces left. Nor is B challenging A's prediction and estimate that this amount will last twenty-four days. Notice also that B's comparison in 16 is not directly a comment on the content of A's affirmation and explanation in 05: "We smoke a lid in two or three days." The parallel would be for B to comment, "That's like drinking eight or nine kegs in a week," or, more directly yet, to comment, "That's like drinking a keg in less than one day." But B's statement concerns drinking eight or nine kegs *every* week. The focus is not on how much time it takes to consume a single keg or lid but on how many lids or kegs are consumed over a given time period. Whereas A's statement in 05 could be heard as conditional on the possession of a lid, B's reply has no such conditional quality. Somewhere in A's remarks B has found grounds for attributing the proposition that his three roommates together are in the habit of smoking a lid *every* two or three days.

But this proposition is still short of the virtual standpoint B calls out and challenges. What makes that proposition troubling is not its truth or any other aspect of the acceptability of asserting it but its revelation of a deep-background intention: namely, the intention to *continue* smoking a lid every two or three days and indeed, to take measures to assure this continuation.[3] That this is A's intention follows from the activity in which A's utterances are made. The reason that A is taking inventory and announcing how much marijuana is left and how long it will last is that A is determining when the group will have to buy more marijuana so that they can continue smoking on a regular schedule without running out. The proposition that A, C, and D together smoke a lid every two or three days is a constraint on, and demand for, a plan for future conduct. The role of this proposition emerges from A's responses to B's comments in 02 and 04. B's sarcastic agreement in 02 ("Heh yeah, I guess *so*") cuts in right after A says, "That should last us." It overlaps with A's continuation "for a couple of days at least" and does not respond to it. Taken by itself, the phrase "That should last us" is the sort of assessment one makes to imply that a task is finished. B's agreement orients to the implication that there is no need for further worry, that eight ounces is a more than ample supply of marijuana. In turn 03, A redoes his continuation, this time in a way that suggests something else: there is no need for immediate worry, but the supply is not all that large. It will run out soon enough—in twenty-four days to be exact.

At this estimate, B expresses incredulity. B implies that this number grossly contradicts his own estimate and that he cannot understand the basis for calculating that eight ounces would only last twenty-four days. In turn 05, A explains the basis for his calculation, and in doing so in a matter-of-fact way, A makes it clear that he sees nothing remarkable or troubling about the basic "facts" used to determine when the current supply will be exhausted. So, the virtual standpoint to which B's contra-argumentation in 16 is directed has been reconstructed by B himself, and the relevance of his contra-argumentation can be recognized and accounted for only by understanding how the broader practical activity authorizes this reconstruction.

Another analytic problem posed by this example is how to account for the argumentative force and relevance of turns 16–21. Recognizing and accounting for their argumentative force and relevance requires seeing how, for the purposes of the conversational activity, these utterances function as speech acts. B's argument in 16 carries more than just the force of an assertion to the effect that smoking this much marijuana is excessive. While the comparison that B makes could, in some contexts, be heard as a socially and interpersonally neutral observation, it is not heard that way in this context. B's comparison amounts to an act of criticism and ridicule, an effort to censure the behavior of A, C, and D.

The force of B's comparison as both argument and criticism relies heavily on seeing the implications of the social meaning of drinking kegs. For this group of roommates, drinking kegs of beer had a strong stereotypical association with the social life of "fraternity boys," a life-style and class of persons held in deep contempt by all four roommates. To use this comparison is to suggest that A, C, and D are like fraternity boys, and like them in terms of an activity (the keg party) that they themselves have repeatedly singled out for ridicule. It is because this background is called up that B's comparison has argumentative force in the first place. Because B's comparison ridicules A, C, and D, it has the argumentative force that it does (rather than, say, the kind of argumentative force that might be heard were B's utterance to be taken as a laudatory expression of admiration). B is arguing that smoking this amount of marijuana is morally objectionable in the same way that drinking kegs is morally objectionable, and it is therefore an activity worthy of the same sort of ridicule. This latter inference is strongly signaled by the ridiculously exaggerated terms of the comparison (three kegs per person per week). The factual accuracy of the comparison is not intended to be an issue.

For the purposes of reconstructing and evaluating B's argument as a challenge to A's standpoint, the force of B's argument as a criticism might be ignored. But doing so would make the sense and force of the subsequent exchange quite opaque, or at least unaccountably irrelevant. Taken as an argument against the assertion that it is objectionable to smoke a lid every week, C's argument in 17 makes an irrelevant criticism. It stands as a classic case of argument ad hominem (cf. van Eemeren and Grootendorst 1992a, 11–113; 1992b). But this evaluation rests on reconstructing the discourse in terms of assertions taken more or less at face value, when it is clear that for the participants the discourse must be understood at a deeper pragmatic level. Taken in terms of the practical activity to which the roommates are orienting, C's utterance has its force and relevance as a criticism leveled against B's criticism. C's argument alludes to B's own peculiar substance abuse, implying that smoking two packs of cigarettes every day is the moral equivalent of smoking marijuana in the amounts at issue. As an argument, C is challenging B's right to pass judgment on the others' substance abuse, and that issue has a direct bearing on the appropriate performance of an act of criticism.

Moreover, by coming as a criticism, C's argument does more than simply refute B's argument. It is a "put-down" that spoils B's argumentative identity. It is the kind of tu quoque argument that places B in a morally compromised state from which he cannot easily continue to argue—even in his own self-defense. This kind of predicament is reflected in the decidedly weak denial that he offers in 19 and 21. What C has done is the kind of argumentative move that ordinarily would count as a fallacy of procedure. But it would count as a fallacy not so much because it asserts irrelevant propositional content or contains an error of reasoning but because arguments by criticism carry an illocutionary force that tends to shut down discussion.[4] And that problem is both visible and accountable in terms of the practical activity in which the argument occurs.

A dialectical reconstruction of this dialogue as a series of assertions is certainly possible, but it should be clear that to extract a set of indirectly performed assertions from the text, it is first necessary to see the text as an exchange of speech acts. Each act in each such exchange is arguable on a large number of separate underlying assumptions, and only after the participants themselves have accomplished the reconstruction of one of these as a virtual standpoint is it possible for an analyst to find the assertiveness of the original arguable act. So, we can see that it is largely because of participant follow-ups that the analyst is able to select among the possible standpoints at issue in any arguable act. What standpoints can be reasonably attributed to any conversationalist depends on the practical activity in which those standpoints are called out. Likewise, seeing the relevance of any line of argument depends on finding its place and role in the practical activities which the argumentation is designed to regulate.

The importance of activity and purpose to any account of argumentative discussion is illustrated from a slightly different angle by considering the exchange in example 5.3 below (from Goodwin 1985). Example 5.3 contains an ill-formed case of argument. What makes it ill formed is that the virtual standpoint taken up and argued, while certainly among the beliefs of the first speaker, has no pertinence to her purpose in speaking.

In turn 02, P calls out S's belief that "those people" are Spanish, treating it as a virtual standpoint. S accepts the attributed commitment to the belief and challenges P's counterclaim, abandoning her own original speech act. Although any competent speaker can see that S must believe that "those people" are Spanish, any competent speaker can also see that the dispute over this is off-track and digressive as regards the purpose of S's telling P that those people

Example 5.3

(P and S are two young urban black girls.)

01 S: Pam those Spanish people gonna tell on you!

02 P: They ain't Spanish. They Portariccan.

03 S: How you know they Portariccan.

04 P: They TALK Portariccan.

(whoever they are) are going to tell on her. What makes this example different from example 5.2, where A was challenged to defend an implicit belief with less connection to the actual text than S's belief that the people referred to as Spanish are in fact Spanish?

S's first turn could be decomposed into two simple propositions: "those people are Spanish" and "those people are going to tell on you." The two simple propositions are not equivalent in function, however, for one is asserted and the other is just used to make the assertion. "Those people are going to tell on you" triggers a chain of inferences that convey acts of warning and, perhaps also, criticizing, reprimanding, taunting, and the like. This is the primary point of the utterance. Pam is going to get in trouble for what she has done because those people are going to tell on her.

Although "those people are Spanish" is not asserted, it can be reconstructed as a virtual standpoint in the same way that virtual standpoints were reconstructed from the earlier cases. But even as a logical presupposition of what S *has* asserted, its only role is to identify which people are being referred to, and the success of this identification is already presupposed by P's objection that "those people" are not Spanish but Puerto Rican. S's commitment to "those people are Spanish" is easily inferable from her speech, but not in a way that has a substantive bearing on the appropriateness of any primary speech act(s) she might be performing. Whether those people that S refers to are Spanish or Puerto Rican is irrelevant to whether or not they are going to tell on Pam, whether or not Pam will get in trouble as a result, whether or not Pam has done anything she deserves to get in trouble for, and so on. The truth of the proposition that those people are Spanish is no more relevant to the issues at hand than is the truth of the proposition that the addressee's name is Pam. Assigning the attribute "Spanish" to "those people" works to fix the intended referent in the same way that "Pam" works to obtain the attention of the intended addressee.

Once "those people" have been successfully located by means of some form of reference, it really does not matter whether the form of reference is correct or not.

Taking into account only the reconstructible assertions attached to an utterance, it would be difficult to give any principled account for why the argument in example 5.3 is so obviously irrelevant, while superficially similar arguments are relevant. By taking into account the pragmatic function of S's utterance, we can see that P's dispute is quite literally pointless—even though S is committed to the truth of the proposition, and even though S could very well be incorrect in her attribution. P's objection has no bearing on the point of S's utterance as a speech act, nor does it point to the failure of S's attempt at reference. The proposition that those people are Spanish can be argued, but not argued in a way that is relevant to the purposes of the exchange projected by S's utterance.

Hierarchical Organization of Standpoints

One implication of the way in which virtual standpoints are reconstructed by ordinary arguers from practical activity contexts is that these standpoints are organized hierarchically with respect to some superordinate activity. There is some superordinate speech act whose characteristics define a disagreement space structured in terms of the beliefs, wants, and intentions implicit in the act. Such an act typically has no particular standpoint associated with it, but a complex of beliefs reconstructible from it, any one of which might function as a virtual standpoint once challenged by an antagonist. This suggests that seemingly disjointed and otherwise divergent lines of argument can be coherently and systematically related by virtue of their common connection to the status of some superordinate speech act.

In connected discourse, argumentation often involves consideration of a series of separable standpoints. On the surface, these standpoints may appear to pursue quite unrelated issues. The importance of seeing standpoints as being reconstructed from a disagreement space created by the practical activities of conversation is that it reveals an underlying systematicity to the standpoints that are made an issue in conversational argument. Consider the following excerpt from a telephone conversation between two college-aged women friends.

This conversation, like the one in example 5.2, can be seen to divide into two episodes, the first encompassing the first five turns, and the second beginning (and ending) with the sixth turn. The

Example 5.4

01	A:	I'm getting fat again.
02	B:	You are *not*.
03	A:	*Yes* I am.
04	B:	You've got *no* buns.
05	A:	I've got the puffy stomach though.
06	B:	Don't worry about it. No one but you can even notice it.

standpoint taken by A in 01 is first addressed by B as a simple assertion of fact and is debated back and forth in terms of evidence for and against A's being fat. But in turn 06, B does not address the standpoint "I am getting fat." Instead, B seems to reconstruct a different virtual standpoint contained in A's first utterance, namely, A's concern for how she will look to others.

To be sure, there is a shift in the argument here. But there remains a continuity of orientation in B's two lines of argument. The shift in 06 is not of the same order as if B had said something grossly irrelevant: "You took only thirty minutes to complete your biology exam" or "You know, I saw Jane yesterday and she's really getting fat too." Here, we would have much more difficulty in finding an argumentative relevance in B's turns.[5] What gives unity to B's two lines of argument and the two standpoints she reconstructs is the pragmatic point of A's saying, "I'm getting fat again." She is not simply asserting a fact; she is making a kind of complaint whose point is to express concern and dissatisfaction, and to seek sympathy or reassurance. It is the point of A's speech act that structures the disagreement space from which B extracts both standpoints.

Once this pragmatic organization of the argumentation is seen, we can readily imagine B pursuing still other lines of argument. For example, B might call out and challenge the virtual standpoint that B is an appropriate person for A to ask for sympathy: "Well, you should talk. Look at me. I can't even *fit* into my clothes anymore." Or B might call out the virtual standpoint that A has a right to complain about her situation because A is not responsible for bringing about her problem: "What do you expect when you eat four Dove Bars a day?" Even seemingly "helpful" suggestions can be seen as having argumentative force because of the way they minimize the problem, dismissing A's concern and blunting the point of her seeking reassurance: "Just wear loose clothes," or "You can always go on a diet." Such suggestions implicitly challenge the standpoint that the problem is a serious one worthy of concern.[6]

Felicity Conditions and "Issue Structure" in Argumentation

The concept of a speech act not only allows us to see that there is an underlying unity in the way ordinary arguers reconstruct seemingly diverse standpoints from an arguable utterance; speech act theory also can provide a basis for formulating how the content of a large part of this disagreement space is structured. The fact that arguments occur not only by, but over, speech acts has an important organizational consequence; namely, the global organization of the argumentative exchange will be structured by the "issues" that are associated with the type of act giving rise to the argument. Roughly speaking, the issues correspond to felicity conditions for the performance of the arguable speech act, and these issues subsume indefinitely complex sets of subordinate propositions.[7] One of the principal advantages of a theory of argumentation based on the speech act is that it emphasizes that when disagreement occurs, it is not always or in the first place over the truth or justifiability of propositions but over the propriety or acceptability of acts. The issues concern not only matters of evidence, or of the relevance and completeness of evidence, but very frequently matters of rights, obligations, desires, intentions, expectations, understandings, feelings, and relationships. Whatever act serves as the arguable, the felicity conditions for the performance of that type of act define a set of issues for argument over the act. The felicity conditions for the disputed act provide an organized basis for a series of individual arguments in a coherent discussion.

For example, arguments developing around prototypical requests are organized by the felicity conditions for requesting (see, e.g., Searle 1969; Labov and Fanshel 1977; Jacobs and Jackson 1983).

The speaker, S, says (or does) something that counts as an attempt to get the hearer, H, to agree to perform an action, A; and:

1. S wants H to do A. (sincerity condition)
2. The elements associated with the performance of A (e.g., time, place, objects) exist and/or are mutually agreeable. (preparatory condition)
3. H has the ability to do A. (preparatory condition)
4. H is willing to do A. (preparatory condition)

5. *H* would not do *A* in the absence of the request; that is, *H* would not do *A* as a matter of course. (preparatory condition)

6. There is some good reason to perform *A*, i.e., some need for *A* or benefit from its performance. (preparatory condition)

When a speaker makes a request or performs any other recognizable speech act, the addressee may demand justification in terms of any or all of the corresponding conditions or may object to the act's performance on the grounds that one or more conditions fail. The speaker may defend the act by affirming the satisfaction of the conditions. The addressee may defend a rejection of the act or the performance of a conflicting act by negating one or more conditions. The felicity conditions define the general grounds upon which an act must be defended and upon which it may be challenged; "reasons" offered for acceptance or rejection, agreement or disagreement, compliance or noncompliance, are particularized versions of these general grounds.

Since each distinguishable type of illocutionary act has its own set of felicity conditions, the specific issues involved in any argument will depend upon the characteristics of the arguable act. Although argument may be conducted primarily by means of challenge and assertion or assertion and counterassertion, the underlying issues raised by the challenge or addressed by the assertion are not always felicity conditions for asserting but felicity conditions for whatever act type provoked the disagreement—for example, a statement, an offer, a complaint, an insult, a question, a compliment, a request, or an assertion. These conditions define what lines of argument are relevant and what are irrelevant in a dispute over any given type of act.

In the next section the heuristic value of felicity conditions will be displayed in an extended case study. The previous examples in this chapter have dealt with ordinary argumentation in conversational dialogue. The discourse to be analyzed below appeared in print, and while it presumably reflects more careful planning and editing on the part of the disputants than what is ordinarily found in spontaneous argumentation, it still reflects ordinary argumentation and its practical structuring.

Case Study: Responses to an Editorial Opinion

The case study to be analyzed here is an extended argument involving multiple participants: an editorial column in a college newspaper, and a series of letters responding to it. All contributions to this extended argument appeared in the *Oklahoma Daily*, the student-run newspaper of the University of Oklahoma. The controversy was sparked by a feature story entitled "OU's band is becoming a nuisance," written by the newspaper's sports editor, Doug Ferguson (Feb. 27, 1986, 7). Over the week following the appearance of this story, fourteen responses appeared in the "Letters to the Editor" column, all critical. Ferguson's story opened with a proposal to "get rid of the band" and continued with a wide-ranging critique of the band's conduct and performance. The fourteen letters written in response to it took up a series of issues explicit or implicit in Ferguson's piece.

Both the original article and the letters appeared to have been written to convey serious arguments, and the letter writers, in particular, appeared to have been trying to produce carefully reasoned positions. The arguments appearing in these letters were neither unusually good nor unusually poor, but whether or not they typify the quality of ordinary argument, they do typify how ordinary argument comes about and the way that issues structure argument when it occurs. Because the body of materials is too lengthy to reproduce in full, we begin with a brief descriptive summary of the original article and the letters responding to it.

Ferguson's article appeared the day after the University of Oklahoma lost a close basketball game against Kansas University, ending the team's forty-eight-game home winning streak. Ferguson argued that the band had failed in its responsibility to rally fan support for the team and implied strongly that this lack of fan support robbed OU's team of its "home court advantage." In analyzing the band's failure, he noted a poor musical repertoire and a general lack of responsiveness to the team and its fans. The following brief excerpts represent well the tone of the article:

This column isn't going to set well with the musicians who get prime seats for OU basketball games, but Monday night's game was the last straw. The band hurts more than it helps. For that matter, I'm not quite clear where it actually helps. Is it a crowd motivator? No way. Is it an entertainment piece? Rarely. The band does nothing more than make noise. Not the noise that distracts the visiting team, but the noise that distracts everybody. I'm not criticizing the sound that comes out of the instruments, nor each individual's musical ability. But there is a difference between sound and noise. The band has a repertoire that includes "Boomer Sooner," "Oklahoma!" and one or two school themes; the rest is a disgrace. . . . One reason why OU basketball fans are among the worst in the Big Eight conference is the band. . . . Unless the band starts earning its seats, I think we ought to tune them right out of Lloyd Noble Center. Does the band not have an obligation to rally the fans? It's a powerful tool that can involve the student body actively better than the cheerleaders, better than anybody. But it doesn't. It spends the entire game shouting immature obscenities and entertaining themselves.

The letters written in response to the article took up a large number of issues, summarized below in order of frequency:

1. Is the band to blame for the fans' lack of enthusiasm? (mentioned 8 times).
2. Are the musical selections played appropriate? (mentioned 7 times).
3. Was Ferguson's article appropriate/fair/responsible? (mentioned 6 times).
4. Is the band's performance adequate? (mentioned 4 times).
5. Is Ferguson competent (as a journalist or as a music critic)? (mentioned 4 times).
6. Is Ferguson's opinion representative? (mentioned 3 times).
7. Does the band live up to its obligation? (mentioned 3 times).
8. Does the band really shout obscenities? (mentioned 3 times).
9. Do the band and the press deserve their reserved seats? (mentioned 3 times).

An appreciable proportion of the argumentation concerned a series of assertions made by Ferguson: that the band is responsible for lack of fan enthusiasm, that the crowd is not entertained by the band's performance, and that the band spends much of its time shouting immature obscenities. None of the letters simply challenged or refuted assertions, but many of them mentioned one or more. For example, one letter from a member of the band raised the following list of objections to Ferguson's article ("To drum home the point," Feb. 28, 1986, 14):

1. the band's obligation is to support the team and its coaches, not specifically to rally the fans;
2. the fans are impossible for anyone to motivate;
3. some of the musical selections criticized by Ferguson were performed at the request of the players or the coaches;
4. some of the musical selections criticized by Ferguson were performed to communicate a point (e.g., to suggest that the referees were incompetent);
5. the band is not allowed to perform while the ball is in play.

For the most part, this letter consisted of direct contradictions of claims made by Ferguson. Several letters, including one signed by

the members of the basketball team, consisted primarily of contradictory statements of opinion:

When we start down the ramp, it is awesome to hear the band kick into
"Boomer Sooner." When we are warming up, the music the band plays helps
psych us up for the game, and the only time the crowd gets excited is when
we do dunks. . . . We think that what the band plays is jazzy and has a great
rhythm to it. ("Team plays up band," Mar. 4, 1986, 8)

Neither of us are in the band, but all we've heard about the band in the
stands have been compliments. ("Don't beat the band," Feb. 28, 1986, 14)

Although assertion and counterassertion figured prominently in
the series of letters, as noted before, none of the letters treated
Ferguson's article as just an assertion or series of assertions. The
letter writers clearly saw the assertions offered as part of some
broader act, so our first analytic problem is to arrive at some characterization of the act.

This is no small task. The central fact about speech acts, that
what a speaker says is not the same as what the speaker does in
saying it, gives rise to a fundamental fact about communication,
that what a speaker is doing in saying something is always to some
degree indeterminate. In Ferguson's article, one possibility is that
what he was doing was making a proposal, namely, to get rid of the
band. Such proposals (termed propositions of action in many argument textbooks) are widely considered to depend for their validity
on the following conditions (see, e.g., McBurney and Mills 1964):

1. Something is wrong with the current state of affairs.
2. This problem may be attributed to a cause, C.
3. Eliminating C would in fact remedy the problem.
4. Eliminating C would not create any additional problems.

The first three conditions are an exceptionally accurate outline of
what Ferguson said in the column. What is wrong is that the fans do
not support the team; the cause is that the band distracts the fans
instead of rallying them to support the team; getting rid of the band
would make Lloyd Noble Center a more hostile arena for visiting
teams. But despite the direct statement of the proposal and the
apparent fit between the content of the article and the issues appropriate to defense of a proposal, the characterization of this article as
having made a proposal is not very satisfactory. Ferguson cannot
possibly have imagined that the university would consider eliminating the band. The proposal is readily recognizable as a vehicle for the
performance of a different sort of act, namely, an act of criticism.

Ferguson's point and purpose in the article was not to suggest seriously the elimination of the band but to call the band to account for its unsatisfactory performance.

Ferguson's article is thus "officially" a proposal to get rid of the band and "unofficially" a criticism of the band. Most of the argumentation he offered can be given a coherent reading on either interpretation of what he was doing. The arguments that establish the rationale for the proposal serve equally well as backing for the criticism. Possibly, some readers understood Ferguson to be making a serious proposal, but this does not seem likely. The letters responding to Ferguson's article made no mention of the proposal, nor did they take up obvious lines of argument pertinent to the third and fourth issues mentioned above. When the letters offered any explicit characterization of Ferguson's column, it was described as having maligned, accused, insulted, or criticized the band. Furthermore, some of the issues raised in the letters make sense only as responses to criticism. Tentatively, then, we analyze the exchange of views as an argument over a criticism rather than as an argument over a proposal. We reserve for later discussion the complexities raised by the possibility of multiple characterizations of the arguable.

Our position on the relationship between speech act preconditions and issue organization suggests that if Ferguson's article counts as an act of criticism, it must satisfy the felicity conditions for this kind of criticism or be accountable for satisfying them. Argument over the article should likewise be structured around issues which represent particularized versions of these conditions. The felicity conditions for this kind of criticism may be formulated as follows:

The speaker, S, says or does something that counts as a negative evaluation of the actions or attributes of the target, T, and:

1. S holds a negative opinion of the action or attribute. (sincerity condition)

2. S has adequate grounds for this opinion. (preparatory condition)

3. S has whatever qualifications are necessary (knowledge, training, access to pertinent information, etc.) in order to form an opinion on T's actions or attributes. (preparatory condition)

4. S has a right to evaluate T's actions or attributes by virtue of being affected by them or by virtue of some special role; in either case, S must have some constructive intention. (preparatory condition)

5. T may be held accountable for the actions or attributes (i.e., they are dependent upon T's skill and/or will). (preparatory condition)

Both Ferguson's article and the letters responding to it should show attentiveness to these issues in their argumentation. We consider whether and how each of the preparatory conditions enters into the exchange of views. One expected result of this analytic effort is that the contradictions of Ferguson's assertions, along with a wide range of additional objections, should be seen to be subsumed by issues related to the act of criticism. The justifiability of individual assertions put forward in the performance of the criticism should be challenged only where the assertions have some bearing on the validity of the criticism.

S has adequate grounds for his criticism. A major component of Ferguson's argument concerned this condition. The grounds for the criticism were spelled out clearly: the band produces distracting noise, has a "disgraceful" repertoire, conducts itself in an immature fashion, fails to perform its primary task of rallying the fans to intimidate opponents, and so forth. Most of the specific assertions made by Ferguson, in fact, pertained to the first of the four preparatory conditions. A number of the letters disputed these grounds, as indicated above, either by contradicting Ferguson's opinion or by contradicting specific facts offered as backing for Ferguson's opinion.

S has the qualifications necessary to form a justified opinion of T's actions or attributes. The letters called Ferguson's qualifications into question both directly and indirectly. Some of these attacks are textbook cases of argument ad hominem, but from the pragmatic point of view of the speech act being addressed, they are not necessarily impertinent. Is it appropriate to challenge Ferguson's criticism on the grounds that he lacks the qualifications necessary to defend the criticism? Yes, if the argument is over the act of criticism rather than over the propositional content per se. The most direct of the attacks on Ferguson's qualifications appear below:

Without personally attacking Mr. Doug Ferguson, allow me to say I am surprised *The Daily* would allow one of its editors to write on a topic that he or she did not fully understand or comprehend. Unfortunately, it is apparent that this is what has taken place. (" 'Three Blind Mice' serves purpose," Mar. 3, 1986, 8)

You're the type who wouldn't know the difference between Beethoven's 9th and Dvorak's 9th. You would much rather hear someone banging on a bass drum to get a basketball crowd fired up. If you had wanted an ape banging on a drum you should have gone to Oklahoma State. ("Sounding the same note," Mar. 4, 1986, 8)

Mr. Ferguson, your education in journalism appears to be sadly lacking. Sir, an opinion is meant to be placed on the editorial page, not in the sports column. . . . Since you seem to be unable to discern the difference between sports and editorial, how can you tell the difference between music and noise? ("Pride members proud," Mar. 4, 1986, 8)

Flatulent ignorance published is piteous. . . . Before you further malign the Showmen, get your facts straight. Ask more than one person about their opinion. Isn't getting the story right what journalism school is all about? ("Get the facts," Mar. 4, 1986, 8)

One interesting feature of these responses is that they are not particularly responsive to the content of what Ferguson had to say about the band's musical quality. His argument was not primarily about musical quality but about the appropriateness of the band's performance for its presumed purpose. Another noteworthy feature of some of the responses is that they indict Ferguson's critique of the band by pointing to defects in his performance of his own role as sportswriter. Of course there is no connection between Ferguson's skill as a journalist and his musical judgment. Nevertheless, these responses contribute to a defense of the band by calling into question Ferguson's own credibility and judgment, on which the critique depends.[8] These arguments are often considered fallacious because they fail to address the truth or falsity of what has been claimed. From a communicative point of view, they have an intelligible role in the dialogue as grounds for challenging the act of criticism.

S *has a right to evaluate* T's *performance and a constructive intention in doing so.* Like any other speech act, criticism should be purposeful. Usual purposes include remediation of an undesirable condition or correction of a substandard performance. This preparatory condition has to do with whether or not the critic has a legitimate interest in whatever is being criticized. Presumably, Ferguson felt no need to defend his right to evaluate the band's performance, since his role as sports columnist permitted both reporting and commentary on matters related to sports. Moreover, if the band were indeed indirectly responsible for lost basketball games, Ferguson shared with all the fans a stake in how well the band performed.

Several of the letters raised arguments around this condition. One suggested that Ferguson could remedy the situation by simply not coming to games (implying that what is wrong is not the band's performance but Ferguson's attitude):

If you don't like what you see at an OU basketball game, then why don't you quit coming and ruining everyone else's time. No one is making you come and sit through all of our "noise." ("The final word on Sooner Showmen," Mar. 6, 1986, 8)

The implication is that the criticism is gratuitous, a theme which is developed more directly in another letter:

Tell me, who are you going to rip next week, the poms, cheerleaders or Top Daug? ("'Three Blind Mice' serves purpose")

Other letters questioned whether criticism of the band does in fact fall within the scope of Ferguson's role as sports columnist:

Does Mr. Ferguson's position as sports editor give him the right to degrade such a fine spirit group as the Sooner Showmen? ("Band has warmed up," Mar. 3, 1986, 8)

. . . who are you to be criticizing music? You are a journalism major, not a music major. ("The final word on Sooner Showmen")

Finally, the letters responded to Ferguson's criticism with gratuitous criticisms of their own—of the newspaper, the journalism school, and Ferguson himself. If these retaliatory criticisms are relevant at all, their relevance is not to the content of Ferguson's article but to broader pragmatic issues of rights and right conduct.

The related issue of whether or not Ferguson's intentions were constructive also gets some play in the letters, in the form of countercriticism of Ferguson for divisiveness.

I guess what I am really trying to express in this letter is the need for the band and fans to stick together and support our fine basketball team. With the Big Eight and NCAA tournaments just around the corner, the Sooners do not need to have their fans divided. Mr. Ferguson, your article did just that. ("To drum home the point")

As for the timing of your article, I don't believe it could have come at a worse time. If you want a "coalition" between the band and students, why don't you go find one that makes you happy. The one we have now seems to be doing just fine without your two-cents worth. ("The final word on Sooner Showmen")

A valid objection to Ferguson's critique need not question the truth of what is claimed. What is claimed apparently must be not only true but also constructive and consistent with the speaker's role.

T *may be held accountable for the actions or attributes.* Criticism presupposes that whatever is being criticized could have been otherwise. Circumstances not under the control of the target or not the responsibility of the target ought not be made the basis for a criticism of the target. Ferguson's article critiques several distinguishable aspects of the band's performance, and each point of critique received one or more responses related to accountability.

First, Ferguson was taken by the readers to be attacking the quality of the musical performance, even though he was careful to deny any such intention. One way of responding to this sort of attack is to treat it as just an assertion about the quality of the performance and to try to contradict it. But Ferguson did not merely imply that the performance is poor, he also implied that the band is somehow blameworthy. (Not all poor performances are critiqueable, of course, and that is why this condition is included.) Arguments about how hard the band works to prepare for games, which occurred in four separate letters, have no obvious relevance to a refutation of Ferguson's presumed claims about the band's musical performance. Their relevance is to the issue of whether or not the band deserves censure.

Second, Ferguson criticized the band directly for its choice of musical selections. Of all the points raised in his column, this was the second most commonly attacked. Although some of the responses defended the musical selections (e.g., arguing that "Three Blind Mice" is played as a commentary on the referees, of whom there are three on the floor at any given time), most of the responses simply pointed out that the band does not choose what to play but simply obliges the pompon squad, the coaches, or the players.

Third, Ferguson criticized the band for failing to arouse the crowd. Eight separate letters argued that the band is not to blame for the fans' lack of enthusiasm. The letters uniformly accepted the fact that the fans are unsupportive, and the letters rarely questioned Ferguson's assertion that the band is unable to motivate the fans. Instead, the letters denied that the band could be held accountable for its inability to motivate the fans, by arguing that nothing could motivate the fans:

Don't insult the band because of the lack of enthusiasm of the fans. They do a good job in an impossible situation. ("Don't beat the band")

It is important to notice that unless the letters are analyzed as responses to an act of criticism, rather than as responses to a set of specific assertions, the relevance of the responses is very difficult to explain. They do not deny the assertions which compose the "grounds" for Ferguson's criticism but deny that these grounds satisfy the conditions for valid criticizing.

Conclusions

Within an ideal model of critical discussion, the acceptance or rejection of a standpoint should be determined by what grounds there are for belief or disbelief in it. The disagreement space shaped by such a commitment, although related to the disagreement space shaped by practical decision making, interpersonal influence, and relationship negotiation, is not the same space. In the natural attitude, people conduct argumentation with attention to the practical consequences of speech, making an orientation to resolution of dispute over any identifiable proposition subordinate to the pragmatic import of the disputed issue.

We argue with things others say in a fashion that is determined by the speech acts through which the arguments are conveyed and by the activity type in which virtual standpoints are contained. Ordinary arguers are naive reconstructors of argumentation, and their reconstructions provide a crucial grounding for any normative reconstruction of argumentation. We have tried to show that one advantage of locating normative reconstructions in ordinary arguers' reconstructions of speech acts is that the problems of identifying issues and analyzing lines of argument become tractable. More important, such an understanding of argumentation allows us to make sense of ordinary disputants' practices, and to make sense of them in terms of a pragmatic model of relevance in discourse.

An issue raised in passing is the general question of what a speaker is responsible for defending when a conversational act has been challenged. Our position might seem to presuppose that the "type of act" being performed in the "arguable" is an unproblematic reflection of the speaker's intent, so that the issues which might be raised against the arguable are in some sense under the control of the speaker. Empirically, however, a speaker may end up defending issues well removed from the act intended. Our observations suggest that among the many negotiations that might be involved in the opening stage of argument, one of the most consequential may be the negotiation over what act the speaker is to be taken as having performed in the confrontation stage.

For example, both the column and the letters to the editor analyzed in this chapter hang together neatly as an act of criticism and a series of challenges to that act. The column could have been taken up as a quite different sort of act, however, and in fact the article is "officially" a proposal and not a criticism. This is important, for if the article gets taken up as a proposal, the directly relevant issue is whether there is or is not a problem with the band, not whether

Ferguson himself is in a position to evaluate the problem, while if the article gets taken up as criticism, Ferguson's qualifications and motives become quite central.

Presumably, Ferguson did not intend to get involved in defending his own competence, judgment, and motivation. His circumstance typifies much of ordinary disputation, with its unanticipated openings for disagreement and its unforeseen implications for argumentative roles. For any conversational act, multiple interpretations of speaker intent may be plausible; for any one interpretation of speaker intent, there will be a spreading substructure of issues, any one of which may become the focus of dispute. This suggests that the naive reconstructions of ordinary arguers are always to some extent negotiations and that the normative reconstructions of analysts are always to some extent tentative and open-ended.

Notes

1. Transcription notation is explained in note 2 to chapter 3.

2. The conversation was tape-recorded with the knowledge and permission of all parties present to provide materials for a classroom assignment. Ethnographic information was supplied by one of the participants (B) to aid in understanding the transcript.

3. It should be added that part of what makes A's standpoint the subject of argument is precisely that A takes its legitimacy for granted and apparently feels no need to assert it at all. Unlike an assertion, which has the preparatory condition that it not be obvious that the listener would accept that proposition in the absence of its assertion, A presupposes the acceptability of his standpoint—and that is part of what B's incredulity and subsequent argumentation is directed toward.

4. There are alternative ways of dealing with this kind of predicament. A stereotypical alternative is to react with an aggravated form of counterattack that leads the discussion into an escalating spiral of blame and counterblame (see Jabobs, Jackson, Stearns, and Hall 1991). But this is hardly a less troublesome procedure for resolving a dispute.

5. We do not mean to imply that argumentative relevance could not be found, only that it would be more difficult to do so. Given the right assumptions, virtually *any* utterance can be interpreted as argumentatively relevant. We could, for example, try to hear the former response as somehow implying that A is not really concerned about her being fat but is anxious about how she did on her exam, and so it is not really a sincere complaint. Or for the latter response, we could try to hear the argument that A should not complain, because Jane has the same problem—or perhaps she should take comfort in this fact. These interpretations are clearly stretching it, and these readings make the utterances sound distinctly artificial. But we do not close off the possibility that a natural argumentative reading could somehow be constructed.

6. Here it is interesting to note that in constructivist research on comforting messages addressed to persons in distress, it has been shown that "helpful" suggestions have properties of denial similar to straightforward denials of the factual basis for a complaint. See Burleson 1984.

7. Whether or not felicity conditions exhaust the content of the disagreement space is an open issue. In part, the issue is not so much a straightforward empirical one as much as a conceptual issue. What, for example, counts as a speech act? In example 5.2, has A performed the speech act of making a determination, or is this best thought of as a global speech event? Or should implicatures be thought of as a different class of issues altogether? When speech acts can be addressed by issues not clearly listed in previous accounts of felicity conditions, is that because felicity conditions do not exhaust the range of relevant issues, because the specific list of felicity conditions is wrong, or because the speech act does not fit the canonical form? (See Jacobs 1989.) Entailments of felicity conditions are notoriously open-ended, further emptying empirical content from the claim that felicity conditions define the content of possible lines of argument (see Labov and Fanshel 1977). At present, it seems safest to treat a list of felicity conditions simply as a useful heuristic for categorizing lines of argument around any particular speech act.

8. In his study of "degradation ceremonies," Garfinkel (1956) points out that speakers themselves must be morally secure before they can successfully accuse others.

6

Mediation as Critical Discussion

While conversational argument may display many of the features of a critical discussion, some higher-order conditions for such a discussion may still be unfulfilled. In entering into argument, ordinary arguers may lack the motivations or abilities presupposed by the ideal model of critical discussion, so that second-order conditions are not fulfilled. They may, for example, be more concerned with winning the argument or with simply reaching a settlement than with ensuring the resolution of the dispute by justifying or refuting the proposition concerned. Or they may be unwilling or unable to assess the acceptability of an argument independently of their personal stake in the conclusion it supports. Or they may be unable to follow the structure of an argument, to express their standpoint clearly, or to proceed through a discussion in an orderly fashion.

The circumstances of real argumentation may also diverge from the conditions presupposed by the model of a critical discussion in such a way that third-order conditions are not fulfilled. A model of critical discussion is free to focus on the ideal performance of speech acts with one single function; ordinary arguers engaged in actual argumentation concentrate on just one goal at the risk of endangering other functions that their speech acts should fulfill.[1] A model of critical discussion, in its basic form, assumes unconstrained deliberative resources, for example, unlimited time and ready access to relevant information; ordinary arguers engaged in actual argumentation generally confront difficult constraints on time and on availability of evidence. A model of critical discussion presupposes general equality between disputants; ordinary arguers engaged in actual argumentation regularly face conditions of power inequality. A model of critical discussion presupposes that an unresolved disagreement is a neutral outcome; in actual argumentation one party's interests or standpoint may be invoked by default in the absence of any achieved agreement, as when an unresolved argument for change favors the party defending the status quo.

Such considerations suggest that there is an inherent gap between the real and the ideal and that a model of critical discussion cannot straightforwardly return to the circumstances from which it was abstracted without creating practical paradoxes. For the ordinary arguer, a model of critical discussion is not so much a set of prescriptions for engaging in actual argumentative conduct as it is a set of standards against which actual practice is to be compared.

How to bridge the gap between the real and the ideal can be seen as a kind of "engineering" problem. "Real-izing" an ideal procedure requires comparison of actual conditions with normative assumptions and, wherever a mismatch is found, the creation of a structure or a technique that will alter the conditions or compensate for them. The construction and application of these engineering solutions can be quite self-conscious and highly institutionalized, as with procedures for legal adjudication. But engineering solutions can be found even at the most mundane levels of conversation. Many of the techniques and practices of ordinary conversation can be seen as more or less tacitly applied solutions to the practical problems facing the ordinary arguer.

Third-Party Dispute Mediation

One engineering solution for overcoming the practical problems facing ordinary arguers is to use a third party as a dispute mediator. This is becoming an increasingly prominent alternative in the United States to the resolution of disputes by means of formal court action.[2] In mediation, a neutral mediator (usually a trained volunteer, but sometimes a paid professional) guides disputants in a cooperative search for a resolution to a conflict that they have been unable to resolve on their own.

Mediation differs from arbitration and legal adjudication in that, theoretically, the mediator does not argue for or resolve the case but serves only to facilitate a discussion by which the disputants may search for their own settlement. The role of the mediator is to regulate the process of discussion without affecting the content. Rather than shifting the functions of advocacy and judgment to other parties (e.g., attorneys, judges, arbitrators), mediation attempts to implement a process (via the mediator) whereby the disputants can effectively engage in these functions themselves.

The situation of the mediator illustrates well the problems of translating an ideal model into actual practice under less-than-ideal circumstances. The integrity of mediation is believed to depend upon the neutrality and substantive nonparticipation of the mediator, yet these demands seem to conflict continually with others. A mediator's mandate is to settle cases, but to do so without imposing decisions (Silbey and Merry 1986).

Mediators must respect the voluntary participation of the parties, but they may have to overcome the resistance of one or both parties to consensus decision making. They must remain impartial with respect to competing positions and uninvolved in the advocacy of those positions, but the resolution of differences may be seemingly blocked by unjustifiable proposals, evasion of issues, bogus objections, and the like. If one of the disputants persists in these practices, the mediator may be faced with the choice of "taking sides" or letting the process become a mere contest of wills. And while mediators must be substantively neutral and leave the disputants to identify issues relevant to their dispute, if left unrestricted, disputants may get lost in squabbles, personal recriminations, and unresolvable differences of opinion that sidetrack discussion and block progress.

The mediator's engineering task is to intervene in the discussion in a way that can satisfy these competing demands. How can a mediator manage arguments without making arguments? How can a mediator provide for a fair and just resolution of the dispute without making the decision? The solutions at which mediators arrive are ultimately discursive. The institution of mediation and the role of the mediator can be given concrete form and body only by finding ways of talking that satisfy more or less successfully these paradoxical requirements.

While much of the practice of mediation appears to be reflectively applied, formally trained, and explicitly codified in manuals, these discourse strategies remain largely tacit. They depend upon the background of tacit pragmatic competence that mediators bring to the job. Through these discourse strategies real mediators try to live up to the standard of the ideal mediator and put philosophy into practice.

Engineering Solutions in Discourse

In the following sections we examine transcripts of mediators employing two particular discourse strategies: the use of formulations and the use of questions.[3] Because mediators cannot engage in argumentation with the disputants, they have to find other ways to manage the substance and force of the arguments. Formulations and questions can be used to do work that in other circumstances might be done by openly asserting standpoints, challenging positions, conceding points, making arguments, and so on. Examining how these formulations and questions work reveals the ways in which the resources of natural language can be used to enforce argumentative ideals within actual practice.

Formulations

While mediators should not argue for or against disputant standpoints or tell disputants what to argue, mediators are given license to clarify what the disputants are arguing and to project alternative trajectories for the discussion.[4] In discharging their responsibility to provide for clear communication and procedural order, mediators will often formulate the standpoints and arguments of the disputants and the possible options for moving along with the discussion. Officially, such formulations have straightforward informative and procedural functions—clarifying positions, summarizing the status of an issue, identifying points of agreement and disagreement, closing up one stage of discussion and moving into the next, and so on. In performing these functions, however, formulations can also give substantive shape and direction to an argument, and in that respect formulations can serve as a technique for mediators to manage the substantive character and argumentative force of a discussion without entering into the discussion as an advocate.

Examples 6.1 and 6.2 illustrate this possibility. Consider first the mediator's contribution in turns 036 and 038 of example 6.1.

The mediator's formulation in 036 and 038 effectively clarifies what the wife's objections are all about and puts the discussion back on track toward finding a mutually acceptable settlement. He seems to speak as an impartial voice of the wife. She helps to construct the formulation with her overlapping extension (in 037) and then she confirms its acceptability with her restatement in 039.

The mediator's intervention also occurs at a point of visible confusion and at a point where the argument between husband and wife

Example 6.1

023 M: Whatever ((Pause)) your situation, this child should be
         seeing both of you frequently. And I mean, the the
         younger children are, the b- the more often, the more
         frequent, the visits should be. No necessarily long

024 H: Well I tried to make an effort to see her everyday but
         her mother kind of kept her away ((Pause)) or
         ((Pause)) or I couldn't go see her or else she would say
         that she wasn't going to be home or she didn't want
         company, but I'd, I would go and see her at lunch, the
         same as before I would always go home for lunch and we
         both worked the same distance and I always, came home for
         lunch, took her downstairs and made lunch for her?

025 W: Oh I love to comment on some of those (   ) you would
         come down and see Rachel without telephoning that you
         were coming, you were coming in during Rachel's dinner
         time

026 H: I never stopped her from eating dinner (   )=

027 W: =Okay look it's very distracting for her, when her Dad's
         there, and she's gonna play, for her to sit down and eat
         her dinner. And that you're not only distracting her
         you're distracting the rest of the family.

028 H: But your mother   used
              [   ]
029 W: And it's very inappropriate for you, to show up
         without telephoning

030 H: But your mother used to tell her (   ) that if she didn't
         want to eat to get away from the table. And it was just
         like that.

031 W: It is just like that she's finished
              [   ]
032 H: Alright so what is the problem then
                                 [
033 W: When
         she's finished eating she's excused from the table.
         ((Pause)) But, let's stick with the issue which is, you
         were showing up (without) telephoning

034 H: If you said that=

035 W: =and also, if my mother had something to do in the
         evening you, according to the court's regulation you're
         there at her convenience. Not she there at your
         convenience.

Example 6.1 (Continued)

036 M: So uh what are you what are you saying
Constance uh, is that is this a way of saying that, that
if, there can be some kind of understanding and some kind
of arrangement, that uh you, that would put some kind of
uh, safeguards   then you would you would=
        [   ]   [   ]

037 W: Reasonable boundaries on him

038 M: =have no objection to his uh seeing the child.
                      [   ]

039 W: (   ) I don't
have any objections as long as its reasonable
                      [   ]

040 M: Alright now what
kind of of um, controls would you uh put on it what uh=

041 W: =specified hours specified days ((Pause)) and a
telephone call to ((Pause)) confirm

---

threatens to career out of control. The wife has already raised two particular problems—the husband's coming over without telephoning (025, 029) and his presence during dinnertime, which distracts both the family and the daughter (025, 027). The husband has just asked, "Alright so what is the problem then" with his presence during dinner (032), and the wife has replied with, "But, let's stick with the issue which is, you were showing up (without) telephoning" (033). So there is reason to believe that the argument is getting difficult to follow even for the disputants. Then after saying, "let's stick with the issue," the wife cuts off the husband's reply and seemingly raises a whole new complaint in 035 (note the "and also" preface). The formulation comes off as doing just the kind of job mediators are there to do.

The difficulties in this segment, however, involve more than just problems of clarity and procedural order. The substance and force of the wife's objection are also involved, and this is reflected in the functions of the mediator's formulation. Part of the confusion in this excerpt can be seen to result from the way in which the wife seemingly makes several distinct objections. The threat of procedural disorder comes in part from the force of her objections. In bringing the discussion back into line, the mediator's formulation actively shapes the substance and the point of these objections.

First, this formulation actively synthesizes the propositional content of the wife's complaints. Rather than being a laundry list of distinct and negatively focused complaints, the wife's position is represented as a way of saying that if there were some kind of reasonable arrangement, she would have no objection to the husband's visiting the child. It is not at all obvious that this is anything more than a post hoc formulation that the wife happens to find acceptable.

Second, notice how this excerpt started. The mediator in 023 is engaged in a kind of counseling typical of the preliminary stages of mediation, where the mediator actively tries to establish the principle that any visitation agreement should be in the best interests of the child. In 024 the husband takes the mediator's remarks in a way that is tinged with personal defensiveness and with blame on the wife ("but her mother kind of kept her away"). The wife's entry in 025 with "Oh I love to comment on some of those" signals a personal counterattack.

The mediator's formulation shifts the potential force of the wife's contributions from that of complaints that establish blame and moral censure to that of objections that suggest criteria for an acceptable proposal. The mediator is, in effect, reinstituting the activity frame he was working from in 023 and from which the husband and wife digressed (a common occurrence; see Jacobs, Jackson, Stearns and Hall 1991). This frame leads the disputants out of a concern for personal defense and blame to consideration of proposals for settlement, which is what the mediator elicits next in 040.

Consider one more case of a mediator "actively" shaping the standpoints and arguments of the disputants through the use of formulations. In example 6.2 the positions of the disputants are twice summarized. Both summaries occur at points of potential impasse. The husband (Bill) wants more frequent visits with the children for longer periods of time. The wife (Betty) seemingly resists any change from the current schedule of visits once every other weekend on the grounds that more frequent visits would be too disruptive for the children. That is the focus of the mediator's summary in 201. The mediator then lays out two options for resolving their impasse. After some intervening discussion (deleted from the example) the summary in 263 is made. By this time Bill has proposed a visitation schedule of one day per weekend, with visits switching between Saturdays and Sundays, and the mediator is openly suggesting that the disputants consider some kind of temporary plan.

Superficially, at least, the two formulations in 201 and 260 provide a balanced, two-sided summary of the current standing of the dispute. But these summaries can also be seen to do more than simply

Example 6.2

---

201 M: Uh huh. Well, ah, there're two points here. One is that you ((Bill)) emphasize the quality ah time you and the children have, and your ((Betty)) point of view is that ahm this arrangement would be disruptive for the children. Okay. So your point of view is ahm ah I can't disagree with it, if it's disruptive it's not a good plan. At the same time I have to agree with Bill that Bill needs quality time with the children. But you're saying that the plan he's proposing might be difficult for his children.

202 W: Mhm,

203 M: Now, there's no way to resolve this ((Pause)) ah, unless, something's put into practice,

204 W: Mhm,

205 M: then you see the results. Ah, the other, ah, approach is ah, for you to go to the, Center for Legal Psychiatry for the therapist there will talk with the children

206 W: Mhm we'll make that decision

207 M: and they'll be able to get more, ah deeper into the feeling the thinking,

208 W: Mhm

209 M: of the children. Because right here you see one thing, Bill sees another thing,

210 W: Mhm

211 M: and ah, over there, and ah, maybe hopefully they will see the whole picture and then make a recommendation to the court. ((Pause)) So I think that because the two of you are at, have different points of view,

212 W: Mhm

213 M: ah, maybe at this point we cannot work out a permanent plan.

214 W: Mhm

215 M: Now, if you want to avoid going to the Center for Legal Psychiatry what we could do is develop a permanent I mean a temporary plan, and

((Intervening discussion deleted))

Example 6.2   (Continued)

260 M: . . . ah, but I think that perhaps what we should do is
develop a ninety day temporary plan,

((Pause))

261 H: I can do that,

((Pause))

262 W: I'll listen

[

263 M: And one, there're two suggestions here one is that,
ah it can be every other weekend? or or it could be every
other Saturday every other Sunday. And that way they
don't have to wait fifteen days to see you? And you
don't have to wait fifteen days to see them.

---

mark the progress of the discussion to that point. The phrasing and
positioning of the mediator's comments subtly align the mediator
with Bill's position. Notice in 201 that Betty's reason is presented as
a subjective "point of view" and is reported in the frame of a
conditional statement that withholds judgment as to its truth ("*if
it's disruptive it's not a good plan*"). Bill's reason is reported with no
qualification and comes as an assertion of the mediator of what Bill
"needs." Moreover, the mediator says "I can't disagree" with Betty's
point of view but says "I have to agree" with Bill. Being unable to
oppose a position (Betty's) is not equivalent to being obligated to
agree with a position (Bill's).

A similar asymmetry of presentation occurs in 263, where Bill's
suggestion has a rationale attached to it. Betty's suggestion has no
rationale reported. Moreover, Bill's rationale is not explicitly presented as Bill's (rather than as the mediator's assertion). Its authorship is implied in a way that leaves a margin of equivocality.

Likewise, the mediator's presentation in 203–15 does more than
simply describe the current state of the discussion and lay out the
options for where to go from here. The mediator's formulation does
perform this procedural task, but the way in which these options are
presented and explained also further insinuates the weakness of
Betty's position and presses her to make concessions.

What the mediator has gently put out on the floor is something
like this: Neither Bill nor Betty is going to be able to assemble an
argument that convinces the other—Betty sees one thing, Bill sees
another thing. Instead of continuing to argue, they should try to

resolve their impasse by agreeing on a temporary visitation schedule to see how it would work out (which would mean Betty giving up her resistance to any change in the current arrangement). The reason they should do this is that if they do not work something out, they will have to go through the Center for Legal Psychiatry, which will take the decision out of their hands and may force on them a visitation arrangement that would be far less acceptable than the one they might settle on if they explore the possibilities of a temporary arrangement. It might also be insinuated that, if either party is making insincere or bogus arguments (e.g., Betty's insistence that any change in the current visitation schedule will be too "disruptive" for the children), the center will surely see through this argument when the therapist talks to the children. So those arguments should be abandoned now.[5]

By summarizing the positions of the parties in this way, and by presenting the summaries in the context of future trajectories for the discussion, the mediator in effect adds force to Bill's position, but without openly advocating Bill's case.[6] So, by formulating positions and presenting alternatives, mediators not only can clarify arguments and give direction to a discussion but also may perform tasks that could be pursued more directly by simply making arguments or advocating standpoints. But they can do this without overtly taking over the responsibilities for advocacy or decision making. Those responsibilities remain with the disputants. This use of formulations, then, can be taken as one engineering solution to the problem of how to manage discussion in a way that moves parties toward resolution of differences without entering into the role of advocate.

Questions

Another common means whereby mediators perform many of the tasks that could be accomplished more directly by making arguments is by asking questions. Questioning allows mediators to do many of the tasks of an advocate without having to advocate or challenge any particular standpoint or line of argument. By their very nature, questions raise issues and open up possible standpoints. The phrasing of questions and their positioning in the discourse align the questioner more or less forcefully with those standpoints.

Questions elicit answers. Through lines of questioning the mediator may get the respondent to commit to answers that could serve as common premises for arriving at some conclusion. The advantage of this technique is that, through their answers, the disputants are the ones who make the assertions, so that the mediator has not publicly advocated any standpoint or made a personnal commitment to any argument.

Consider the mediator's questioning of Betty in example 6.3, which occurs some time before the summaries in example 6.2.

Betty's comments in 119 come at the close of a series of turns in

Example 6.3

---

119 W: . . . Ah ((Pause)) at any rate, that's it. I just
think they need some sense of stability and if they're
janked back and forth like you know sharing a broom eh
they're not going to have any sense of stability.
There's no ongoing bond. There's no ongoing anything
it's just well janked back and forth that's totally
disruptive to their living lives. They can't handle
that?

120 M: What about Bill's concern that this (could be a mutual
decision).

121 W: I want Bill this is you know this is I I assume why we
are here I want Bill to be close to them I want them to
have time with them, with him, but I also want them to
have a good stable (operating). And that's first and
foremost in my mind. =

122 M: = Okay. How would you modify modify this ((PAUSE))
proposal then,

123 W: What I would modify it to is every other weekend and
maybe t an two evenings a week, I don't know
((Exasperated))

((Pause))

124 M: Then you say then, every other weekend and two evenings a
week.

125 W: Uhm hm

126 M: Which evenings would you suggest.

((Pause))

127 W: Probably Tuesday and Thursday because if he had them on
the weekend he'd be bringing them back Sunday night so
there's no point in running again in running right over
again Monday night (.) Uh that's just a suggestion, I
don't know, I don't know what's

---

which she has strongly rejected an initial proposal for joint custody made by Bill. (The series began with M: "What do you think of this proposal?" W: "I think it's incredibly confusing and totally disruptive." M: " 'Kay. Would you elaborate on that?") Turn 119 amounts to a shutdown of any further argument over the proposal. Notice the phrase "at any rate, that's it," the repetition of phrases, the return to the initial claim that the plan is "totally disruptive," the intense and absolutistic evaluations ("no ongoing anything"), as well as the nebulous grounds for rejection. Betty's response to Bill's proposal threatens to create an impasse at a very early stage of the mediation session.

The mediator keeps the discussion moving through a two-step series of questions, beginning with 120. The force of the questioning pushes Betty into reluctantly accepting the burden for keeping the session alive. This is done without any explicit challenges, overt demands, or open arguments by the mediator.

Turn 120 questions a pragmatic presupposition of the mediation activity itself. The assumption that any settlement will be based on a "mutual decision" is basic to the mediation process. To reject that assumption is to reject mediation. In effect, the mediator is asking, "Are you willing to entertain alternative custody arrangements at all, or are you going to veto any new proposal?"

Notice that it is the contextual positioning of the question—and not the sentence phrasing itself—that conveys this meaning. The meaning of the question comes from broaching the subject in the slot directly following Betty's rejection. To raise the issue at all at this point is to suggest that there is something about Betty's previous remarks that calls into question her commitment to this assumption. Turn 120 is thus the kind of question where, if a suspicion of bad faith was in the air, that suspicion could be seen to motivate the question. It is a suspicion that, presumably, Betty would wish to deny. At the same time, the question allows Betty to clarify favorably the force of her arguments, that is, to make clear that her arguments reject the particular visitation proposal, not any proposal in principle.

In this way, Betty is "set up" to supply just the affirmation that she does provide in 121. By doing so, she publicly commits herself to a mutual decision. Notice that the mediator immediately follows Betty's turn with "Okay," a move that locks in what she has done. He then brings out the implication of Betty's affirmation. Since she is committed to a mutual decision "then," she would offer for Bill's consideration a modified proposal that overcomes her own objections.

Making this proposal is not something demanded or even called for by the mediator; using a how-question with the "would" modality implies that the decision to do so has already been made by Betty herself. Betty's proposal, however, is clearly given reluctantly. Notice the exasperated tone, the use of "maybe" and "probably," the repeated "I don't know," and the qualifier that "that's just a suggestion." But it is a proposal that is given by Betty, and it involves concessions which will be difficult for her to withdraw and still maintain the appearance of acting in good faith.[7]

Throughout this exchange the mediator has engaged in tasks that could have been accomplished through overt argumentation. Here questioning substitutes for such argumentation. By avoiding overtly argumentative speech acts, the mediator has avoided taking on commitments and expressing intentions that would have damaged his role as an impartial and substantively neutral discussion leader. He avoids asserting that Betty's rejection is an act of bad faith or committing himself to the claim that Betty does not accept that the decision should be a mutual one. He avoids committing himself to the proposition that Betty would be unwilling to entertain or offer alternative proposals. He likewise avoids commitment to any assumption that he and Betty disagree about anything. The mediator is nevertheless also able, by obtaining clarification, to obtain commitments to premises and to elicit acts that follow from those commitments.

Now consider a more extended series of questions by a mediator—questions that have a more confrontational character. Here, questioning is used much more openly to perform argumentative tasks. These three segments in example 6.4 are drawn from a postdivorce custody session in which the husband (Richard) is seeking return of his sixteen-year-old daughter (Vanessa), who ran away to her mother's following a suicide attempt. In these segments, the mediator is ostensibly eliciting and clarifying the wife's (Tammy) point of view and exploring the possibilities for a mutually agreeable settlement. But the direction of the questioning seems in effect to build a case that the daughter needs therapy and that Tammy should act to get the daughter into therapy by getting her to go back to her father.

Segment 001–23 opens after Richard has described a psychiatric evaluation the daughter underwent following the suicide attempt (a few months before she ran away). Segment 030–55 returns to the questioning after a brief side argument between Richard and Tammy. Segment 071–101 occurs near the end of the session, again after the husband and wife have been arguing.

The mediator's questions and Tammy's answers are shadowed by a scenario whose circumstances could be described and assembled into the following argument: Vanessa has serious problems, as indi-

Example 6.4

001 M: Were you ever included Tammy in these evaluative processes?

002 W: Uum, hum yes

003 M: How did you feel about it? What's it like the psychiatric process?

004 W: (   )

005 M: Why not?

006 W: I can't really say because to me it didn't really say anything when we were there at all. She tended to clam up and just wouldn't talk. He did most of the talking.

007 M: How did you feel about the uh how did you feel about the psychiatrist and what they're doing. What they're trying to do =

008 W: We really weren't in there that long. I think the main thing that we were talking about then was uh percentagewise on tennis shoes and not buying expensive things. She wanted uh I think she wanted a bike or something

((Pause))

009 W: I don't know

010 M: Are you saying that you were impressed or you were not impressed?

011 W: I weren't no I was not.

012 M: Do you think that Vanessa needs some intervention? some help? some therapy?

013 W: The thing that I see wrong with Vanessa since she's come home to live with me she defies authority she just wants her own way

014 M: Is that good or bad?

015 W: Bad. I've had my hands full, believe me   ((Pause))   And I know he has too when she was there. She uh she ran away. I've had my hands full.

016 M: How do you feel about her coming back to live with her dad at this point?

017 W: Vanessa and I have sat down and talked about it. We talked about it on the way here. I'm gonna cry

Example 6.4 (Continued)

018 M: That's okay

019 W: He's better for her because he's stricter but she's not
happy there and I'm scared to death she's going to try
and kill herself again but basically he is better for
her. But she says she don't want to go back.

020 M: Is is there some way you and Richard can figure out
something some kind of a of a arrangement where let's say
Vanessa were to live with dad and you and Richard were
kinda work at to get her on a (   )
[   ]
021 W: We've tried that

022 M: You're smiling Richard

023 H: Well yeah because this whole thing is a big circus to me

((Intervening discussion deleted))

030 H: . . . At least he's getting through to her. I just like
the whole program But I couldn't get she allowed Vanessa
to come back and live with her. Ah yeah you wanna come
back sure. Go ahead and cry on my shoulder I'll feel
sorry for you. Vanessa's the best actress in the world.
See when she was living with me I got her a casting
director out in Hollywood. She's a good actress.

031 M: Tammy you were saying when you were driving over here
this morning you and Vanessa had a conversation. (   )
Did Vanessa also feel that it would be best for her to
live with dad?

032 W: No.   She told me that she could not communicate with him
at all

033 M: How do you propose to negotiate this thing this issue
between you and Richard. Because you both are saying,
correct me if I'm wrong, you both are saying that it
probably would be in Vanessa's best interest if she were
to live with dad.

034 W: Uh uhm

035 M: But Vanessa you know she wants to live with mom at this
time. What can you do as mother, as parent what can you
do (   )? To help Vanessa work through this
problem.

036 W: Well she's better she's better with him that he's
stricter than I am. But she's better with me because we

Example 6.4 (Continued)

do communicate and sit and talk. So he's got one point
and I have the other point.

037 M: Do you think that Vanessa needs some therapy?

038 W: Yes

039 M: Do you think it would be a solution that if she were to
continue living with you but the same time concurrently
have some therapy?

040 W: uh hun

041 M: Is she receiving any kind of therapy kind of counseling
right now?

042 W: No

043 M: Has she been living with you for how long now?

044 W: Since   October
        [   ]
045 H: five months

046 M: Five months. In the five month period of time she has
had not had any kind of counseling at all?
((Pause))

047 M: She has experienced some difficulties though, right?

048 W: Uh not anything bad except that she just wants her own
life

049 M: Uh huh. You think that she should be seeing somebody
right now?

050 W: I don't know

051 M: She's been with you X amount of months you must have an
opinion

052 W: Uh when she was seeing someone before to me he wasn't
doing her any good. That's just you know didn't she uh
run away?

053 H: When?

054 W: When she was seeing him   ((Pause))   I think she'd been
seeing Dr. Wendell for about a month or so. Right

055 H: I don't recall. Where'd she run to?

((Intervening discussion deleted))

Example 6.4 (Continued)

071 M: Tammy you're saying that uh what is in the best interest of Vanessa?

072 W: If it
    [

073 M: That's what you're saying =

074 W: Right if it's best then she's to go back

075 M: Are you saying that you're going to leave it up to her? Leave it up to the court or are you going to have a say so
  [

076 W: I just want her to be happy and I know if she goes back there she won't

077 M: Yeah Tammy but the question is are you going to leave it up to her? Or leave it up to the court or are you going to help decide this issue? =

078 W: I wish we could get it solved right now. Vanessa doesn't want to go to court she doesn't want to get on the witness stand she doesn't want to go against him she doesn't want to go against the man I'm married to now

079 M: How can you avoid all that then?

080 W: By settling now
    [

081 M: How can both of you avoid it not just you but can both of you?
  [

082 W: Bring Vanessa in and talk to her. She's going on 17 she's not a baby

083 M: Richard if we were to interview Vanessa and if she were to say you know I want to live with mom what would you do?

084 H: I know what she's gonna say

085 M: What would you do? Would that would that would it change anything?

086 H: No =

087 M: It won't? =

088 H: It doesn't change the environment and guidelines she's exposed to now. It doesn't change that what Vanessa wants

Example 6.4 (Continued)

089 W: What kind of environment is she exposed to (   ) I was
          married to you 22 years was I a good wife and mother or
          not? Wasn't I? You've told me that a thousand times
          that I was

090 H: Another point that was missed when we talked about the
          schooling thing

091 M: The uh ((Pause)) What you're saying though is you're
          going to leave it up to Vanessa?

092 W: I think she's old enough to make up her own mind. The
          girl's going on 17 years old

093 M: But don't you feel that she may need some counseling

094 W: Yes

095 M: You're also going to leave it up to her to to decide to
          get into counseling or are you going to would you some
          advice yourself?

096 W: I can do it myself the reason why he did it all he has
          insurance to pay for it I don't =

097 M: But in the last five months she's been living with you have
          you done anything to get her involved into counseling
          kind of therapy sessions? =

098 W: No

099 M: Why not?

100 W: I felt like when she was with me she did not need a
          psychiatrist like I said the only thing she's done since
          she's been in my home she defies authority. She's normal
          average 17 year old girl she likes to go out to the
          ballgames you know she doesn't smoke she doesn't drink

101 M: Are you going to have to come to court? And have it
          resolved in court

cated by her attempted suicide. Therapy or counseling could help
solve those problems. Therefore, Vanessa should be in therapy. However, Vanessa will not enter therapy on her own, and there is little
reason to think that Vanessa will receive therapy if she continues to
live with her mother. Deciding the issue through the courts is
undesirable. Therefore, the best alternative is for the parents (and
Tammy in particular) to find a way to convince Vanessa to go back to
living with her father, who will then get her into therapy.

This is roughly the "case" that hangs over this series of questions. It emerges from the content, phrasing, and sequencing of the mediator's questions and from the pattern of the wife's answers. If the potential for such a case is not apparent at the start, presumably it is increasingly apparent as the series unfolds.

This case is only projected, not established. The mediator never comes out and makes this case; he merely questions the wife in a way that leads her to take a stand with respect to this case. The wife repeatedly answers in ways that would contradict this interpretation of the situation. She clearly resists Richard's proposal that Vanessa be returned to his custody. Her answers often contradict the answers projected by the phrasing of the mediator's questions. Tammy offers considerations that mitigate against certain conclusions that might reasonably be drawn. She sometimes gives noncommittal, even evasive answers or shifts ground in her answers, and she withdraws prior answers, seemingly to escape undesirable conclusions. Indeed, part of the way in which this case is made manifest is as a projection of something that Tammy is trying to avoid by the way she answers.

The thing to see is not that any particular case is definitively established or even argued, only that potential cases are being assembled and negotiated through the questions and answers—and this is something that both Tammy and the mediator are orienting to.

For example, the mediator's questions in 003, 005, 007, and 010 all provide Tammy with the opportunity to say something positive about the psychiatric evaluation sessions or to take a stand on the evaluation made. Those answers, if given, could establish the mutual premises that Vanessa has problems and that therapy would help Vanessa cope with her problems. Questions 012 and 014 shift more directly to the issue of Vanessa's need for therapy. But while Tammy's answer suggests that Vanessa's behavior is "bad," she does not directly claim that Vanessa needs therapy. That claim comes in answer to the question in 037, though Tammy subsequently withdraws that claim in answer to the questioning in 047, 049, and 051, when it becomes apparent that admitting Vanessa's need for therapy is incompatible with resisting Vanessa's return to her father. Then again in answer to the question in 093, she admits that Vanessa may need some counseling, though once again, in 100, Tammy backs away from that claim when it again becomes apparent that this admission is incompatible with resisting Vanessa's return to her father.

Likewise, question 016 begins to address matters relevant to the other major part of a potential case, namely, whether the daughter is better off living with her father or with her mother. Tammy's answer in 019 raises a fundamental conflict. On the one hand, Tammy admits that Richard is better for the daughter (see also 033–34, though this admission is subsequently withdrawn when, in 035, the mediator uses it to suggest that Tammy should help convince Vanessa to go back). On the other hand, Tammy does not want to force Vanessa to go back to her father because Vanessa does not want to go back and because Tammy is afraid that Vanessa will get depressed and again try to commit suicide (019, 076).

Other questions raise two related issues: the willingness of Tammy to convince Vanessa to live with Richard (020–21, 035–36), and how to avoid having to go to court (075–81, 101). A particularly problematic set of questions, as far as the wife's standpoint is concerned, are those that display the apparent unlikelihood of Vanessa getting into therapy while continuing to live with her mother. Twice, in 037–46 and again in 093–99, the series of questions and answers assembles evidence of inconsistency in Tammy's admission that Vanessa needs therapy and Tammy's claim that Vanessa could receive therapy while living with her.

By raising issues and pressing for clarification, the mediator's questions also function to give shape and substance to a potential argumentative case. Although an argumentative reading can be drawn from the sequencing and phrasing of the questions, the questions also make sense as efforts on the part of the mediator to press the wife into clearly and consistently expressing a position on the issues, and to find out how she can take apparently incompatible positions. By asking questions, the mediator has not clearly advocated a case; he has merely gotten Tammy to take a stand with respect to considerations relevant to making such a case.[8] Nevertheless, the way these questions function parallels the way overt argumentative interaction functions to assemble and negotiate the substance of an actual argumentative case.

Many of the questions in example 6.4 have a confrontational style that can approximate another function of argumentation, namely, not merely raising and shaping the materials for premises, but pressing for assent to those premises and to the conclusions they support. That is, by pressing for a clear, unequivocal answer to a question and by phrasing the question in a way that more or less strongly suggests a particular answer, questions can be used to get a disputant to answer in ways that commit them to propositions that support a particular standpoint, that withdraw commitments, or that at least make the disputant take a standpoint. Consider two specific patterns that have this appearance.

The first pattern appears in the questioning in turns 001–15. Here is a pattern of progressively more pointed questions. Both the phrasing of the questions and the way the answers are followed up project as the "preferred response" one that makes a positive evaluation of therapy for Vanessa. In 007 the mediator reformulates his initial question in 003 after Tammy seemed unimpressed with the evaluation sessions. The question in 007 now focuses on a lesser basis for approval: what the psychiatrist was "trying to do" rather than on what the psychiatrist actually did do.

Then, in 012, the mediator rephrases the question in terms of what the daughter needs, framing it almost as a rhetorical question by the seemingly incredulous repetition of "some intervention? some help? some therapy?" Notice that "some" here calls for a kind of minimal admission. Both times that the mediator asks questions with bald either-or alternatives (010, 014), the questions come after Tammy has supplied opinions that would not warrant the proposal that Vanessa should be in therapy.

The mediator's questions thus create multiple opportunities for Tammy to answer in a way that would provide grounds for concluding that Vanessa should be in therapy. These opportunities are created by shifting the focus of the questioning across multiple possible grounds for arriving at such a conclusion, and simply by virtue of the mediator's repeated failure to accept Tammy's answers as providing closure.

The increasingly pointed projection of a positive answer about the value of therapy goes hand in hand with an increasingly pressing call for any kind of definite answer at all. A striking feature of this series is the persistently noncommittal, seemingly evasive quality of Tammy's answers. The wife has to be pushed into answers that take any stand, pro or con, with respect to the issue of Vanessa's getting into therapy.

While in 004 Tammy apparently provides a minimal answer that expresses a negative opinion of the evaluation sessions (see M's follow-up: "Why not?"), in 006 she "can't really say" why she feels that way. Turns 008 and 013 both avoid direct answers to the mediator's questions, and 008 is followed up with an "I don't know" in 009. The only clear, direct, and unequivocal answers Tammy gives come in 010–11 and 014–15 in response to the mediator's closed-choice, either-or questions that finally pin her down. By forcefully pressing for a clear, unequivocal answer, the mediator thus does something that looks much like the work that gets done in pushing forward an argument: establishing the conditional relevance of assent or dissent, given the issuing of an argument.

The second pattern with a confrontational quality comes in the series of questions in 037–46, which is then virtually repeated step by step in 095–99. Both series are a good approximation of a "confrontation sequence" (Bleiberg and Churchill 1975; Jacobs 1986). Such sequences have been noticed to function as a strategy for getting people to participate (wittingly or unwittingly) in exposure of flaws in their own position.[9]

In this case, the question sequences seem designed to confront Tammy with the following dilemma: Tammy agrees that her daughter needs therapy (037–38, 093–94), and Tammy claims that by living with her, Vanessa could be provided therapy (039–40, 095–96). The problem with this position is that Vanessa has already been living with Tammy for five months and has not been receiving therapy of any kind (041–46, 097–99).

The incongruity of Tammy's actual practice, given her stated position, is emphasized in both series by using forms of expression that emphasize the degree of inaction ("any kind of therapy," "any kind of counseling at all," "have you done anything") and that emphasize the length of time (the figure of five months is repeated twice in 046 and used again in 097). And both series end with aggressively confrontational questions that express incredulity. In both series, the final question has the practical effect of pushing Tammy to withdraw her commitment to one of the prior claims— either that Vanessa needs therapy or that by living with her mother, Vanessa can get that therapy.[10]

The asking of questions thus functions not merely to perform such tasks as probing, clarifying, and organizing but also to perform important argumentative tasks. Questioning can give shape and substance to potential cases and can push for answers in ways that parallel the way in which assent and dissent are made conditionally relevant by making an argument.

Conclusions

The use of formulations and questions, then, appears to have important argumentative functions within mediation. These devices offer strategies that are sensitive to the multiple and sometimes paradoxical demands placed on the conduct of the mediator. They are interesting because they illustrate how institutional ideals must ultimately be realized through the practical engineering of discussion at a very mundane and detailed level of discourse. It is not enough simply to say in the abstract that mediators ought to manage the process of discussion but not its substance, that mediators ought to facilitate the search for a settlement but not impose a settlement. Concrete techniques must be fashioned to do this. The techniques of formulating and questioning stand as exemplary of how people can employ the resources of ordinary language to approximate an ideal model of a critical discussion under less-than-ideal conditions.

Formulations and questions appear to be well suited to doing the job of compensating for problems in the way that disputants argue for and against positions without actually doing the arguing for the disputants. These techniques provide mediators with a kind of "functional substitute" for open argumentation and advocacy. That is, they provide ways of doing some of the tasks which argumentation and advocacy are directly designed to do, while avoiding some of the commitments that follow from pursuing these tasks in open, on-record fashion.

It should be clear that formulations and questions have this potential because managing the process or procedures of argumentative discourse inevitably affects the substance and force of what is said. This may be an unintended consequence of otherwise innocent efforts at clarification, summarization, and procedural guidance. But it can also become a strategic possibility that is actively exploited by the mediator. If used adroitly, these techniques enable mediators to help fashion the substance and force of arguments while dancing around the role of advocate.

Notes

1. For example, ideals of clear and efficient communication will often be incompatible with the need to protect the face of the addressee (Brown and Levinson 1987).

2. Throughout the United States there are now thousands of mediation programs provided by various kinds of public and private organizations, private practitioners, and agencies at all levels of government. Programs handle a wide range of cases, including family and neighborhood disputes, small-claims disputes, academic and employment grievances, labor-management disputes, pre- and post-divorce custody and visitation disputes, insurance and contract disputes, environmental disputes, and even cases involving felony offenders and their victims. For a general overview, see Roehl and Cook 1985.

3. See note 3 to chapter 4 for full details on mediation transcripts analyzed in this chapter. Transcription notation is explained in note 2 to chapter 3. M, H, and W designate mediator, husband, and wife respectively. All names have been changed.

4. Mediators are given license to advocate that, as a general principle, any settlement should be "in the best interests of the child." This comment rarely, however, leads to specific objections to proposals put forth or agreed upon by the disputants. More often, mediators present this principle in a way that is distanced from any particular proposal. Repeatedly emphasizing

the interests of the child has more than substantive consequences for discussion, however. It also performs the procedural function of creating a "win-win" cooperative framework for discussion as opposed to the "win-lose" adversarial framework the disputants often bring with them. This kind of framing function can be seen in 023 of example 6.1, in 120–21 of example 6.3, in 033 and 035 of example 6.4, and in 071 of example 6.4. Mediators also sometimes suggest conventional solutions to standard problems facing the disputants, for example, common ways of scheduling visitations or standard ways of resolving apparent impasses. For a general overview of the management functions ascribed to mediators, see Donohue, Allen, and Burrell 1988.

5. It should also be noted that the mediator's description of alternatives puts pressure on Bill to offer a more acceptable proposal, since all parties know that the evaluation process at the Center for Legal Psychiatry will take months to complete. In the meantime, the current visitation schedule will stay in effect. So, if Bill has a more acceptable proposal to offer, he should do it now. Part of the perceived pressure on Betty results from the "win-lose" adversarial framework the disputants seem to impose on the discussion, from the perception that sticking with the current arrangement would not count as a "settlement," and from the presumption of change that is carried by the mediator's suggestion (later made explicit in 260) that the disputants consider a temporary visitation schedule. Any change in the current schedule means that Bill will leave with more than he started and Betty with less. The very suggestion of a trial visitation schedule suggests that the mediator believes that the likelihood of harmful disruption for the children is not serious enough to preclude testing to see whether that harm will occur.

6. In fact, later on in this session the mediator explicitly raises this issue of "something, ah, of concern that you might feel that I'm taking Bill's side." He denies this: "It's not that I'm taking his side." He instead claims that all he is doing is "trying to modify" Bill's plan because the original plan was unacceptable, and that is why the mediator is "discussing different options."

7. Compare the pragmatic logic of this sequence to the very similar pattern in 040 and 041 of example 6.1. Here too, once the mediator has gotten agreement with his formulation, he calls for a proposal as a next step that is consistent with the presupposition that *some* proposal would be acceptable, even if the arrangement under discussion is not.

8. In fact, the mediator's own expressed opinion does not unequivocally support this projected case. After the session has broken down in impasse with both Richard and Tammy deciding to settle the issue in court, the mediator closes in turn 146 this way:

"I would suggest at this point that uh we end this session uhm I think to continue would be uhm would be counterproductive I would for it to uh by continuing this session I would hate for it to uh to draw the uh widen the space between you more and more and more. I think that what is needed is that both of you are going to have to have some kind of relationship uh some kind of working relationship for Vanessa. I'm of the opinion that she needs to be seen by someone I think that the one time incident of the attempted suicide is a very serious situation and it needs to be looked at and be dealt with (   ) either by living with dad or by living with you but she has to be seen by someone who can. I'll be in favor of just letting the court decide."

While the mediator expresses the opinion that Vanessa should be in therapy, he does not claim that this means she should live with her father.

9. The technique of "confrontation" in therapy seems designed to get the patient to acknowledge dilemmas and contradictions, to take stands, and to face up to issues when the patient appears to be avoiding them. There is a rather clear parallel in mediation, where the resolution of differences requires that disputants clearly express standpoints and not shift ground in defending those standpoints. See also the discussion of example 3.1 in chapter 3.

10. The argumentative potential of these series seems to be apparent to Tammy and is probably intended by the mediator. Note the pause after turn 046. Normally, the next turn would be expected to be an answer to this question, but instead there is only silence. Tammy has no reply to her apparent dilemma, and the mediator lets it sink in. Then when the mediator reopens the question of Vanessa's needing therapy, Tammy escapes by returning to a theme she voiced earlier in 013: there is no serious problem. When the mediator tries to reestablish the premise that Vanessa needs therapy, Tammy slips away by returning to evasive and noncommittal answers. Notice that the questioning in 093 and 097 virtually repeats the propositions in the earlier line of questioning. But this time the argumentative intent and force of the questions is more strongly signaled by the "don't you" structure of the question in 093 (as opposed to "do you" in 037) as well as through the use of "but" in 097 in reply to Tammy's assertion that she can care for her daughter. And then Tammy escapes her dilemma once again by retreating from the claim that Vanessa has problems needing therapy (100). Note also the oddity of the content and sequencing of turn 101. The mediator cannot come out and say that Tammy is not facing up to the problem; he cannot directly point out that her position is contradictory and unacceptable. The question, however, by directly following Tammy's answer, makes it plain that he sees this line of questioning getting nowhere, which means that there will be no settlement, which means that the issue will have to be resolved by the court.

7

Failures in Higher-Order Conditions in the Organization of Witnessing and Heckling Episodes

The ideal model of critical discussion shares with the classical rhetorical tradition in communication an understanding of the rhetorical situation as one in which discussants knowingly enter into a joint effort to reach a consensus or mutual accommodation of interests based on critical assessment of the relative acceptability of competing standpoints. The design of argumentation is assumed to be fundamentally instrumental in nature, that is, aimed toward the practical end of discovering the basis for collective action, agreement, or understanding. See, for instance, Aristotle's "faculty of observing in any given case the available means of persuasion" (1924, 11.1.2.135b 26), Bryant's "function of adjusting ideas to people and people to ideas" (1953, 413), or Burke's "inducing cooperation" (1950, 43). On this view, rational discussants would be expected to appeal to reasoning and evidence acceptable to themselves and to the other party, adjusting to their interlocutor's frame of reference and establishing a common ground or identification of interests from which they might reason together or otherwise transcend their divisions. They would be expected to conduct themselves in ways that maintain a mutual openness to criticism and to the demand for justification.

These expectations presuppose the existence of second-order conditions in two ways. First, these expectations presume that arguers hold the appropriate attitudes and social commitments associated with the expected conduct. Second, these expectations presume the existence of a rational audience. It makes sense to adjust to an interlocutor's frame of reference and to try to achieve mutually reasoned assent only if that interlocutor is motivated and able to engage in reasoned discussion. Indeed, if this latter presupposition is not satisfied, an arguer will find his or her interlocutor continually failing to live up to standards for reasonable conduct and, in a certain dialectical sense, will find that the opening stage must constantly be reopened (or, perhaps more accurately, that the interlocutors never really move out of the opening stage in the first place).

This possibility of failure in second-order conditions raises several questions that are the focus of this chapter: What are reasonable limits to entering into resolution-oriented argumentation? How do arguers determine whether or not their interlocutor fails to live up to the preconditions for a rational discussant? What are these preconditions? And what, if anything, could be the point of argumentation where these preconditions fail?

Fields of Argumentation

All argumentation is conducted within pregiven contexts of interpretive categories, background beliefs and values, standards of proof and authority, norms of conduct, and so on. These contexts can be thought of, loosely, as argument fields, as institutional frameworks that give content to the conduct of argument (Toulmin 1958; Willard 1983). Fields provide publicly organized patterns of inquiry and deliberation. They give substance to the subject matter, topics, and issues of argumentation, and they provide standards of authority, legitimacy, objectivity, rationality, and acceptability. The field notion, then, stresses that all argumentative deliberation occurs within some sociohistorical context and that all reasoning is reasoning-in-context.

One of the more interesting implications of the field notion is that the same principles that promote the resolution of conflict when argumentation is conducted *within* a field may actually preclude the possibility of resolution when argumentation is undertaken *between* fields. Where fields produce quite different assessments of what is reasonable, factual, authoritative, relevant, problematic, assumable, and so on, arguers from those fields may find themselves continually slipping as they attempt to arrive at some common ground, no matter how tentatively assumable it may be, either in terms of initial premises for making arguments or in terms of procedural agreements for conducting argumentation. Arguers from such fields may, for all practical purposes, find themselves assuming incommensurable positions in a dispute. Both sides may find themselves encountering what appears to be an irrational interlocutor. Under such circumstances, the very idea of entering into critical discussion may appear pointless as efforts to engage in critical discussion dissolve the very conditions for its possibility.

Witnessing and Heckling

These features are neatly illustrated in the speech event of "witnessing and heckling" as it takes place when preachers Jed Smock and Max Lynch visit college campuses across the United States (Jacobs 1982). For our purposes, witnessing and heckling are interesting because they exhibit just the sort of incommensurability of perspectives that might arise from a failure of second-order conditions. In this section, we describe what typically happens in this event. We then turn to the various perspectives the participants themselves use to make sense of what is going on in this event. By showing how participants rationalize what goes on in the event, we are able to display something of a paradoxical phenomenon, namely, the way in which individual-level adherence to standards of reasonableness can produce social-level unreasonableness.

Smock and Lynch travel from university campus to university campus, spontaneously drawing crowds for an afternoon, reproducing a characteristic confrontation with the students at each site. The preachers rail against the sinfulness of campus life and announce "the wrath of God, the vengeance of God, the Hellfire and brimstone" that await the unrepentant.[1] Although large crowds are attracted, the crowds are not moved—at least, not moved to repent. They consistently respond by mocking, teasing, heckling, and challenging Smock and Lynch. There is remarkable standardization in the event from site to site. While new variations in the event are always possible, there is a recognizable uniformity in each party's topics and lines of argument, in their style of conduct, and in the overall tone of the event.

Much of the preaching focuses on the sinfulness of the audience and is openly inflammatory in tone. Smock in particular harps again and again on this point. He paints a picture of the typical college student as driven by carnal desires, "in bondage to lust." In the name of avoiding hang-ups, he claims, they lead lives of "immoral self-indulgence." "Yeah, you have fun," he snarls at the giggling crowd. "Your girl gets pregnant, and you go out and kill the baby and you say, 'Well I *sure had fun.*'"

Smock frames the sinfulness of the audience in both personal accusation and sweeping censure. He frequently picks out individuals in the audience who are smoking cigarettes, laughing or smirking, dressed "shabbily," or wearing fraternity T-shirts. And he implicates the general student body with condemnations of drugs and sex running rampant in the dormitories, drunkenness in the bars ("Some of these girls would rather lie face down in their own vomit than hold a baby to their breast"), or the "ethical relativism" and "existentialism" that is being preached in the classrooms.

He and Lynch regularly argue that the Bible conflicts with feminist and other secular humanist doctrines. According to the Bible, God did not intend for women to assume positions of leadership; their place is in the home raising a family. Smock says that God made woman as a "companion *for* man" and that "any woman who doesn't want a husband is sick." He tells the audience: "The Bible specifically says that women should be modest in their apparel. *But,* there's nothing modest about it when you see . . . the girls going to classes in gym shorts. THERE'S NOTHING MODEST ABOUT THAT! That's ridiculous! That's absurd and disgusting!"

Likewise, Smock condemns homosexuality as an "abomination." He likes to remind the audience of God's destruction of Sodom and Gomorrah ("because they were all queers") or to cite AIDS as a more contemporary demonstration of God's wrath.

Throughout the afternoon, the preachers work in the face of relentless questioning and heckling. The most common form of heckling comes in the form of crowd responses: of laughter, whistling, applause, howling, and hooting. But individual hecklers are also peppered throughout the audience. Much of the individual heckling comes in response to what the preachers say, and some of it has an argumentative force. (After a tirade against bars, one shouted, "Jesus drank wine. He drank wine, didn't he?") But most of the heckling is only distantly connected to any argument. It seems more designed to mock, tease, or fluster the preacher. ("Aww, tell us about fornication. That's more fun." "Do you masturbate or fornicate?" "*You* should have been aborted, Jed.")

While public sympathizers are rare, there are always serious challengers who have not given up from the start on the idea of debating points made by the preachers. These people usually raise the same issues at each session. They challenge the validity of the Bible or the preachers' claims about the Bible. They want to know how the preachers can be so sure that the Bible is true and all other viewpoints are false. They question the preachers' right to condemn other viewpoints. They try to debate the preachers' stands on social issues. Such exchanges, however, rarely seem to go any place. Example 7.1 illustrates the tone of the event.[2]

Preacher and audience quickly find themselves plunging into an intractable conflict. There is comprehensive and endless disagreement over facts, values, norms of conduct, sources of authority, descriptive vocabulary, the relevance of evidence and premises, starting assumptions, issues, and on and on. The participants themselves widely perceive the comprehensive and irresolvable nature of their differences, although that does not keep them from arguing with each other. These disagreements result from the quite different perspectives that fundamentalist and secular audience members bring to bear in participating in the event.

These different perspectives can be treated as distinct fields of argumentation. Each perspective represents a socially sanctioned way of reasoning about the subject matter at issue in the disputes, and each has its own understanding of how reasonable argumentation should proceed in these circumstances.

Standpoints and Perspectives

Although the surface structure of these witnessing and heckling episodes is manifestly argumentative, the episodes are also manifestly incapable of producing resolutions of disagreements. There is a confrontation not only between alternative standpoints but between broader perspectives that frame these standpoints. To understand the peculiar organization of the episodes, it is first necessary to understand the perspectives within which the opposing parties operate. If the preachers are considered as protagonists of a position and the hecklers as antagonists, then it will be the perspectives of these two parties that we must understand.

Participants' perspectives may be partly reconstructed from behavior—from what the participants say and do, partly from interviews focusing on participants' understandings of the event and on their own rationales for their own participation. Individuals participating in these episodes understood the meaning of the event in radically divergent ways, but these understandings divided into three groups, which we may term the secular comic, the secular humanist, and the fundamentalist. Each perspective produces a different dramatic structuring of the event which organizes the perceptions, the accounts, and the performances of those who occupy that perspective. Each perspective supplies a kind of subjective rationality, a way of reasoning about the event so that occupants may find lines of action in the event and assign interpretations to the event in a coherent fashion.

Example 7.1

01 A1:   Do you consider the Devil to be a being?

02 P: A being? You'd have to define what you meant by-
                                               [

03 A1:   Alright.
Do you-   You believe in the Devil right? existing,
right?

04 P: Yes.

05 A1:   Alright. Do you think he's- Is he smart? Can he read
and so forth?

06 P: Sure.

07 A1:   Alll right, HOW DO I KNOW YOU'RE NOT THE DEVIL? then

08 P: How do I?- how do you know?

09 A1:   I mean if you go against my religion, how do I know
you're not the Devil? I mean, you got no credentials.

10 P: You can tell the voice of God from the voice of the
Devil because, you see, you need to know the Bible.

11 As: ((Crowd laughter))

12 A1:   I know the Bible.

13 P: If you don't know the Bible, then you can't tell.

14 A1:   I know the Bible but you're not interpreting it the same
way I do.

15 P: If you don't know- if you don't know- if you don't know
the Bible, then you *can't* possibly tell me. You'll be
confused. You'll even believe some pervert like Sigmund
Freud. Or you'll believe some philosopher like Jean
Paul Sartre. Or you'll believe some ole'- some false
prophet like the Maharishi Mahatma Gandhi and he'll have
you ohming or some other ridiculous thing.

16 Ax: Ohhhhmmmmmmmmmmmmm
            [

17 Ax: Ohhhhhmmmmmmmmmmm
                  [

18 As: Ohhmmmmmmmmmmm
mmmmmmmmmmmmmmmmmmmm
            [

19 P: So you need to know the Bible or
you're bound to be deceived.

Example 7.1 (Continued)

20 Ax: Da-da-da-da::, a-na-na-na:, hey hey hey::, goo-hood
bye:: ((Kiss him good-bye melody))

21 P: That's why the Devil has done all he can to keep the
Bible out of the hands of this generation.   Even by
having the Supreme Court of the United States turn
against the Bible and make it so restricting that in
effect the Bible is almost been outlawed in our public
schools.   Because the Bible- the Bible exposes so much=
            [

22 As: ((Crowd applause; cheers))
            [

23 Ax: Not outlawed,   just not (   )

24 P: =of what you're learning in the classroom today *as* the
lies of the Devil.   So unless you know God's written=
            [

25 Ax: Tell us about women's lib then.

26 P: =Word, you're bound to be deceived.

27 A1:   But I *know* the Word.   It just doesn't mean the same
thing to me as it does to you.   So how do I know you're
not deceiving me?

28 P: Alright.   Now, you'll have to be more specific.

29 Ax: He *is* the Devil!

30 As: ((Crowd laughter))

31 P: What am I saying that you believe contradicts the
written Word?

32 A1:   You keep condemning everybody, saying everybody's going
to Hell.   But you don't know that.
            [

33 P: Oh.   I haven't said *every*one is going to Hell.
I just said quite clearly, earlier, those that raised
their hand and confessed Jesus, if they're sincere, they
have everlasting life.   They're going to Heaven.

34 A1:   But if they, uh, smoke pot and listen to rock and roll
music, fornicate, and I mean you listed just about=
            [

35 Ax: Yeah!
            [

36 Ax: YEAH, Rolling Stones!

37 Ax: YEAH!

Example 7.1 (Continued)

38	A1:	= everything everybody does and everybody's going to Hell so far.
39	P:	We've repeatedly said there's one sin, there's one sin that sends a man to=
		[
40	A1:	Only one's gonna be up there is *you*.
41	P:	= Hell, that's not believing in Jesus.
42	A1:	Is that the only thing you can't do? You can do anything besides that?
43	P:	And then- most people out here probably smoke pot, drink booze, fornicate.
44	Ax:	AMEN!
45	Ax:	Yeah!
46	Ax:	YEAH!
		[
47	Ax:	WHOOOO-EEEEE!
48	Ax:	Hooooyeah!
		[
49	P:	Not all of you do. Of course I know the only reason a lotta these fellas are virgins is not because they don't want any. They want it. They just can't get it.
50	As:	((Crowd laughter; hooting; whistling))
51	Ax:	How do you get it?
52	P:	Well you wanna sin and you can't sin enough sinner.
53	Ax:	Do you believe in separation of church and state?
54	P:	What?

Secular Perspective: Comic and Humanist

The comic and humanist attitudes have a common core generated as a solution to a common interpretive problem. The interpretive problem is how to make sense of the behavior of the preachers, given its manifest irrationality. The preachers seem to be trying to persuade, but they behave in a manner no one would expect to succeed. Interviewees widely reported the attribution that the preachers "want us to repent" and are "trying to get people to believe in religion," but they also made frequent mention of the patently counterproductive tactics of the preachers. The following is a representative interview response by an audience member:

I understand a lot of the things he says, and I agree with him. But I don't agree with the methods he does it with. . . . If he said it in a different manner I think he'd get through to a lot of people instead of making a big joke out of everything. . . . He's alienating them more than anything. (Interview 22-A)

The style and tone of the preachers appear to systematically undermine their very purpose. The audience resents their "holier than thou" attitude and the way they "condemn everybody." The preachers make incredible claims that no one could be expected to believe. They stereotype everyone and use categories that do not even apply.

The preachers antagonize people and receive a shower of abuse in return. Yet they repeatedly and knowingly stage these events. They persist in their caricatures of campus life, in their name calling, and in their hard-line fundamentalism. They make no apparent effort to adjust to the frame of reference of their audience. How does one make sense of such behavior?

Most nonbelievers quickly come to approach the event on the assumption that they are dealing with a morally defective character-type whose conduct is not subject to rational explanation. In interviews, most people were reluctant to volunteer any kind of account for what the preacher must think he is doing. If they did offer some account, it was usually that he was "crazy," a "zealot," a "lunatic," or an "egomaniac." Students widely insisted that the preacher was incapable of reasoned discussion. "He doesn't know sanity. He doesn't know logic. The only thing he knows is hell and brimstone," exclaimed one. Interviewees reported continual frustration in trying to engage the preacher on a "reasonable" level.

You just can't talk rationally to them because they're so *set* in their ways. You just discuss up to a point with them where they won't change their views and then you just leave them. (Interview 08-A)

[We heckle] because you can't argue with him logically. I tried for a year or so and gave up. . . . In this situation I think heckling is the only thing that has any sort of impact. . . . [I came to start heckling] because I tried to discuss things rationally with him and got nowhere. I'd show logical contradictions and he'd just deny them. (Interview 02-A)

Smock's irrationality is something that is taken to be manifest in his stated positions. "This is really heavy," exclaimed one onlooker to another. "*Listen* to him. He's out of it." The students simply cannot accept the idea that a rational person would believe, for example, that he and God would one day "reenter the Earth's atmosphere" to destroy the armies of the Earth with a "super cosmic ray" or that when God drove Adam and Eve from the Garden of Eden (which many take to be a pretty weird story in itself), God also transformed lions from herbivores into carnivores and turned snakes into venomous creatures. Smock's "obvious" misinterpretations of the Bible are taken as further evidence of a defect in his reasoning faculty.[3]

Students also see the preacher as morally perverse. In the eyes of the secular audience members, "he's trying to shove things down everybody's throat." The following interview captures this feeling well. When asked why they heckled the preacher, the interviewees replied:

A: He's making religion a mockery.
B: That's exactly right. He brings it out here and he tries to shove it down people's throats.
A: Yeah. People should be left to their own beliefs.
B: People should find religion in their own way.
A: Religion is a personal thing. Just believe what you want. I mean, that's why there are churches. If you want to go in them, you can. Nobody's forcing you to go in. So you should just leave it at that. (Interview 08-AB)

The students see the preacher's style as deliberately confrontational. Countless times they expressed the feeling that "he's really rude and inconsiderate." They were particularly dismayed by Smock's social intolerance and his authoritarian attitudes. For example, interviewees made statements like:

Where does he get off insulting people like that? Who does he think he is anyway? I don't care how strongly you believe something, that doesn't give you the right to go around calling people names. The guy's a jerk. (Interview 12-D)

He doesn't answer questions at all or he doesn't face issues. He just automatically asks you if you're a believer and if you're not a believer, it's just the end. He doesn't want to have anything to do with you. And it really defeats his own purpose because everybody mocks him. (Interview 11-A)

There have been people here a couple of times who have put questions to him and he just blew them off with, "What are you saying, sinner?" If anybody real serious comes up they blow it off, you know. I don't think he's going about it the right way. (Interview 20-D)

The preaching directly conflicts with widely held beliefs that biblical and ethical doctrine is a matter of personal interpretation, that love for one's fellows means social tolerance, that no one has the moral authority to condemn others for what they believe. The whole moralistic tone of the preaching was seen as "hypocritical," as generating hostility in the audience, and as obstructing reasonable, civil discussion.

Both the comic and the humanist attitudes produce dramatic structurings of the event consistent with this understanding of the preacher, though representatives of these two approaches reason from these beliefs in somewhat different directions. For the humanist, the event is a confrontation over social policy. The character of the preacher is that of a closed-minded reactionary driven to impose his twisted attitudes on others. Students told us the preachers were "racists," "bigots," "sexists," "fascists," and "conservatives"—all labels taken from the sociopolitical framework of a secular morality. These students take the issues discussed seriously.

They see themselves as "fair-minded" and "open" to ideas different from their own. They expect standards of civility and mutual respect, openness to change, a certain level of personal distancing from the issues, and a tentativeness in drawing conclusions—claiming for themselves something like the position of an ideal critical discussant. But this secular ideal for argumentative discussion collapses in the actual event. The humanist arguers quickly find themselves placed in an adversarial relationship with the preacher. They feel thrust into a role of defending basic principles of social justice, their own personal integrity, or the integrity of the process of reasonable discussion itself.

Humanists repeatedly talked about how they felt provoked into "speaking out" and challenging the preacher's views. This motive was usually articulated in ways like the following:

[I argue] because I finally get to the point where, of where I'm tired of the hypocrisy. I feel I ought to say something. (Interview 05-A)

Sometimes you- I have thoughts on my mind. I want to express them. I gotta get it out. It's- sometimes I make an ass of myself, but I don't care. Sometimes I say something very valid. (Interview 15-C)

The aim of the humanists is to refute the preacher's claims through questioning and argument, sometimes simply to enforce their right to question and argue, but above all, to try to "make him face facts." But this effort often degenerates into sarcasm and angry clashes. From this perspective, the preaching becomes a cause for resentment and anger; the irrationality of the preacher is a source of continual frustration. The primary point of these encounters, however, is not so much to persuade the preacher—he is after all "out of it" and probably beyond reason. The point is to "make a point" before the audience and to take a stand against him.

For the vast majority of the audience, however, the event contains no serious issues. It is simply something from which to extract easy entertainment. As one student put it: "I find this very entertaining. It's better than happy hour. Why spend your money getting drunk when you can be over here?" Unlike the humanist, who resists what is going on and sees the preaching as a perversion of a serious forum for the discussion of ideas, the comic accepts what is going on "for what it is" and tries to encourage it. The whole event, like the preacher, thus becomes nothing but a "farce" and a "mockery." Students frequently used terms like "show," "spectacle," and "comedy" to express their understanding of the "absurd" nature of what was going on.

From this perspective, the conduct of the preacher is seen as humorous absurdity that invites mockery. His irrationality becomes a source of teasing and scoffing. With so many other people heckling, the whole thing becomes "just a riot" that is just too much to resist. As one interviewee explained it:

[I came to start heckling because] I saw it was a good time. The first time I saw him people were already heckling and everybody was having a good time, so I started heckling and yelling back too. (Interview 02-B)

Another interviewee said:

When you first come out here you don't know that it's [heckling] acceptable. Then you see a couple of people start doing it, then you see it feels so good to do it. (Interview 13-A)

The widely perceived appropriateness of the heckling is closely tied to perceptions of the preachers. Hecklers openly admit that they are "taunting," "teasing," "tormenting," and otherwise trying to "get to" Smock. Most see it as harmless fun—as "wisecracks" and "pranks." Like small boys poking at a snapping turtle, it occurs to very few that a character of the preacher's type has any rights or feelings worth considering.

Most feel that the preacher is simply getting what he deserves. As one student wrote, Smock had "totally disregarded the feelings and opinions of his audience" and therefore "deserves the worst treatment he can possibly get." Others claim that Smock actually wants to be heckled, that he has perverse psychological needs that are satisfied by provoking such a response. This account was repeatedly offered by hecklers, usually in a humorous frame:

I think he is, uh, kind of on an ego trip really. I think he comes here for the attention, you know, 'cause he *knows* that all these people are gonna be down on him and it's kinda like, uh, well, he talks, uh, he's real righteous, you know, like, and, uh, I don't know. I think he's on a head trip. He's on an ego trip. (Interview 18-B)

I think, I think he does it just for a personal kick . . . because, I don't know, it gives him, it's a new thrill. He was on, he was on the drug scene and now it's a new thrill for him. (Interview 01-D)

In any event, the preacher has turned the event into such a mockery that the only viable response for the audience is to play along and reflect back to him the mockery *he* has created. The position of the comic seems to be: It's no use trying to reason with a guy like this, but at least we can show ourselves that this is all just a joke (and get some fun out of doing so).

Most of the students approach this event with a mixture of amusement and disapproval. It is never really clear to most whether they should laugh or get angry. While these two reactions are relatively distinct, most audience members move back and forth between them as events unfold. Indeed, the blend in perspective is reflected by the incredulity that always lurks behind the serious challenges of the humanists and by the mean-spirited taunting that brings delight to so many of the comics. The usual ambivalent and paradoxical stance of the audience member is well illustrated in the following letter to the editor:

Recently, as I was sauntering past the Nebraska Union I was attracted by the ravings of a madman. As I am a fairly open-minded person and had some free time, I stopped to listen to whatever propaganda he might be espousing.

Many of the students who gathered to listen to this lunatic stood by politely and giggled at the appropriate places. Meanwhile, this idiot told horror stories of how young, pure freshmen women were intentionally intoxicated by vicious, black-hearted frat boys who would steal their virginity, make whores of them and cast them out as broken, useless women.

His encore to this stage of his often-jeered monologue was his, and Jesus', personal endorsement of Ronald Reagan for President.

After several minutes of trying to take this joker seriously, I became convinced that at some time in this pitiful man's life he had taken the wrong combination of dangerous narcotics and turned into the Bible-thumping clown he is today.

Normally, I do not sow criticism upon one who holds views which are different from mine. But as a serious student I cannot help but be affronted by a man who seeks to undermine values I hold dear. He is a man as dangerous as any regent. He is a man who would condone the closing of libraries at a university so that the regents could afford their annual bowl game excursion.

Although there are almost as many factions of deviants as there are of Christians (and I do not claim to speak for all of them), there is one faction I do represent. We the congregation of Dr. Smith's Church of Decadent and Immoral Thoughts wish to formally and publically [sic] protest this insult; this man's demeaning attacks on sex, drugs, lusting and rock 'n' roll. And in his next appearance on campus we will cheerfully pick up the rally cry: "Throw him in the fountain!" (Don Fallon, "Message criticized," *Daily Nebraskan*, University of Nebraska-Lincoln, Sept. 9, 1980, 5)

The Fundamentalist Perspective

For the preachers themselves and for their partisans within the audience, the speech event only remotely resembles what the humanist and the comic see. The fundamentalist sees the event through the categories of biblical drama. Smock and Lynch have been chosen by God to preach the Gospel on college campuses. They liken themselves to the Old Testament prophets and New Testament martyrs and see themselves being persecuted for bearing witness to the Truth.

Within this drama, the preachers are not really engaged in efforts at persuasion at all. They are engaged in acts of witnessing, which are designed to take a stand against sin, to expose it in faithful accordance with the will of God. It is for this reason that Smock shocks the audience by confronting individuals in the crowd and indicting campus life. By using moralistic terms like "lust," "fornication," "whore," or "sinner," he is deliberately exposing these acts for what they are. As he explained in an interview:

I remember I was talking with a woman and she admitted that she was having sexual relations with her boyfriend. "You're going to have to stop fornicating with him. It's God's law." "*Oh!* Don't use that word. It makes our relationship sound so *ugly!*" ((said in falsetto voice)) See, that word, fornication, points it out for the sin that it is. See, your sociologists call it an open marriage. You know, a professor is going to say, "What do you think of an open marriage?" They'll all say that. But they're not going to say, "What do you think of adultery? Do you think it's all right to commit adultery?" Because that word, see, points it out for the sin that it is, whereas an open marriage—that's a neutral term. It's morally neutral.

[Interviewer: So you try to choose those terms?]

Yeah. ((Claps hands)) They're *biblical* terms. They're *piercing.* Jeremiah said the Word of God is like a *hammer,* ((pounds fist on the table)) *smashing* the rock to pieces. Paul said it's quick and it's powerful, and it's sharper than a two-edged sword. That word, "Fornicator!" "Drunkard!" These are sharp words, two-edged, as opposed to saying, "You promiscuous person." "Fornicator!" See the difference?

For the preacher to take a more moderate approach would be to legitimate what is wicked. He will not tone down his indictments. To take a conciliatory stance, to adapt to the frame of reference of the sinner, would be to "prostitute" the Church to the very system that must be replaced. Besides, no one would be saved by that kind of a message; they would only be further lulled into complacency and complicity in the sin of the world. According to Smock:

But you see, other people who try to do what I do, they won't preach against sin. They'll just take a "Smile, Jesus loves you" approach. "So what?" For most people it's just "so what?" See, I don't tell them, "Smile, Jesus loves you." I tell them, "God loves you," but I tell them, "Repent! Mourn! Weep! Your sins have separated you from God. God is angry with you. God does love you and since He loves you, He's angry with you because you've rebelled against Him." This is *Truth*. Uncompromised. Not watered down.

Nor will the preacher debate God's will against the tenets of a secular morality—a fact which many in the audience find so frustrating. The issue is not whether God's way is better—that is a question posed by the Devil to separate people from God. The issue is, What is God's will? When students question the relevance or validity of the Bible or the authority of his representatives, that is the Devil at work. And you do not debate the Devil; you turn your back on him. For Smock, the choice is simple: "I speak absolutely. 'This is the way it is, thus sayeth the Lord. Accept it or reject it.'"

While fundamentalists see the preachers as God's anointed representatives sent to expose the sinfulness of the system and thereby to warn the students, the preachers flatly deny that they are trying to persuade anybody. That is not their mission. Both Smock and Lynch referred to Noah, who got only the members of his own family into the ark after 120 years of preaching. As Lynch put it: "We're always successful when we are true to God's calling. Just by the fact that we're out here we're successful. It's not the response, it's not the numbers, but just preaching." The primary task of the preachers is to "obey God" and to faithfully bear witness to him. They are there to be "a glory to God" by "preaching in righteousness."

When asked if he recognized that the vast majority of the students would never be converted by his method of preaching, Smock replied:

Yeah. The Bible says many are called, few are chosen. Strait is the gate, narrow the way, few there'll be who find it. That's absolutely right. I know most of them will not be converted. See, a lot of people try to water the message down to get more people in. I'm not going to do it. Noah preached 120 years. The only people he got in the ark were members of his own family. That didn't stop him. He just preached in righteousness.

While the preachers dream of a campuswide revival and want the students to be saved, they take for granted that this response is outside their own control. The preachers see conversion as the result of the power of God working through their faithful presentation of his Word. In fact, conversion is not a matter of being convinced of anything. In his autobiographical pamphlet *From DEATH unto LIFE*, Smock explained his tactics by referring to 1 Corinthians 2:4–5: "And my speech and what I preached were not with persuasive words of wisdom but with a demonstration of spirit and power that your faith might be, not in men's wisdom, but in God's power." The preachers describe conversion in terms of the sinner "opening one's heart to Jesus" and being "filled with the Holy Spirit." Conversion involves a decidedly transcendent act by the sinner, enabled by the grace of God. In this sense, the failure of the audience to convert is not a failure of the preachers to adapt but a failure of the audience to be receptive to presentation of the Truth.

From within the fundamentalist perspective, the pragmatic function of witnessing is not so much audience-directed as it is self-directed. It is the fulfillment of a moral imperative rather than an instrumental one. This is best seen by the role heckling plays within the biblical drama. For the fundamentalist, heckling becomes a vivid completion of the drama. It is the basis for the purification of the witness and proof of his salvation. Christian audience members reported that in the face of the hecklers, the presence of God was clearly revealed to them. For example, one of Smock's sympathizers wrote:

Many of us from F.G.S.F. here in Raleigh went with Jed as he travelled in N.C. campuses, and we witnessed as he spoke. Reactions were Scriptural: he has been stoned, beaten, spit-on, harassed, and hated, but God is with him. Many of us experienced God's anointing as never before, but only as we stood before the hostilities in the name of the Lord Jesus. (Bill Wiley, "Jed Smock—Apostle," a letter to the editor of an unknown newspaper reprinted for distribution by Jed Smock)

Indeed, the Bible is filled with passages that warn that faithful witnessing, by its very nature, leads to violent rejection. The Bible instructs the witness to interpret his persecution as a test of faith which, if passed, leads to salvation.[4]

From this perspective, the style and tactics of the preacher become intimately bound up in a test of character. Witnessing becomes a public test of the preacher's willingness to deny his old self and to cut himself free from the old order.[5] Likewise, in exposing the sinfulness of the audience, the witness is subjected to a test of his new character. God's witness must speak out against sin, regardless of the suffering it might bring him in response. In facing his persecutors, a witness must maintain his character as God's appointed messenger. In this way, the event is transformed into a spiritual enactment of faith. It becomes a source of inspiration, not discouragement. Said Smock, "I leap for joy when I am persecuted for the sake of Christ."

Reflexive Structuring of Confrontation

Here, then, is a speech event organized in ways that are quite different from those envisioned by a model of critical discussion. The event itself exhibits a highly stable, almost ritualistic pattern of conflict with no real movement toward consensus and little apparent effort at mutual adjustment. The arguments of the preachers and the hecklers function not so much to unify opposing parties or to convince the addressees as much as to polarize the parties further and to vindicate each participant morally. Rather than working to overcome a lack of consensus, this speech event works to exploit a lack of consensus. Here, participants engage in a combat of selves where argumentative strategy is dominated by a self-expressive function and by moral constraints on the range of choices available for pursuing any instrumentally defined outcome.

It would be easy to analyze and evaluate what is going on as a perversion of the ideals of critical discussion. The conduct of the preacher, who, after all, initiates the event, would seem to be a particularly easy target for criticism on procedural grounds (though the preacher is hardly the only ready target for such criticism). One can also question the intent of the preacher (and perhaps his capacities), suggesting that the self-expressive functions pursued by the witness conflict with those required for critical discussion.

Such criticism would share certain substantive features with the secular humanist perspective, the latter being organized around a willingness to debate the standpoints of the preachers, if only the preachers would grant that these standpoints are in fact arguable. The problem with such criticism is that it ignores the way in which those sorts of judgments beg the very questions that are at issue in the dispute. Underlying this approach would be a failure to appreciate the way in which the organization of the event is an adaptation to its epistemological and interactional circumstances—that is, its second-order conditions.

Specifically, what such criticism ignores is something that the participants themselves recognize implicitly, each from within their own perspective—namely, that argumentation will not work. It is not just that procedural standards have been flaunted, but that there is no apparent way of entering into argumentation over what those standards should be without having already agreed on the very standards that are at issue. There is no reason to expect that following those procedural standards would do any good, even if the parties could come to some sort of agreement on what those standards should be. Each party attributes blame for this to the other. We should see that the intentions of the participants in arguing (to confront, to mock, to witness) and the ways in which participants conduct the argument are not the *cause* of the intractability of the conflict but a *consequence* of it.

What the participants face is a kind of comprehensive disagreement where the longer they stay to listen, the deeper they probe for justifications—and the more they debate, the more alienated they become. The mechanisms of critical discussion are designed to apply conditionally and locally, not comprehensively. The mechanism is conditional in the sense that any particular belief or region of belief can be tested only by assuming the acceptability of the rest of the system. It is local in the sense that doubt can be focused on any particular belief, value, or norm, but not on the entire system of belief and value all at once.[6] In other words, critical discussion requires some common ground, however provisional, for fields to come into alignment on issues and to be modified. And these fields have no obvious common ground.

Reflexivity in Practical Reasoning

Participants in this speech event treat the dramas they see as unproblematically given in their experience of the event. To the parties who see them, the dramas appear to be factual, stable, obvious features of the argumentative transaction itself, not the mere product of the way their perspectives structure action and interpretation. The perspectives, then, supply their occupants with a persuasive guide to the reality of the event. The analytic problem that a multiplicity of perspectives presents the critic is how any perspective can be such a persuasive guide to its occupants while having so little force for the occupants of other perspectives.

Participants are able to sustain this sense of objectivity and exclusivity for their own perspective by the way in which they reason practically from the primitive beliefs of those perspectives so as to preserve the sense of validity for those beliefs (e.g., the fundamentalist beliefs in the sinfulness of the audience and God's appointment of the witness; the secular beliefs in nonreligious standards of

morality and rationality and the sociopolitical—or just humorous—
nature of the issues being discussed).

Participants take for granted the correctness of their dramatic
structurings such that apparent anomalies are treated not as potential disconfirmations but as occasions for the elaboration of secondary beliefs consistent with those dramatic structurings. By virtue of
being able to elaborate these beliefs, those secondary beliefs work
to demonstrate and reaffirm the objective, factual character of the
dramatic structurings that were apparently challenged in the first
place. Underlying the participants' behavior is what ethnomethod-
ologists call a reflexive pattern of reasoning and interpretation
(Leiter 1980, esp. chap. 5; Pollner 1974; Wieder 1974, esp. sec. 2).

This pattern is most visible in the way that the secular audience
members and the fundamentalists work to discredit the claims and
conduct of the other. One would think that the fact of open, sustained, and intense conflict would pose a powerful challenge to the
assumed objectivity of one's own perspective. Participants preserve
their perspective, however, by elaborating beliefs that are consistent
with the drama they perceive and that explain away the argumentative activities of the other parties as being somehow defective. In
this way, each participant's own perspective is reinforced.

The preachers and audience members are able to preserve the
sense of objectivity for their own dramatic structurings of the event
by such interpretive practices as attributing irrational and confrontational character-types to their adversaries, treating them as being
incapable of seeing what is obvious, and accusing them of being
deliberately perverse. Each dramatic structuring of the event provides for such blameworthy character-types and motives within the
overall framework of the drama.

What is particularly striking about the sorts of accounts participants construct to discredit the occupants of other perspectives is
the reciprocal usage of those accounts. By assuming the truth and
self-evident nature of their own beliefs, *all* the participants are able
to see the absurdity of the others' beliefs. By assuming the rationality of their own reasoning, *all* the participants are able to see the
irrationality of the others' reasoning. By assuming the morality of
their own purposes, *all* the participants are able to see the immoral
nature of the others' treatment of them. In doing so, all the participants are able to accomplish for themselves a position in the event
worthy of praise and acceptance. In other words, occupants maintain their own perspective by placing the claims and conduct of
others in ironic contrast to their own, showing how others fail to
live up to the standards and assumptions that their own perspective
takes as given—and to which the claims and conduct of others stand
as a challenge.

How this works within the secular perspective is that the audience assumes the overall validity of their own values and beliefs, and when the preacher's conduct or arguments violate these presupposed values and beliefs, the violation is seen not as a challenge to the audience's own standpoints but as a patent defect in the preacher's performance. The secular humanists issue repeated challenges to the preacher's positions on issues, but although these challenges rest on arguments seemingly reasonable and convincing, the preacher never seems to change his position in any fundamental way.

The audience members never take these failures as evidence of a failure of their own sense of rationality and objectivity; they judge the preacher irrational for refusing to enter into the secular perspective in order to persuade his audience (though they do not enter into the fundamentalist perspective in a search for persuasive adaptation in making their own case). Smock's arguments do not make sense to the audience and seldom have any compelling logic for them; his stated beliefs are crazy and absurd. The secular audience simply cannot believe that Smock really believes what he claims to. Or maybe he does really believe what he says, though the audience cannot accept that a rational person would hold such beliefs. The preacher is seen as confrontational and perverse because his argumentative conduct does not live up to audience standards. His use of biblical labels and bald accusations runs counter to the audience understandings of when civility and mutual respect are called for. His failure to accept any authority other than the Bible and the justification of his absolutist stands in terms of an ordination by God appear to be nothing more than an egomaniacal closed-mindedness. So, even procedural evaluations are grounded in the substantive assumptions of the audience's secular standpoint and serve to reinforce that standpoint.

But the secular audience is not alone in holding its reflexively reasoned accounts. Fundamentalists, like Smock and his supporters, also employ a rich set of interpretive procedures for discrediting the opposition of the audience. For someone like Smock these procedures are particularly interesting, since he has been intimately familiar with the secular perspective of the audience. Key to the fundamentalist reading of the situation is the assumed factual character of the sinfulness of the audience—more specifically, of the audience's attitudes and life-style. This assumption allows the fundamentalist to construct a variety of accounts for opposition to the preacher that do not call into question the justifiability of the preacher's standpoint.

The heckling is evidence of defensiveness; it shows that the hecklers themselves "see" their own sinfulness and fear to have it exposed. Repeatedly, fundamentalists expressed the idea that the heckling was a normal, expectable reaction of those who love their sin. A common theme among fundamentalists was expressed in one letter to the editor where the writer noted, "When the truth is preached, people become angry as their sins are exposed for everyone to see." Smock claimed: "They don't like having their sins exposed. See, a lot of these same people, they'll be bragging about their sexual exploits. And I come up and call them the sinner they are, or the whore or whore-monger, and they're offended. They expose themselves."

The operation of this kind of reasoning is neatly illustrated in the following letter to the editor:

Righteousness needs no defense—its truth is obvious. Those who would reject righteousness would reject its defense. Their sin and folly is evident to all, as in truth, only sin can produce such vehement opposition to righteousness. . . . That people are alienated has always been the case. The message of repentance is always offensive to those who love their sin. Remember that all but John of the early apostles were martyred; search out Paul's ministry to see how the crowds received his preaching with hatred; count the afflictions of the early saints for the sake of preaching. (Brother Cope, "His cup runneth over . . . ," letter to the editor of an unknown newspaper, reprinted for distribution by Jed Smock)

Lynch claimed that many hecklers "feel insecure. Many of them are rationalizing and compensating for that insecurity by outwardly coming against us. You see, they really have a deep need inside that they won't recognize." They are trying to "hide" from their sin through drugs, booze, and heckling. Through such reasoning, the heckling becomes proof of the sinfulness of the audience rather than constituting a challenge to the system in which sin is a sensible concept.

Just as the secular audience members attribute irrational character-types to the preachers as a way of accounting for the lack of reasonable discussion while still preserving the sense of their own rationality, so also the fundamentalist attributes irrationality to the audience. While the audience widely sees heckling as a reaction to the irrationality of the preacher, Smock sees it as proof that the audience has no rational response to his position. According to Smock: "Anyone can come up here and cuss and swear and mock and heckle. And to me, that's a sure indication that they have no rational argument." Smock stated in an interview: "They resort to mockery and ridicule because they can't *reason*. Most of them are not informed enough to reason. See, you've got to know something about the Bible to reason against it. Of course, even then it's very hard to reason against the truth. It's actually impossible."

For the fundamentalist, it is the audience that is closed-minded and perverse. The preacher is able to preserve the assumption that he knows the Bible and is speaking the Truth by using that assumption to see that the audience does not know what they are talking about.

Interestingly, the very same issues that the audience uses to show Smock's irrationality—that he will not justify his faith in the Bible—is turned within the fundamentalist perspective into proof of the audience's irrationality. The audience is seen to be irrational because they refuse to consider the Bible from the premise that it might be true, that it might be the Word of God. They will not even read it. They only challenge the assumption that the Bible is God's Word and demand a justification according to standards outside of God's order. That demand is obviously irrational because such standards are certain to find the Bible lacking precisely because they are outside of God. For the fundamentalist, the only rational approach is to "open your heart" to God and accept him on his own terms.

For the fundamentalist, then, rejection of the preaching is proof that the hecklers are closed-minded. They have already decided to reject God's Word, which is why they reject it out of hand and will not even entertain what is obviously the Truth. In this way, then, the fundamentalist is able to explain the failure of the audience to accept God's Word, while preserving the assumptions of the preachers' rationality and the truth of the Bible.

Likewise, just as the audience is able to use categories like "sexist" and "fascist" to see and explain the apparent perversity of the stands taken by the preachers, so also the fundamentalist employs a set of biblically authorized categories like "sinner" or "Pharisee" to discredit the actions of the audience. Smock said of one group of hecklers who had been persistently questioning him that day:

They're like the Pharisees. Jesus had a group, a religious crowd, that constantly followed him around: the Pharisees that were constantly harassing him, asking him questions—*not* because they wanted to learn and wanted information. Just to try to trick him, catch him in his words, or trip him up in some way. Embarrass him. And that is the attitude with which a lot of the questions were asked.

The applicability of such categories reinforces confidence that the fundamentalist perspective "makes sense," while at the same time the plausibility of that application is warranted by the fact that it is consistent with a fundamentalist perspective. In fact, the biblical vocabulary of motives supplies the fundamentalist with accounts for the audience's heckling that reveal the presence of Satanic forces—for example, describing persons with phrases like "in bond-age to lust," "demon-possessed," and "captivated by a spirit which led them to rebel."

Such attributions work in a way that allows the fundamentalist to accept the appearance of the motives and understandings avowed by the secular audience member, while finding support for the validity of his own perspective in the underlying causes for these motives and understandings. A person may well have doubts about the Bible, but those doubts have been sown by the Devil; some may well think sexual intercourse outside of marriage is just innocent fun, but that is because they have been lured away from God by the ways of the flesh.

A secular audience member might account for Smock's apparent belief that he will one day reenter the Earth's atmosphere with God to destroy the armies of the world by attributing to him "ego needs" that drive him to construct a reality that affirms his potency; in parallel fashion, the preachers account for audience beliefs in terms of underlying causes that discredit the perspectives of the audience by showing them to be rooted in sin and the deceptions of Satan.

Both audience members and preachers are thus reasoning in ways that maintain the consistency between the assumed authority for their perspective as a field of argumentation and the fact that others are apparently not impressed by the force of the arguments generated by their perspective. The very same categories and assumptions that are apparently being challenged are, through a variety of common interpretive practices, used to discredit those challenges (because they are inconsistent with those categories and assumptions). Thus, the perspective under attack is actually reinforced.

Interdependence of Perspectives

It would be a mistake to assume that the apparent incommensurability of the perspectives from which participants argue is sustained simply by principles of internal self-organization. Incommensurability and the apparent closure of each field to the objections and challenges of the other are aspects of the way that representatives of these fields manage their encounters with one another. The integrity of the perspectives themselves emerges from the interplay of the principal parties in the event. This can be seen in two examples.[7]

Smock will discuss issues only with those he takes to be willing to accept the validity of the Bible—at least tentatively. For Smock, such willingness is a basic indication of the sincerity of a potential interlocutor. In so doing, he avoids calling into question a central premise in his perspective. But by discussing issues only with (potential) believers, he demonstrates to the audience his own irrationality and insincerity. Likewise, by questioning the validity of the Bible—or Smock's interpretation of it—the audience presumes the legitimacy of secular standards for judgment and so preserves a central premise in their perspective. For the audience, a willingness to examine critically the validity of the Bible against secular standards is a basic indication of sincerity of a potential interlocutor. But by questioning the validity of the Bible instead of tentatively assuming its truth, the audience proves to Smock their insincerity and irrationality. And by showing their insincerity and irrationality, the audience justifies for Smock his not taking them seriously. By showing his own irrationality and insincerity, however, Smock justifies for the audience their continual challenging of him.

Or again, on the basis of past experience Smock views himself as understanding the attitudes and life-style of campus youth. He has done the things he now accuses the students of doing and can therefore claim to understand their experience. But the experience he confesses is no longer framed in terms of its lived quality for the students, but in terms of a new set of constructs that can be imposed only from outside. So by expressing his understanding of campus life, Smock only proves to the students that he possesses no such understanding. His portrayals of campus life appear caricatured, leading the audience to mock and tease him. But this teasing and mocking only proves to Smock, in turn, that he has struck a nerve, that the audience is trying to hide from the truth of their own sinfulness. Their agitation reinforces his belief that he has correctly characterized what goes on at college campuses, and so he continues.

The interdependence of the two perspectives in this event, the way they continually feed off of one another in their confrontation, sustains the witnessing and heckling indefinitely without resolution.

Conclusions

In terms of the dialectical ideal of critical discussion, the witnessing and heckling in this speech event provide insight into the dynamics of higher-order conditions for critical discussion. Pretty clearly, much if not most of what is said and done in this speech event fails to live up to the standards of critical discussion. All of the parties in this event feel restricted in their opportunities to advance their standpoints or to cast doubt on the standpoints of others. None of the parties appear to accept fully their burdens of proof and rebuttal in justifying their standpoints. Much of what any party says is taken by others to be nonserious, insulting, or otherwise damaging to a climate of reflective mutual engagement.[8]

At first glance, much of what is wrong appears to result from the absence of an essential second-order condition for critical discussion—a serious, resolution-oriented attitude on the part of the participants.[9] To the fundamentalists, resolving a dispute is not the main point—at least, not with the kind of audience they encounter. Given the evident inability and unwillingness of the secular audience to engage in discussion from within a framework that the fundamentalist recognizes as reasonable, the main goal of the preaching is transformed from convincing people to sustaining a faithful witness to the Truth in the face of incorrigible hostility. Argumentation serves at best as a vehicle for resisting the arguments of the audience.

For the comics among the audience, all is just nonserious farce and mockery. Argumentation becomes at best a game exploited for the purpose of making a point that serves to ridicule and taunt the preachers. To a lesser extent, the fulfillment of second-order conditions is also questionable among the secular humanists. Although they see themselves as trying to argue seriously and open-mindedly with the preachers, in fact their cooperativeness is conditional on acceptance of secular tenets which cannot be questioned and is limited because their goal is simply resistance to and exposure of the preacher.

As we stated earlier, however, the absence of a resolution-oriented attitude is best seen as *consequence* as well as *cause* of the failures to engage in critical discussion. The impossibility of the situation for the participants can perhaps best be seen by recalling the pragmatic preconditions for making an argument. We suggested in chapter 1 that among the felicity conditions for undertaking to justify one's standpoint to the satisfaction of a hearer were that speakers believe the following: that the assertions put forward as arguments for their standpoints are true; that those assertions provide acceptable justification of their standpoint; that the hearer will accept the truth of the assertions; that the hearer will accept those assertions as adequate justification of the speakers' standpoint. It becomes quickly apparent to all parties that they will not find a set of assertions that can satisfy the first two (sincerity) conditions while also satisfying the last two (preparatory) conditions.

Likewise, it becomes apparent that, for whatever reason, their interlocutors are not going to put forward arguments that are convincing. For each party, the other party is heard to challenge what is obvious and to assert (and then refuse to defend) what is manifestly absurd. Indeed, this failure is so severe that it appears as a general abandonment of a commitment to the requirement of reasonableness in cooperative discussion, namely, that challenges to an assertion be motivated by reasonable doubt and that assertions be grounded in reasons sufficient to believe the assertion to be true.

The pattern of conflict observed in this event is organized by functions and constraints which closely parallel those discussed by analysts of confrontation rhetoric such as Cathcart (1978, 1980), Gregg (1971), and Burgess (1968, 1970). All three critics point to the way in which confrontation rhetoric fulfills primarily self-expressive needs in a manner that is constrained by moral presuppositions. This study shows how these functions and constraints are grounded in fundamental epistemological divisions between the antagonists.

What this suggests, then, is that there are substantive epistemological limits to the scope of the problem validity and intersubjective validity of critical discussion as a method of dispute resolution. Given as starting points divergent perspectives as extreme as those studied here, progress in resolving differences of opinion may prove to be impossible for all practical purposes.[10] Epistemological divisions may necessarily preclude adjustment, conciliation, or compromise. Under such conditions, patterns of argumentative engagement will feed upon the perspectives of the engaged parties in the self-confirming and polarizing way noticed by Scott and Smith (1969).[11]

One of the paradoxes of failures of such higher-order conditions is that while an attempt to convince an addressee through argumentation may no longer make sense, interlocutors may nevertheless feel impelled to resist one another actively and to demonstrate their moral alienation. Given their divisions, moral constraint and motives of self-expression may come to dominate argumentative choice as divisive and polarizing forces. In a sense, the failure of higher-order conditions for critical discussion may not only preclude the reasonable use of argumentation to resolve differences of opinion; it may also demand the use of argumentation in order to enact an "agonistic ritual" (Cathcart 1978, 1980). This study, then, amplifies the pessimistic evaluation of critics concerning the natural trajectory of encounters between parties locked in confrontation.[12]

Notes

1. Remarks in quotations come from interviews, field notes, or transcripts of recordings of the event.

2. Specific audience members are identified by number. Unidentified

individuals are marked as Ax; entire groups are identified as As. Crowd response is indicated only by editorial directions—the outbursts are usually so chaotic that individual contributions are generally drowned out or not describable. Smock is identified as P. Transcription notation is explained in note 3 to chapter 2.

3. In fact, very few in the audience have actually read the Bible. Their familiarity is with selected passages and secondhand interpretations. Smock frequently polls the audience and generally finds that between 4 and 8 out of 200 to 300 students claim to have read all of the New Testament. Fewer have read the Old Testament. Yet, interviewees widely assert that they know the Bible. Remarks like the following are common: "I think the man is terribly misinterpreting the Bible. . . . Any person who has read the Bible will know that this man is absolutely off the wall. . . . I don't think his interpretation is legitimate, period" (interview 16-B). "He incorrectly quotes the Bible all the time, heh-heh. I mean perceptively. He just takes things out of context, and with Jed it's obvious. He does it all the time, and it's intentional, and people point it out to him and he just skips over it and goes on to something else" (interview 19-C).

4. The Bible instructs Christians that they will suffer so that "the proof of your faith, being more precious than gold which is perishable, even though tested by fire, may be found to result in praise and glory and honor at the revelation of Jesus Christ" (*New American Standard New Testament*, 1 Peter 1:7).

5. In this sense, the retelling of autobiographical material to an audience functions less as a proof to the audience than as an act of commitment by the speaker.

6. See Swanson's (1977, 208–10) discussion of the mundane and critical stance within the natural attitude.

7. In both cases there is an interlocking of incompatible interpretations similar to the clash of moral imperatives described by Burgess (1968, 1970) or the punctuation problems discussed by Watzlawick, Beavin, and Jackson (1967).

8. Despite the fact that all sides see these failures, we have cast them here in terms of the perspectives of the participants rather than as objective circumstances. This is in part to recognize that who is responsible for these failures is not agreed upon and because part of what is at issue in this event is precisely what are the preconditions for and proper application of such standards as critical openness, accepting burden of proof, showing mutual respect, and so on.

9. The participants would also question the argumentative competence of their would-be protagonists, though not their own. While this perception has a great deal to do with what is wrong here, its contribution to the argumentative knots in this event is somewhat different from the lack of a discussion-minded attitude, which is openly admitted by all the participants.

10. One can never rule out in principle the possibility that with enough patience, forbearance, and goodwill, participants could make progress. Any particular case will always involve a practical decision that progress is not

going to occur. It is also important to recognize that the appearance of incommensurable perspectives does not imply closed perspectives *in general*, only that the perspectives are for all practical purposes closed to one another. Closure is best seen as a relational feature of the interaction between interlocutors rather than as an intrinsic property of any particular perspective or way of arguing.

11. Scott and Smith (1969, 8) observe: "the response mechanisms turned to by those whose presuppositions could not contemplate confrontation often seem to complete the action sought by those who confront, or to confirm their subjective sense of division from the establishment. The use of force to get students out of halls consecrated to university administration or out of holes dedicated to construction projects seems to confirm the radical analysis that the establishment serves itself rather than justice. In this sense, the confronter who prompts violence in the language or behavior of another has found his collaborator. 'Show us how ugly you really are,' he says, and the enemy with dogs and cattle prods, or police billies and mace, complies. . . . [The art of confrontation] may provoke the response that confirms its presuppositions, gratifies the adherents of those presuppositions, and turns the power-enforced victory of the establishment into a symbolic victory for its opponents."

12. As Burgess (1970, 129–30) observes: "A metamoral critic also can understand from a strategic view why moralistic rhetorics increase in intensity of confrontation as crisis deepens, even until personal and cultural consequences may be virtually disregarded. . . . Ultimately, the more clearly advocates perceive threats to their moral world and the more openly they are attacked by voices from an alien world, then the narrower are their options for strategic choice and invention, resulting in a striking lack of adaptability *within* rhetorics that can prevent resolution of conflict *between* rhetorics. In the extremity, this is indeed the stuff of which martyrs and martyred movements are made."

8

Directions for Elaboration
of the Model

In chapters 1 and 2, we introduced an ideal model of argument that describes the ideal structuring of discourse for the function of coming to consensus over a disputed claim. In chapter 3, we discussed the analytic tools needed for the application of this ideal model to actual argumentative discourse. In chapters 4, 5, 6, and 7, we examined a series of issues that arise in the attempt to make the application to empirical observations. These empirical explorations have direct or indirect implications for each of the five main components of a comprehensive study of argumentation: the philosophical, the normative, the analytic, the empirical, and the practical. In this brief concluding chapter, we consider some of these implications.

Implications for Philosophical Concepts
of Reasonableness

Our approach locates argumentative reasonableness in procedures for critical discussion rather than in the form of reasoning or in the substance of initial premises per se. We take this notion of reasonableness to be a pragmatically specialized variant of the same notion of cooperative rationality that lies behind Grice's (1975) conception of a cooperative contribution to the purpose of a conversational exchange (i.e., the Cooperative Principle).

A critical rationalist position locates reasonableness in publicly negotiated procedures for discussion (intersubjective validity), while maintaining a pragmatist standard for successful resolution of a dispute that transcends the local beliefs of any given individual or group (problem-validity). This pragmatist standard sees resolution as more than simple achievement of agreement, as an outcome of a process of full and free critical examination of the basis for competing standpoints. Reasonableness, then, is located in the self-correcting capacities of a discussion procedure and not in the security of substantive starting points.

The existence of intractable disagreements like those between preacher Jed Smock and his student hecklers presents something of an empirical challenge for our position. At the very least, the existence of such "deep disagreements" sets a limit in principle on the problem-solving validity of any procedural conception of argumentative rationality (Fogelin 1985; Woods 1990). Intractable disagreements of this kind are indeed well known to argumentation theory and often discussed as the problem of incommensurability or field-dependency (cf. Brown 1977; Kuhn 1970; Rorty 1979; Toulmin 1972; Willard 1983).

An initial survey of such disagreements suggests that participants have simply not entered into discussion with a resolution-minded attitude, that instead they have come to the discussion with interests they treat as privileged and as beyond debate. Closer examination, however, suggests that the failure to engage in a progressive discussion is less the result of a failure of resolution-mindedness than it is a source of the seemingly aberrant attitudes and motives adopted by the participants.

Such cases exhibit the substantive grounding of critical discussion. Any intersubjectively acceptable discussion procedure must be negotiated against a substantive background that is taken for granted. Where critical rationalism sees reasonable argumentation provided by abstract procedures for dialectical resolution of a difference of opinion, those procedures can be implemented only against a background of prior agreements.

It is interesting and significant that participants are regularly drawn into the witnessing and heckling episodes with a willingness in principle to engage in argumentation. In what should be the opening stage, however, both preacher and heckler seem to take stock of the other's actions and substantive beliefs and determine that the other is not an appropriate interlocutor. The situation is such that they cannot satisfy simultaneously the sincerity and preparatory conditions for argument (or as experienced by participants, they cannot be persuasive without misrepresenting their own beliefs). The misengagement is so great that each side sees it as evidence that the other side fails to meet basic requirements of sincerity and rationality.

In part, the problem is that some measure of common ground is necessary in practice in order for participants to judge it reasonable to enter into critical discussion at all—to see that some sort of movement toward resolution is even plausible. But this problem is not just a practical question of how individuals judge the sincerity and rationality of their interlocutor. Some measure of common ground is also necessary in principle in order for participants to negotiate a procedural basis for critical engagement. Where substantive differences are so extensive that parties cannot even engage in procedures to negotiate procedures, argumentation cannot really get started. If argumentation is undertaken anyway, it can be expected to degenerate quickly in just the sort of ways we have observed.

Implications for Normative Models

In the ideal model, it is assumed that participants begin a critical discussion with a mutual recognition of a difference of opinion and with certain interactional commitments that can be summed up as "resolution-mindedness." The ideal model recognizes no interactional objectives other than disagreement-resolution, it recognizes no prioritization among participant interests, and it recognizes no positions as exempt from challenge and refutation. It is further assumed that all moves within such an idealized discussion will be of certain restricted types; in the argumentation stage, for example, speech acts will fall within the class of assertives. It is not claimed that real argumentative discourse is like this, but only that this is what argumentative discourse would be like if exclusively tailored for disagreement-resolution.

As our empirical analyses make clear, actual argumentative discourse may only poorly approximate critical discussion in this idealized sense. Our initial efforts at reconstructing conversational argument as critical discussion showed two things. First, while argumentative moves can be reconstructed even from ordinary discourse far removed in appearance from a normative ideal of argumentative communication, it is clear that a great deal of ordinary argumentation does not take place through straightforward exchange of assertive acts; indeed, it often seems designed to create a purposeful indefiniteness of force and meaning. As argued in chapter 5, arguments must be reconstructed (naively by participants as well as reflectively by analysts) from broader activity contexts that serve to structure a disagreement space with respect to some other interactional purpose.

Second, while the objective of disagreement-resolution can be found in a wide variety of cases, this objective is always intertwined with other interactional objectives. The quality of a dispute seems to depend on the way in which disputants manage these multiple demands. Some objectives may be pursued in ways that make them only incidental to the resolution-orientedness of an exchange, but others may enter into an exchange in ways that work at cross-purposes with resolution. In extreme cases (such as the mediation discussed as example 4.1) participants set themselves against resolution by working not only *for* themselves but *against* their coparticipants. Moreover, these two features are interrelated.

From the standpoint of the ideal model, the fact that assertives occur indirectly, by way of other kinds of acts, may appear as an obstacle to genuine resolution, to be repaired through precization or other clarifying moves. From the standpoint of the participant, however, this characteristic is a strategic resource to be guarded and exploited. Recall the conversation between Mrs. Lee and the Mormon missionaries (example 3.1), and the maneuvering of Mrs. Lee to avoid direct answers to questions recognized as having the potential to limit her later options (cf. example 6.4). We can see that in ordinary argumentative contexts, participants are not purely resolution-minded but are involved in a balancing of argumentative objectives with other objectives, including the protection of privileged positions. We can see that this factor regularly gives rise to strategic maneuvering as the participants seek to fulfill their argumentative obligations without sacrificing their other objectives.

Hence, one challenge for the theory proposed here is to give an account of argumentation occurring under less-than-ideal conditions and conducted by less-than-ideal participants. The theory might be extended toward an accommodation of the means by which people approximate critical discussion—or fail to do so—under practical limitations and constraints.

One direction for such an extension might be toward elaboration of a concept of argumentative strategy. Strategy may seem irrelevant to the concerns of normative theory. Compared with the theoretical picture of ideal discussion conducted under ideal conditions, the concept of strategy evokes images of evasion, concealment, and artful dodging. Such things are and should be excluded from an ideal model of critical discussion, but strategy also encompasses means employed to enforce an ideal in the face of nonideal conditions.

For example, we saw in chapter 6 that mediators of custody and visitation disputes must devise means to correct or compensate for the obstacles disputants bring to the discussion. These means, which are creative solutions to the problems presented by practical circumstances, are efforts to affirm the values underlying the ideal model and to realize the ideal in practice. Mediator strategies are designed to transform a degenerative form of argument—one in which parties often seek interpersonal objectives that *preclude* resolution—into something closer to the ideal. The idealized picture of the mediator is a reasonably good approximation of the code of conduct constituting our first-order conditions for critical discussion. But the mediator has no resources for shaping of the argument other than discourse, and the mediator must operate within the same discursive possibilities as the disputants themselves, maneuvering for commitments by disputants so as to create strategic opportunities of his or her own.

A paradoxical feature of the mediator's role is that the mediator participates in the construction of arguments without taking on any commitments, so that the mediator "advances" positions and lines of argument without having to acknowledge and defend the sorts of commitments that interlocutors might like to challenge. In other words, the mediator's lines of argument enjoy a special sort of privilege that comes from a pragmatically based immunity from challenge. The paradox in this arrangement is that the mediator's privileged position grows out of an assigned role as a manager of the first-order rules. The strategic requirements of the mediator's position stand as exemplary of a class of argumentative problems in need of analysis, namely, problems arising from situations in which parties to a dispute labor under less-than-ideal conditions to approximate an ideal discussion procedure.

Implications for Analytic Methods

One of the consequences of applying a strategy of maximally dialectical analysis to the reconstruction of argumentative discourse is that a very wide range of discourse can be rendered suitable for analytic inspection. Especially in reconstructing the discourse in example 4.1, the method of normative reconstruction has proven to be quite powerful. Precisely the power of the method, however, raises additional issues for developing further an approach to the analysis and critique of ordinary discourse.

A strategy of maximally dialectical analysis self-consciously erases indeterminacy of force and meaning, deliberately resolves ambiguity in the direction of normatively preferred meanings, and charitably assumes legitimate argument wherever it should occur.

Doing so allows the analyst to show exactly to what assertions disputants are committed if they are acting in accordance with the requirements of a discussion oriented toward the resolution of a difference of opinion. In so reconstructing the best possible case from the materials at hand, analysts inevitably take on themselves a burden of interpretation much stronger than the one assumed by everyday interlocutors. This is done, in part, to satisfy the demands of the analytic tools currently available for evaluating the propositional form and substance of an argumentative case. It is also done in lieu of a developed theory of communicative obligation for argumentative discourse.

For instance, the normative reconstruction provided for example 4.1 stands not just as a charitable rendering of the case implicit in Genie and Fred's argumentation. That reconstruction also stands as an ironic contrast to the way in which Genie and Fred managed their discussion, and does so precisely because their argumentation could be reconstructed in a way that was not readily apparent. There is a digressive quality, a lack of orderly responsiveness, and an appearance of pointless nit-picking that ought to be kept in view.

Or again, the contributions made by the mediators examined in chapter 6 constitute a kind of implicit communication not easily treated within the general framework of conversational implicatures and communicative intentions presented in chapter 1. They constitute a kind of "off-record" communication in which the implicature is strong enough to be identified, but not so plain and obvious as to constitute a publicly accountable act (Brown and Levinson 1987). Clearly, from a normative point of view, such slipperiness in communicative intent opens the possibility for procedural abuses as well as strategic opportunity.

The reconstructive problems facing a critic of these sorts of discourse seem to be qualitatively different from those facing the critic who attempts to reconstruct the missing premise in "He is an Englishman. He is therefore brave" (Grice 1975, 44–45). What would be helpful here is a more developed empirical account of communicative responsibilities. It should not assume that just because analysts can reconstruct a better case than would appear at face value, disputants have no ongoing responsibility to improve the clarity of their case.

Implications for Empirical Description

A descriptive theory depends at some level on normative assumptions, if only to differentiate between relevant and irrelevant phenomena. There are, as D. O'Keefe (1987) has pointed out, an infinite number of true descriptions of discourse. Descriptions built without reflection on their underlying normative presuppositions run the risk of allowing superficial, peripheral, or incidental characteristics of interaction to dominate the description of argumentation. The task of simply choosing cases for analysis is but one example. Without some preexisting normative model that identifies relevant and irrelevant cases, the theorist may be led to focus on extremely superficial indicators of conflict rather than on underlying functions and structures of argument.

Consider the range of possible ways one might set about describing argumentative discourse. One might choose to focus on the evident competitive and strategic aspects of argumentation, proceeding by classifying argumentative tactics and establishing through experimentation or observation which of these are most effective in winning the argument. Much of contemporary persuasion research takes this course, offering nonevaluative comparisons among different message types or among messages differing in some specific feature (for a representative summary of the research, see O'Keefe 1990, esp. chap. 9). This research has often had an overt practical purpose, centered on the improvement of outcomes *at the level of the individual persuader*. But such research, taken as a body, promotes other sorts of consequences for practice, some of which are quite undesirable from a normative perspective. Specifically, the strategic variables isolated in the research represent choices—sometimes unreflective ones—about what is important in the process of invention, oftentimes superficial features of form and presentation rather than deeper issues of argument quality and rationality.

Some might suppose that the only important criterion for the quality of a description is its fidelity to the subject matter—its accuracy. Our view is that descriptions can be better or worse, not only in terms of their accuracy, but also in terms of their practical significance. In a series of essays on "practical discipline," Craig (1983, 1987, 1989) has proposed that communication theory be understood always as having a practical dimension, whether by intention or not. According to this view, *any description of a communication process whatsoever has potential consequences for practice*, some of which will be unintentional and unanticipated. Craig's argument is not that any description has practical utility but that even in the absence of explicit efforts at application, the description will unavoidably shape practices by the values it expresses and the issues that it raises. In part, this result can be seen as an outgrowth of the meaning ascribed to the communication process by any particular description of it, and of the courses of action this suggests to communicators. For example, as Craig (1983) suggests, the *description* of persuasion implicit in strategically oriented work has the unintended practical consequence of shaping persuasion as a competitive enterprise rather than as, say, the creation of social consensus through free testing of ideas.

As communication scholars, we cannot choose *whether* to have consequences for communication practice; we can, perhaps, choose *what kind* of consequences to encourage. We can adopt the course chosen by much persuasion research, that of treating the substantive focus of our research as evaluatively neutral and choosing what to describe without regard for practical consequences. The paradox of such a choice is that our partial and selective descriptions of discourse within such an approach may change the quality of that very discourse. If practitioners were to take their cue from the portrayals of persuasion implicit in strategically oriented research (as they evidently do in such fields as politics and marketing), some would gain strategic advantage. But to the extent that the research draws attention mainly to superficial issues of form and presentation rather than to issues of content and justification, the broader consequence one would expect would be degradation of the quality of public decision making.

A quite different choice presents itself to the discourse analyst, especially within normative pragmatics. Instead of being indifferent to the characteristics of communication selected for study, letting methodological preferences and a rather restricted conceptualization of outcome implicitly choose characteristics for us, it is possible to treat communication self-consciously as a set of practices whose characteristics must be described and critiqued against some defensible standard of argumentation quality. To accomplish this aim, description cannot be an autonomous enterprise but must be integrated with normative theorizing.

Our decision to position the study of argumentation within a general normative pragmatics permits a dual commitment to *usefulness* and *adequacy* in description. The ideal model serves to focus attention on those aspects of argumentation that have some pertinence to the function of disagreement resolution, creating links with interests in validity, soundness, or other aspects of argument quality. But the model does not restrict us to finding in discourse only that which the model prescribes. On the contrary, the model helps us to notice and to understand the significance of a wide range of argumentative patterns exhibiting widely varying degrees of correspondence with the idealization of critical discussion. The model does not prevent our seeing what argumentative practice is actually like. This fact should be evident from the empirical analyses presented throughout, in which observed arguments are set up in contrast to what the model portrays as ideal. It is precisely in the contrast that some of the most interesting observations are to be made. The model's function is thus to help us to notice what is, from a certain point of view, most important about argumentative practice.

Implications for Practical Research

Our commitment to an empirical approach based on a normative theory offers a distinctive set of practical applications; furthermore, it reflects a distinctive view of practicality. This view of practicality is closely aligned with Craig's concept of practical discipline, mentioned briefly above. In our view, practical research rests on two foundations: normative theory, which embodies the end states to be sought from practical interventions, and empirical description, which identifies the starting states and materials from which these end states must be fashioned.

Practical research may be seen as directed toward the development and testing of plans for making real argumentation look as much as possible like ideal argumentation. Such plans depend upon two descriptions: a description of ideal performance, but also a description of actual performance. While normative theory can, to some extent, build an idealization of argumentation on hypothetical ideal conditions, practical theory must be built on a careful recognition of real-world constraints and limitations.

Our view of critical discussion and its requirements permits a rather flexible approach to practical application. The objective of any application is to bring actual argumentative practice into closer alignment with ideal argumentative practice. How this is done depends on what is thought to be the practical obstacle to ideal critical discussion. Is the obstacle found in inadequate skills on the part of the arguers? Is it found in competition between the aim of disagreement-resolution and other aims? Is it found in a failure of second- or third-order conditions? Different obstacles require different interventions, and our ideal model with its associated levels of preconditions allows us to focus alternately or collectively on individual, procedural, and contextual obstacles.

One way of improving argumentative practice is to try to transform individual arguers into ideal critical discussants, by equipping them with skills and encouraging attitudes required for ideal participation. This sort of application is one we share with approaches to argumentation centered on reasoning. Training people in argumentation techniques is indeed possible from within the theoretical and reflective approach we have described. So far, this approach has been applied primarily to the teaching of the analysis and evaluation of argumentative discourse and the identification of fallacies (van Eemeren and Grootendorst 1991, 1992a).

It is also possible to approach the improvement of practice at a social rather than an individual level, crafting procedural solutions to practical problems that do not depend so much on individual skills and attitudes as on the structured contexts in which argument takes place. In lines of work centered on discourse rather than on persons—that is, on properties of communication systems—practical research may involve efforts to engineer the communication process itself to conform to some desired model. Consider the problem of engineering the process of arguing, of making real argument resemble ideal critical discussion. Taking critical discussion as a standard for performance, what could be done to bring actual communicative practices into line with the standard? At a general level, there might be no way to do so. Within certain social contexts, however, it is possible to construct procedures that will emulate critical discussion, for the betterment of the process.

A good approximation of the process of engineering ideal argument can be found in the procedures underlying third-party mediation. The basic practical premise behind such mediation is that people involved in disputes have the capacity to resolve their own disagreements rationally and cooperatively if structures can be created around them to compensate for the natural deficiencies in their performance as arguers. The presupposed description of ordinary disputation is as important to the theory of mediation as is the description of ideal disputation, for it generates assumptions about what it would take to transform the ordinary into the ideal or near-ideal, revealing the obstacles in the path of ideal argumentation. To see this point, one need only contrast the assumptions behind mediation with the assumptions behind related processes (such as arbitration and adjudication), namely, that disputants cannot both argue and judge the dispute, that they cannot separate their own wishes from an evaluation of the validity or justifiability of a position.

The practical theory behind mediation has two components: a prescribed method for organizing disputation, and a prescribed role for the mediator. Note that the theory does not have a component prescribing attitudes or behaviors for the disputants, it being assumed that the attitudes and behaviors of the disputants can be shaped by the structures prescribed for the process.

The prescribed method for organizing disputation is modeled closely after stage models of problem-solving group discussion, such as Dewey's Reflective Thinking Sequence. Mediators are trained to walk disputants through an ordered series of discrete steps (identification of the problem, generation of possible solutions, evaluation of alternatives, etc.) and to try to complete each step before allowing progression to the next. Specific techniques are often prescribed for dealing with impasse, such as returning to an earlier stage in the process to generate some new alternatives.

The prescribed role for the mediator apparently owes no debt to any articulated normative theory but is nevertheless based on an implicit normative ideal. The mediator's role, as portrayed in the literature, is to create conditions for rational discussion between the disputants, and it is the set of conditions that are desired that compose the underlying normative theory. Among those most frequently discussed in the literature are bilateral commitment to resolution of dispute through discussion, voluntary participation by both parties, unrestricted opportunity to raise concerns and make suggestions, approximate power equality between disputants, and consensus decision. It is not assumed that these conditions hold prior to mediation; as mentioned before, it is the mediator's job to try to create these conditions.

Practical theories of argument always presuppose some description of argument and some normative ideal, whether or not they rely on articulated theoretical positions. The theory of mediation takes as its normative ideal something much like the pragma-dialectical model of critical discussion. The description of argument it presupposes is essentially an implicit theory of why people fail to resolve disputes on their own: because they have competitive rather than cooperative motives, because they are unable to state their own positions clearly or to understand their opponents' positions, because they are unable to separate means from ends, and so on. The theory of mediation is a set of instructions for eliminating or compensating for the natural defects of disputants. Its institutions and practices may properly be seen as a kind of engineering achievement.

A brief illustration will flesh out the sense in which mediation practices may be seen as efforts to engineer argument. The general approach to the engineering problem is to compare actual conditions with normative assumptions, and wherever a mismatch is found, to create a structure or a technique that serves to alter the conditions or to compensate for them. We consider here how mediation attempts to cope with one specific threat to rational discussion, namely, the existence of power inequality between disputants.

Mediation theory takes as ideal a discussion in which both parties have equal power. Real disputants engaged in real disputes rarely satisfy this precondition for rational discussion. One way of responding to this situation is to try to eliminate power differences, which is not a practical response, even if it were possible in principle. Another way of responding—also not practical—is to abandon hope of rational discussion. Meditation theory responds to the situation by trying to find ways to neutralize or limit the influence of power on the discussion. The mediator, through control of the resources of language and situation, can even things up and reduce the possibility that the weaker party will be coerced into accepting an unfavorable resolution.

In divorce mediation, for example, an issue of widespread professional concern is the inequality that commonly exists between husband and wife. The husband is frequently in control of the wife's financial welfare, and in some instances, there may be a history of physical domination. In transcripts of divorce mediation, we have observed a number of techniques that have been devised at an institutional level or invented at an individual level for the purpose of compensating for power inequality.

For example, to prevent husbands from using family finances to coerce unfavorable custody and visitation arrangements, some mediation programs demand a rigid separation between discussion of property division and discussion of child custody. Separate hearings are held on each set of issues, within different agencies. If disputants attempt to raise property issues in mediation, mediators simply insist that such issues must not be discussed in the mediation session but must be taken up before a judge. It is worth mentioning, in passing, that wives are often in a position to coerce unfavorable property settlements from husbands, using visitation as a lever. For example, in one transcript we reviewed, the wife claimed that the level of support offered by the husband would force her to move to a distant state to live with her relatives. In these cases, too, the mediator has the obligation to try to force a separation of the two sorts of issues. In the case of this virtually on-record threat, the mediator's strategy was to insist that the husband and wife discuss visitation plans for two different scenarios: one assuming the move and the other assuming no move.

When inequality arises not from external circumstances but from differences in ability to argue one's case, the mediator may intervene in a variety of ways. If one party is afraid to speak in the presence of the other, the mediator can request separate caucuses and can take on the job of summarizing the weaker party's position to the other party. In one case we reviewed, the wife said almost nothing, while the mediator confronted the husband on numerous issues, explaining that he was "speaking for" the wife.

In extreme cases of inequality, where corrective measures do not seem to guard adequately against coercive resolutions, the mediator's prescribed course of action is to redirect the case from mediation to adjudication, where the legal rights of each participant are safeguarded and the legal position is evaluated by a judge.

Forcing a separation of issues that might be used coercively, controlling the expression of positions in mediation, and controlling the accessibility of the mediation process itself are three ways mediators can create a simulation of a rational discussion. What is of interest about each technique is that they do nothing about the power imbalance itself but concentrate instead on neutralizing its effect on the discussion. Practical theory is based not on a compromise between real and ideal, but on creative bridging of the gap between the two.

This creative bridging is an ongoing process within mediation. Much of what has been devised within this field must be regarded as successful engineering. These engineering achievements, however, continually raise questions that properly belong within the domain of normative theory, rather than within the domain of practical theory.

For example, efforts to engineer argumentation through the intervention of a "neutral" third party can and should be evaluated for their ability, in principle, to serve their supposed function. As a single example, one technique that mediators frequently use is to meet objections to proposals not with exploration of the merits of the proposal but with minor repairs designed to compromise between competing wants. As a means of reaching agreement, this may be quite effective, but that does not mean that rational decision-making has taken place. Such a tactic might lead to the optimal proposal being passed over for bogus or trivial reasons. In the absence of systematically applied normative critique, the correlation between the tactic and the outcome is the only basis for evaluation.

Assuming that argumentation theorists cannot choose whether to be practical, but only how to be practical, we argue for an approach built explicitly on normative theory integrated with description of actual communication practices to generate practical theory and interventions. Normative theory often has the appearance of a set of prescribed behaviors, and it is tempting to lapse into thinking that a normative theory of argumentation is a set of directives which instruct people in how to argue. But a set of idealized behaviors under ideal conditions is not a practical theory, because such idealizations do not by themselves pinpoint the obstacles to their own realization. Our view suggests that the applicability of normative theory to practice is to be sought not in the translation of the theory into a bundle of instructions and prohibitions but in the critique of practice and the identification of opportunities for better alignment of actual practices with ideal practices. Within such an approach, both explicit normative theory and relevant description of discourse are crucial, since it is the comparison between normative models and actual circumstances of practice that generates structures and strategies useful in improving practice.

References

Akmajian, A., R. A. Demers, A. K. Farmer, and R. M. Harnish. 1990. *Linguistics: An introduction to language and communication*. 3d ed. Cambridge: MIT Press.

Aristotle. 1924. *Rhetorica*. Trans. W. Rhys Roberts. In *The works of Aristotle*, 11 vols., ed. W. D. Ross, 11:1–218. Oxford: Clarendon Press.

Atkinson, J. M., and J. Heritage, eds. 1984. *Structures of social action: Studies in conversation analysis*. Cambridge: Cambridge Univ. Press.

Austin, J. L. 1962. *How to do things with words*. Cambridge: Harvard Univ. Press.

Bach, K., and R. M. Harnish. 1979. *Linguistic communication and speech acts*. Cambridge: MIT Press.

Bakeman, R., and J. M. Gottman. 1987. *Observing interaction: An introduction to sequential analysis*. Cambridge: Cambridge Univ. Press.

Barth, E. M., and E. C. W. Krabbe. 1982. *From axiom to dialogue*. Berlin: De Gruyter.

Bleiberg, S., and L. Churchill. 1975. Notes on confrontation in conversation. *Journal of Psycholinguistic Research* 4:273–78.

Blumer, H. 1969. *Symbolic interactionism*. Englewood Cliffs, NJ: Prentice-Hall.

Brashers, D. E., and R. A. Meyers. 1989. Tag-team argument and group decision-making. In *Spheres of argument: Proceedings of the sixth SCA/AFA conference on argumentation*, ed. B. E. Gronbeck, 542–50. Annandale, VA: Speech Communication Association.

Brown, H. I. 1977. *Perception, theory, and commitment: The new philosophy of science*. Chicago: Univ. of Chicago Press.

Brown, P., and S. C. Levinson. 1987. *Politeness: Some universals in language usage*. Cambridge: Cambridge Univ. Press.

Bryant, D. C. 1953. Rhetoric: Its function and its scope. *Quarterly Journal of Speech* 39:401–24.

Burgess, P. G. 1968. The rhetoric of black power: A moral demand? *Quarterly Journal of Speech* 54:122–33.

———. 1970. The rhetoric of moral conflict: Two critical dimensions. *Quarterly Journal of Speech* 56:120–30.

Burke, K. 1950. *A rhetoric of motives*. Berkeley: Univ. of California Press. Rev. ed., 1969.

Burleson, B. R. 1984. Comforting communication. In *Communication by children and adults: Social cognitive and strategic processes*, ed. H. E. Sypher and J. L. Applegate, 63–104. Beverly Hills, CA: Sage.

———. 1989. The constructivist approach to person-centered communication: Analysis of a research exemplar. In *Rethinking communication*, vol. 2: *Exemplars*, ed. B. Dervin, L. Grossberg, B. J. O'Keefe, and E. Wartella, 29–46. Newbury Park, CA: Sage.

Cappella, J. N. 1979. Talk-silence sequences in informal conversations. Part 1. *Human Communication Research* 6:3–17.

———. 1980. Talk and silence sequences in informal conversations. Part 2. *Human Communication Research* 6:130–45.

———. 1990. The method of proof by example in interaction analysis. *Communication Monographs* 57:236–42.

Cathcart, R. S. 1978. Movements: Confrontation as rhetorical form. *Southern Speech Communication Journal* 43:233–47.

———. 1980. Defining social movements by their rhetorical form. *Central States Speech Journal* 31:267–73.

Clark, H. H. 1979. Responding to indirect requests. *Cognitive Psychology* 11:430–77.

Clark, H. H., and S. E. Haviland. 1977. Comprehension and the given-new contract. In *Discourse production and comprehension*, ed. R. O. Freedle, 1–40. Norwood, NJ: Ablex.

Clarke, D. D. 1983. *Language and action: A structural model of behaviour*. Oxford: Pergamon.

Cohen, P. R., and H. J. Levesque. 1990. Rational interaction as the basis for communication. In *Intentions in communication*, ed. P. R. Cohen, J. Morgan, and M. E. Pollack, 221–55. Cambridge: MIT Press.

Cohen, P. R., and C. R. Perrault. 1979. Elements of a plan-based theory of speech acts. *Cognitive Science* 3:177–212.

Copi, I. M. 1965. *Symbolic logic*. 2d ed. New York: Macmillan.

Coulter, J. 1983. Contingent and a priori: Structures in sequential analysis. *Human Studies* 6:361–76.

Coulthard, M. 1977. *An introduction to discourse analysis*. London: Longman.

Craig, R. T. 1983. Galilean rhetoric and practical theory. *Communication Monographs* 50:395–412.

———. 1987. What would a practical theory of language and communication look like? Paper presented at the annual meeting of the Speech Communication Association, Boston.

———. 1989. Communication as a practical discipline. In *Rethinking com-*

munication, vol. 1: *Paradigm issues,* ed. B. Dervin, L. Grossberg, B. O'Keefe, and E. Wartella, 97–122. Newbury Park, CA: Sage.

Crawshay-Williams, R. 1957. *Methods and criteria of reasoning: An inquiry into the structure of controversy.* London: Routledge & Kegan Paul.

Delia, J. G., B. J. O'Keefe, and D. J. O'Keefe. 1982. The constructivist approach to communication. In *Human communication theory: Comparative essays,* ed. F. E. X. Dance, 147–91. New York: Harper & Row.

Dennett, D. 1990. Three kinds of intentional psychology. In *Foundations of cognitive psychology: The essential readings,* ed. J. L. Garfield, 88–110. New York: Paragon House.

Donohue, W. A., M. Allen, and N. Burrell. 1988. Mediator communicative competence. *Communication Monographs* 55:104–19.

Duncan, S., Jr., and D. W. Fiske. 1977. *Face-to-face interaction: Research, methods, and theory.* Hillsdale, NJ: Lawrence Erlbaum Associates.

Edmondson, W. 1981. *Spoken discourse: A model for analysis.* London: Longman.

van Eemeren, F. H. 1987a. Argumentation studies' five estates. In *Argument and critical practices: Proceedings of the fifth SCA/AFA conference on argumentation,* ed. J. W. Wenzel, 9–24. Annandale, VA: Speech Communication Association.

———. 1987b. For reason's sake: Maximal argumentative analysis of discourse. In *Argumentation: Across the lines of discipline,* ed. F. H. van Eemeren, R. Grootendorst, J. A. Blair, and C. A. Willard, 201–15. Dordrecht: Foris.

van Eemeren, F. H., and R. Grootendorst. 1982. Unexpressed premisses. Part 1. *Journal of the American Forensic Association* 19:97–106.

———. 1983. Unexpressed premisses. Part 2. *Journal of the American Forensic Association* 19:215–25.

———. 1984. *Speech acts in argumentative discussions.* Dordrecht: Foris.

———. 1988. Rules for argumentation in dialogues. *Argumentation* 2:499–510.

———. 1989. Speech act conditions as tools for reconstructing argumentative discourse. *Argumentation* 3:367–83.

———. 1990. Analyzing argumentative discourse. In *Perspectives on argumentation,* ed. R. Trapp and J. Schuetz, 86–106. Prospect Heights, IL: Waveland Press.

———. 1991. The study of argumentation from a speech act perspective. In *Pragmatics at issue,* ed. J. Verschueren, 151–70. Amsterdam: John Benjamins.

———. 1992a. *Argumentation, communication, and fallacies: A pragma-dialectical perspective.* Hillsdale, NJ: Lawrence Erlbaum Associates.

———. 1992b. Relevance reviewed: The case of *argumentum ad hominem. Argumentation* 6:141–59.

van Eemeren, F. H., R. Grootendorst, and T. Kruiger. 1987. *Handbook of argumentation theory: A critical survey of classical backgrounds and modern studies.* Dordrecht: Foris.

Ferrara, A. 1980. An extended theory of speech acts: Appropriateness conditions for subordinate acts in sequences. *Journal of Pragmatics* 4:233–52.

Fisher, W. R. 1978. Toward a logic of good reasons. *Quarterly Journal of Speech* 62:1–14.

Fogelin, R. 1985. The logic of deep disagreement. *Informal Logic* 7:1–8.

Frentz, T. S., and T. B. Farrell. 1976. Language-action: A paradigm for communication. *Quarterly Journal of Speech* 62:333–49.

Garfinkel, H. 1956. Conditions of successful degradation ceremonies. *American Journal of Sociology* 61:420–24.

———. 1967. *Studies in ethnomethodology.* Englewood Cliffs, NJ: Prentice-Hall.

Gibbs, R. W., Jr., and S. M. Delaney. 1987. Pragmatic factors in making and understanding promises. *Discourse Processes* 10:107–26.

Gibbs, R. W., Jr., and R. A. G. Mueller. 1988. Conversational sequences and preference for indirect speech acts. *Discourse Processes* 11:101–16.

Goffman, E. 1959. *The presentation of self in everyday life.* New York: Anchor.

———. 1974. *Frame analysis.* New York: Harper & Row.

Goodwin, M. H. 1985. The serious side of jumprope: Conversational practices and social organization in the frame of play. *Journal of American Folklore* 98:316–30.

Gregg, R. B. 1971. The ego-function of the rhetoric of protest. *Philosophy and Rhetoric* 4:71–91.

Grice, H. P. 1975. Logic and conversation. In *Syntax and semantics,* vol. 3: *Speech acts,* ed. P. Cole and J. L. Morgan, 41–58. New York: Academic.

———. 1989. *Studies in the way of words.* Cambridge: Harvard Univ. Press.

Grootendorst, R. 1987. Everyday argumentation from a speech act perspective. In *Argument and critical practices: Proceedings of the fifth SCA/ AFA conference on argumentation,* ed. J. W. Wenzel, 165–75. Annandale, VA: Speech Communication Association.

Habermas, J. 1970. Toward a theory of communicative competence. In *Recent sociology,* vol. 2: *Patterns of communicative behavior,* ed. H. P. Dreitzel, 114–48. New York: Macmillan.

———. 1979. *Communication and the evolution of society.* Trans. Thomas McCarthy. Boston: Beacon Press.

———. 1981. *The theory of communicative action.* Vol. 1: *Reason and the rationalization of society.* Trans. Thomas McCarthy. Boston: Beacon Press.

Halliday, M. A. K., and R. Hasan. 1976. *Cohesion in English.* London: Longman.

Hancher, M. 1979. On the classification of co-operative illocutionary acts. *Language in Society* 8:1–14.

Heider, F. 1953. *The psychology of interpersonal relations.* New York: John Wiley.

Heritage, J. 1984a. A change-of-state token and aspects of its sequential placement. In *Structures of social action: Studies in conversation analysis,* ed. J. M. Atkinson and J. Heritage, 299–345. Cambridge: Cambridge Univ. Press.

———. 1984b. *Garfinkel and ethnomethodology.* Cambridge: Polity Press.

Horn, L. 1984. Toward a new taxonomy for pragmatic inference: Q-based and R-based implicature. In *Georgetown University Round Table on Language and Linguistics, 1984: Meaning, form, and use in context: Linguistic applications,* ed. D. Schiffrin, 11–42. Washington, DC: Georgetown Univ. Press.

Jackson, S. 1986. Building a case for claims about discourse structure. In *Contemporary issues in language and discourse processes,* ed. D. G. Ellis and W. A. Donohue, 129–48. Hillsdale, NJ: Lawrence Erlbaum Associates.

Jackson, S., and S. Jacobs. 1980. Structure of conversational argument: Pragmatic bases for the enthymeme. *Quarterly Journal of Speech* 66:251–65.

———. 1989. About coherence. In *Communication yearbook 12,* ed. J. A. Anderson, 146–56. Newbury Park, CA: Sage.

Jackson, S., S. Jacobs, and A. M. Rossi. 1987. Conversational relevance: Three experiments on pragmatic connectedness in conversation. In *Communication Yearbook 10,* ed. M. L. McLaughlin, 323–47. Beverly Hills, CA: Sage.

Jacobs, S. 1982. The rhetoric of witnessing and heckling: A case study in ethnorhetoric. Ph.D. diss., Univ. of Illinois at Urbana-Champaign.

———. 1985. Language. In *Handbook of interpersonal communication,* ed. M. L. Knapp and G. R. Miller, 313–43. Beverly Hills, CA: Sage.

———. 1986. How to make an argument from example in discourse analysis. In *Contemporary issues in language and discourse processes,* ed. D. G. Ellis and W. A. Donohue, 149–68. Hillsdale, NJ: Lawrence Erlbaum Associates.

———. 1987. The management of disagreement in conversation. In *Argumentation: Across the lines of discipline,* ed. F. H. van Eemeren, R. Grootendorst, J. A. Blair, and C. A. Willard, 229–39. Dordrecht: Foris.

———. 1988. Evidence and inference in conversation analysis. In *Communication Yearbook 11,* ed. J. A. Anderson, 433–43. Newbury Park, CA: Sage.

———. 1989. Speech acts and arguments. *Argumentation* 3:345–65.

———. 1990. On the especially nice fit between qualitative analysis and the known properties of conversation. *Communication Monographs* 57:243–49.

Jacobs, S., and S. Jackson. 1981. Argument as a natural category: The routine grounds for arguing in conversation. *Western Journal of Speech Communication* 45:118–32.

———. 1982. Conversational argument: A discourse analytic approach. In *Advances in argumentation theory and research,* ed. J. R. Cox and C. A. Willard, 205–37. Carbondale: Southern Illinois Univ. Press.

———. 1983. Speech act structure in conversation: Rational aspects of pragmatic coherence. In *Conversational coherence: Form, structure, and strategy,* ed. R. T. Craig and K. Tracy, 47–66. Beverly Hills, CA: Sage.

———. 1989. Building a model of conversational argument. In *Rethinking communication,* vol. 2: *Exemplars,* ed. B. Dervin, L. Grossberg, B. J. O'Keefe, and E. Wartella, 153–71. Newbury Park, CA: Sage.

Jacobs, S., S. Jackson, S. Stearns, and B. Hall. 1991. Digressions in argumentative discourse: Multiple goals, standing concerns, and implicatures. In

Understanding face-to-face interaction: Issues linking goals and discourse, ed. K. Tracy, 43–61. Hillsdale, NJ: Lawrence Erlbaum Associates.

Jose, P. E. 1988. Sequentiality of speech acts in conversational structure. *Journal of Psycholinguistic Research* 17:65–88.

Kauffeld, F. 1987. Rhetoric and practical necessity: A view for the study of speech acts. In *Argument and critical practices: Proceedings of the fifth SCA/AFA conference on argumentation,* ed. J. W. Wenzel, 83–95. Annandale, VA: Speech Communication Association.

Kreckel, M. 1981. *Communicative acts and shared knowledge in natural discourse.* London: Academic.

Kuhn, T. S. 1970. *The structure of scientific revolutions.* 2d ed. Chicago: Univ. of Chicago Press.

Labov, W., and D. Fanshel. 1977. *Therapeutic discourse: Psychotherapy as conversation.* New York: Academic.

Leech, G. N. 1983. *Principles of pragmatics.* London: Longman.

Leiter, K. 1980. *A primer on ethnomethodology.* Oxford: Oxford Univ. Press.

Levinson, S. C. 1979. Activity types and language. *Linguistics* 17:365–99.

———. 1983. *Pragmatics.* Cambridge: Cambridge Univ. Press.

Littman, D. J., and J. F. Allen. 1987. A plan recognition model for subdialogues in conversation. *Cognitive Science* 11:163–200.

McBurney, J. H., and G. E. Mills. 1964. *Argumentation and debate: Techniques of a free society.* New York: Macmillan.

Maines, D. R. 1981. Recent developments in symbolic interaction. In *Social psychology through symbolic interaction,* 2d ed., ed. G. P. Stone and H. A. Farberman, 461–86. New York: John Wiley.

Nofsinger, R. E., Jr. 1975. The demand ticket: A conversational device for getting the floor. *Speech Monographs* 42:1–9.

O'Keefe, B. J. 1988. The logic of message design: Individual differences in reasoning about communication. *Communication Monographs* 55:80–103.

O'Keefe, D. J. 1977. Two concepts of argument. *Journal of the American Forensic Association* 13:121–28.

———. 1987. Message description. Paper presented at the annual meeting of the Speech Communication Association, Boston.

———. 1990. *Persuasion theory and research.* Newbury Park, CA: Sage.

Pearson, J., and N. Thoennes. 1984. A preliminary portrait of client reactions to three court mediation programs. In *Reaching effective agreements,* ed. J. A. Lemmon, 21–40. Mediation Quarterly, no. 3. San Francisco: Jossey-Bass.

Perelman, C., and L. Olbrechts-Tyteca. 1958. *The new rhetoric: A treatise on argumentation.* Notre Dame, IN: Univ. of Notre Dame Press.

Perrault, C. R., and J. F. Allen. 1980. A plan-based analysis of indirect speech acts. *American Journal of Computational Linguistics* 6:167–82.

Pike, K. 1967. *Language in relation to a unified theory of the structure of human behavior.* The Hague: Mouton.

Pollner, M. 1974. Mundane reasoning. *Philosophy of Social Science* 4:35–54.

Roehl, J. A., and R. F. Cook. 1985. Issues in mediation: Rhetoric and reality revisited. *Journal of Social Issues* 41:161–78.

Rorty, R. 1979. *Philosophy and the mirror of nature.* Princeton, NJ: Princeton Univ. Press.

Rosaldo, M. Z. 1982. The things we do with words: Ilongot speech acts and speech act theory in philosophy. *Language in Society* 11:203–37.

Sanders, R. E. 1987. *Cognitive foundations of calculated speech: Controlling understandings in conversation and persuasion.* Albany: SUNY Press.

Saville-Troike, M. 1982. *The ethnography of communication: An introduction.* Oxford: Basil Blackwell.

Schegloff, E. A. 1988. Presequences and indirection. *Journal of Pragmatics* 12:55–62.

Schegloff, E. A., G. Jefferson, & H. Sacks. 1977. The preference for self-correction in the organization of repair in conversation. *Language* 53:361–82.

Schiffrin, D. 1987. *Discourse markers.* Cambridge: Cambridge Univ. Press.

Schutz, A. 1973. *Collected papers.* Vol. 1: *The problem of social reality.* The Hague: Martinus Nijhoff.

Scott, R. L., and D. K. Smith. 1969. The rhetoric of confrontation. *Quarterly Journal of Speech* 55:1–8.

Searle, J. R. 1969. *Speech acts.* Cambridge: Cambridge Univ. Press.

———. 1975. Indirect speech acts. In *Syntax and semantics,* vol. 3: *Speech acts,* ed. P. Cole and J. L. Morgan, 59–82. New York: Academic.

———. 1976. The classification of illocutionary acts. *Language in Society* 5:1–24.

———. 1990. Collective intentions and actions. In *Intentions in communication,* ed. P. R. Cohen, J. Morgan, and M. E. Pollack, 401–15. Cambridge: MIT Press.

Searle, J. R., and D. Vanderveken. 1985. *Foundations of illocutionary logic.* Cambridge: Cambridge Univ. Press.

Silbey, S. S., and S. E. Merry. 1986. Mediator settlement strategies. *Law and Policy* 8:7–32.

Sperber, D., and D. Wilson. 1981. On Grice's theory of conversation. In *Conversation and discourse: Structure and interpretation,* ed. P. Werth, 155–78. New York: St. Martin's Press.

———. 1986. *Relevance: Communication and cognition.* Cambridge: Harvard Univ. Press.

Stech, E. L. 1975. Sequential structure in human social communication. *Human Communication Research* 1:168–79.

Stubbs, M. 1981. Motivating analyses of exchange structure. In *Studies in discourse analysis,* ed. R. M. Coulthard and M. M. Montgomery, 107–19. London: Routledge & Kegan Paul.

———. 1983. *Discourse analysis: The sociolinguistic analysis of natural language.* Chicago: Univ. of Chicago Press.

Swanson, D. L. 1977. A reflective view of the epistemology of critical inquiry. *Communication Monographs* 44:207–19.

Taylor, T. J., and D. Cameron. 1987. *Analyzing conversation: Rules and units in the structure of talk.* Oxford: Pergamon.

Toulmin, S. E. 1958. *The uses of argument.* Cambridge: Cambridge Univ. Press.

———. 1972. *Human understanding.* Vol. 1: *The collective use and evolution of concepts.* Princeton, NJ: Princeton Univ. Press.

———. 1976. *Knowing and acting: An invitation to philosophy.* New York: Macmillan.

Vanderveken, D. 1985. What is an illocutionary force? In *Dialogue: An interdisciplinary approach,* ed. M. Dascal, 181–204. Amsterdam: John Benjamins.

———. 1990. *Meaning and speech acts.* Vol. 1: *Principles of language use.* Cambridge: Cambridge Univ. Press.

Wallace, K. R. 1963. The substance of rhetoric: Good reasons. *Quarterly Journal of Speech* 49:239–49.

Watzlawick, P., J. H. Beavin, and D. D. Jackson. 1967. *Pragmatics of human communication.* New York: Norton.

Wenzel, J. W. 1980. Perspectives on argument. In *Proceedings of the [first] SCA/AFA conference on argumentation,* ed. J. Rhodes and S. Newell, 112–33. Annandale, VA: Speech Communication Association.

Wieder, D. L. 1974. *Language and social reality: The case of telling the convict code.* The Hague: Mouton.

Willard, C. A. 1983. *Argumentation and the social grounds of knowledge.* University: Univ. of Alabama Press.

Woods, J. 1990. Standoffs of force five. Unpublished manuscript. Netherlands Institute for Advanced Study in the Humanities and Social Sciences, Wassenaar.

Wootton, A. 1976. *Dilemmas of discourse.* New York: Holmes & Meier.

Zimmerman, D. N. 1988. On conversation: The conversation analytic perspective. In *Communication Yearbook 11,* ed. J. A. Anderson, 406–32. Newbury Park, CA: Sage.

Index

Farmer, A. K., 59 (n. 19), 185
Farrell, T. B., 3, 188
Felicity conditions, 3–6, 17 (nn. 3, 4, 5, 8), 18 (n. 15), 54, 92, 166; as basis for reconstruction, 92; as ideal model, 16; as structure of disagreement space, 104–5, 116 (n. 7); for arguing, 4, 166; for criticizing, 109; for requesting, 4, 104–5. *See also* Essential condition; Sincerity condition; Preparatory condition; Propositional content condition
Ferrara, A., 3, 17 (n. 8), 53, 187
First-order conditions, 31, 32, 33, 174; as code of conduct, 30, 31
Fisher, W. R., 34 (n. 1), 188
Fiske, D. W., 51, 53, 54, 58 (n. 12), 187
Fogelin, R., 35 (n. 4), 171, 188
Formulations, 120; as functional substitutes for argumentation, 139
Fourth-order conditions, 35 (n. 10)
Frentz, T. S., 3, 188
Functional substitutes for argumentation, 139
Functionalization, 13–15

Garfinkel, H., 53, 116 (n. 8), 188
Generic speech act conditions, 8. *See also* Speech acts; Felicity conditions
Gibbs, R. W., Jr., 17 (n. 2), 53, 188
Goffman, E., 7, 46, 188
Good reasons, 34 (n. 1)
Goodwin, M. H., 100, 188
Gottman, J. M., 53, 185
Gregg, R. B., 167, 188
Grice, H. P., xii, 6, 7, 10, 16, 18 (nn. 11, 13), 49, 55, 57 (n. 6), 170, 175, 188, 191
Grootendorst, R., xi, xiii, 4, 8, 11, 16, 17 (nn. 3, 5, 8), 18 (n. 15), 19 (nn. 18, 20, 21, 22), 26, 35 (nn. 2, 7), 38, 48, 49, 56 (n. 4), 58 (n. 11), 68, 99, 179, 187–89

Habermas, J., 35 (n. 9), 188
Hall, B., 35 (n. 5), 115 (n. 4), 123, 189
Halliday, M. A. K., 42, 188
Hancher, M., 53, 188
Harnish, R. M., 17 (n. 2), 18 (nn. 14, 15), 59 (n. 19), 185
Hasan, R., 42, 188
Haviland, S. E., 59 (n. 20), 186
Heider, F., 35 (n. 10), 188
Heritage, J., 44, 53, 56 (n. 2), 72, 185, 188

Higher-order conditions, 30–35 (n. 10), 117, 142, 167
Horn, L., 53, 188

Ideal model, xii, 14, 20, 22, 25–30, 32, 33, 34, 44, 45, 48, 114, 142, 170, 172–74, 177, 178; and actual practice, 34, 38, 117–19; as basis for reconstruction, 24, 44–45, 48, 62, 88; required features of, 26
Illocutionary act, 5, 17 (n. 3), 19 (n. 22), 105; complex illocutionary acts, 5
Illocutionary force, 2–3, 16 (n. 1), 17 (n. 2), 100
Implicature, 7–8; in reconstruction, 49
Incommensurability, 144, 164, 169 (n. 10), 171. *See also* Deep disagreements
Indirect speech acts, 17 (n. 2), 18 (n. 13), 51, 60, 80, 170, 173
Inequality, 34, 118, 180–82. *See also* Higher-order conditions
Instrumental rationality, 6
Interdependence of perspectives, 165, 168
Intersubjective validity, 14, 167, 171
Issue structure of argument in conversation, 104

Jackson, D. D., 59 (n. 18), 168 (n. 7), 192
Jackson, S., xi, xiii, 3, 6, 10, 16, 18 (nn. 11, 16), 19 (nn. 18, 19), 35 (n. 5), 44, 55, 104, 115 (n. 4), 123, 189
Jacobs, S., xi, xiii, 3, 6, 10, 16, 17 (n. 7), 18 (nn. 11, 16), 19 (nn. 18, 19, 22), 35 (n. 5), 44, 55, 56 (nn. 2, 5), 57 (n. 6), 59 (n. 19), 104, 115 (n. 4), 116 (n. 7), 123, 138, 144, 189
Jefferson, G., 10, 56 (n. 2), 191
Joint activity, 7
Jose, P. E., 53, 190

Kauffeld, F., 59 (n. 19), 190
Kennedy, Senator Edward M., vii, ix, x
Krabbe, E. C. W., 14, 35 (n. 8), 185
Kreckel, M., 51, 190
Kruiger, T., 19 (n. 20), 187
Kuhn, T. S., 171, 190

Labov, W., 54, 104, 116 (n. 7), 190
Leech, G. M., 53, 59 (n. 20), 190
Leiter, K., 160, 190
Levesque, H. J., 2, 186

About the Authors

Frans H. van Eemeren is Professor of Discourse and Argumentation Studies and Dean of the Faculty of Arts and Humanities at the University of Amsterdam.

Rob Grootendorst is Associate Professor of Discourse and Argumentation Studies and Chairman of the Department of Speech Communication at the University of Amsterdam.

Sally Jackson is Associate Professor of Communication in the Department of Communication at the University of Arizona.

Scott Jacobs is Associate Professor of Communication in the Department of Communication at the University of Arizona.

About the Series

STUDIES IN RHETORIC AND COMMUNICATION
General Editors:
E. Culpepper Clark, Raymie E. McKerrow, and David Zarefsky

The University of Alabama Press has established this series to publish major new works in the general area of rhetoric and communication, including books treating the symbolic manifestations of political discourse, argument as social knowledge, the impact of machine technology on patterns of communication behavior, and other topics related to the nature or impact of symbolic communication. We actively solicit studies involving historical, critical, or theoretical analyses of human discourse.